BX 1790

CHURCH AND STATE

BEHIND THE IRON CURTAIN

CZECHOSLOVAKIA, HUNGARY, POLAND, ROMANIA
WITH AN INTRODUCTION ON THE SOVIET UNION

prepared
under the general editorship of
VLADIMIR GSOVSKI

1 9 5 5

Published for the Mid-European Studies Center
of the Free Europe Committee, Inc.

by

FREDERICK A. PRAEGER
New York

TABLE OF CONTENTS

(For detailed Tables of Contents *see* under each section)

PREFACE

THE present publication contains studies prepared by members of the Mid-European Law Project which is financed by the Free Europe Committee, Inc., is under the administration of L. Quincey Mumford, Librarian of Congress, and Dr. W. Lawrence Keitt, Law Librarian of the Library of Congress. It is under the immediate direction and editorship of Dr. Vladimir Gsovski, Chief of the Foreign Law Section, who is assisted by Dr. Kazimierz Grzybowski of the staff of the Project and by Mr. Edmund Jann and Dr. Fred Karpf of the staff of the Foreign Law Section. The staff of the project is composed of lawyers from Bulgaria, Czechoslovakia, Hungary, Poland, Romania, Yugoslavia, Estonia, Latvia and Lithuania, who are refugees from their native lands.

The aim of the present study is to describe the actual position of the church in countries behind the Iron Curtain. It covers Czechoslovakia, Hungary, Romania and Poland. Another volume covering the Soviet Union, Bulgaria and Yugoslavia is under preparation. In seeking for truth, the legislation enacted behind the Iron Curtain was read in the light of the sum total of official material available, such as decrees, regulations, court decisions, declarations of officials, and the general press of each country. Official statements of church leaders in each country were also used wherever available. The authors of each national report refer to the history of churches in their countries where it is required for the understanding of present developments. It is emphasized that the views expressed in the reports are those of the authors.

Although the Church and State in the Soviet Union will be covered in detail in the companion volume, the main events in this field in the Soviet Union and the ideas of its Communist leaders form the background of development in the countries

vii

covered by the present one. Hence, an introduction is supplied, which, without intending to be complete, outlines such situations in the Soviet Union as may throw some light on the policies pursued toward the church by the present governments of Czechoslovakia, Hungary, Poland, and Romania.

An acknowledgment is expressed to Mrs. Rebecca Notz, Legal Analyst, Legislative Reference Service of the Library of Congress, who revised the index.

Introduction

SEPARATION OF CHURCH FROM STATE IN THE SOVIET UNION

by Vladimir Gsovski

The laws and decrees relating to the Church in Czechoslovakia, Hungary, Poland and Romania were prepared and enacted by leaders trained in the Soviet Union or inspired by the ideas that motivate the government of the Soviet Union. Political and legal terms used by them designate concepts which are at variance with the traditional meaning we have for these terms and they conform with Soviet ideas. This is especially true of the separation of Church and State as declared in the laws of some of these countries.[1]

The idea of separation of Church and State in America emerged from the struggle for religious freedom and tolerance. This principle does not imply suppression of worship but is designated to safeguard liberty in the exercise of one's faith. The State is presumed not to be hostile or beneficent to any specific Church, but is equally benevolent to every Church.

But the legislators of Soviet Russia were inspired by quite different ideas. Thus, beginning with the first Decree "On Separation of the Church from the State and the School from the Church" issued January 23, 1918 (in the third month of the Soviet regime), such a separation was not aimed toward religious freedom or tolerance, but was designed to undermine the very existence of the Church in Russia.

This was made clear in retrospect in the publication of the Central Institute for Antireligious Correspondence Courses, printed by a Soviet Government printing office in 1932.

"It is necessary to emphasize that the Soviet Decree concerning the Separation of Church from State and the School from the Church, was from the beginning directed *against religion*. In the question of religion, the Soviet Government never carried a double-dealing policy of equal cooperation with religion and atheism. It would be wrong to represent the whole matter as if our government kept away from the problems of religion, washed its hands and left the matter to its natural course. * * *

Therefore, this Decree cannot be considered otherwise than as a *measure deliberately directed against religion*. The advocates of 'non-religious education in schools' understated the historical role of this Decree, and have misinterpreted it. In fact, according to their opinion, the Soviet Government is neither for nor against religion. No, this is not true. Soviet power fights against religion: In the first place, by means of the separation of all the Churches from the State and then by means of organization of *antireligious education* in the schools and antireligious education of the people at large. It is not that the antireligious work of our Commissariat for Educaiton contradicts separation of Church from State, on the contrary, it follows from it. And vice versa. If, after having separated the Church from the State, our government would not have developed at the same time by all the means at its disposal antireligious propaganda, then * * * religion would have been developed and to an extent strengthened in new refined forms. * * * Therefore, it would be treason to the dictatorship of the proletariat, treason to the spirit and sense of the Decree on Separation of the State from the Church to fail to organize the fight against religion on a union-wide scale by the force and the means of the government itself. * * * In a few words, the analysis of the Decree may be summarized as follows: *If the capitalistic separation of Church and State leads to the free and highest development of religion, the Soviet separation of Church and State leads to the free and final death of religion.*" [Italics supplied][2]

Hostility toward religion, clearly stated in this excerpt, is deeply rooted in the communist philosophy of the Soviet leaders. For Lenin,

"The saying of Marx: 'Religion is the opium of the people,' is the cornerstone of the Marxist point of view in the matter of religion. Marxism has always viewed all contemporary religion and churches, all and every kind of religious organization as agencies of bourgeois reaction, serving as a defense of exploitation and the drugging of the working class." [3]

For Engels the paramount human belief in God was merely "a fantastic reflex." Said Engels:

"Now all religion is nothing else than the fantastic reflex in the minds of men of those external forces which dominate their everyday existence, a reflection in which the earthly forces assume the form of supernatural forces." [4]

Lenin went on to develop this idea:

"God (as He appeared in history and life) is before all a complex of ideas produced by the stupefying oppression of man both by outer nature and class exploitations,—a complex of ideas which strengthens this oppression and lulls the class struggle." [5]

"The religious oppression of humanity is but the product and reflex of economic oppression within society * * *." [6]

For Lenin a good Church was worse than a corrupted one. It is religion itself and not the occasional abuses by the members of Churches that is attacked by Lenin. He says:

"Any religious idea, any idea of a 'good God', any coquetry even with a 'good God' is an abominably nasty thing which is met especially tolerantly (often benevolently) by the 'democratic bourgeoisie' and is just for that reason the most dangerous abomination, most odious infection." [7]

In Lenin's writing, antedating communist rule in Russia, there are passages in which he insisted that the State of that time should recognize religion as a "private affair" of a citizen. However, he made plain that his aim was to deprive the Church of support given by the pre-revolutionary State. He did not expect from his party and party-dominated State any neutrality toward religion.

"The [Communist] Party," said Lenin, "while demanding of the State the declaration of religion as a 'private affair' in nowise should consider the problems of the fight against the dope of the people, religious superstition, to be a private affair." [8]

Lenin vehemently condemned the attempts made by some of the Russian Marxists in 1908-09 to create a link between socialism and religion. According to Lenin:

"The party of the proletariat must be the spiritual leader in the struggle against all kinds of medievalism, including the official religion, and against all attempts to renovate it or to justify it in a new or in another way." [9]

The following passage from Lenin's article "Socialism and Religion" was recently quoted in a *Pravda* editorial of July 24, 1954, as expressing a permanent principle:

"The [Communist] Party as a union of consciously progressive fighters could not and should not take an irrelevant attitude toward unconsciousness, darkness and obscurantism in the form of religious creeds."

A comprehensive antireligious program was adopted at a special conference on antireligious propaganda of the Communist Party of the Soviet Union and its Central Committee held on April 27-30, 1926. It called for "exposing the class essences of religious belief . . . exposing religion in its role, in Western Europe, America and in the Orient, as the servant of capital." It asserted the "anti-scientific nature of religion," and that religion, "distorting and perverting the toiler's concept of the world, the laws of nature and the development of human society . . . imposes upon the toilers a false concept of the world." The program stated, "where religion is victorious, Communism is weak. The Communist regime will only come into being in a society freed from religion." [10]

All religions were equally condemned by this program, but Christianity was especially disapproved. The third point of the program reads:

"The struggle with religion must be carried on by exposing religious morals as a morality imposed in a special manner upon the toilers by the ruling class. (Contemporary Christianity, for example, as a system of morals, represents by itself nothing but such a concept of duty as is in the interest of the ruling exploiters. The morals proposed to the toilers by Christianity are bourgeois—exploiters' morals, training the exploited classes for all those qualities which, from the point of view of the exploiter, his victim should have: silence, passiveness, meekness, patience). It is necessary to condemn categorically, as the worst type of popery, every effort of approachment of Christianity to Communism. Religion must be rejected for good, without reservation and camouflage. * * * It is necessary to point out the harmfulness to the class interests of the toilers of religious emotions and sentiment."

The same hostility and determination to fight religion is also stated in *Pravda* as late as July 24, 1954.

"The victory of the socialist ideology does not mean, however, that in our society the remnants of the bourgeois concept of life and the survival of the ideology and ethics of private owners are totally liquidated. These survivals do not and will not die out by themselves, they must be fought persistently with full force. One of the most tenacious and harmful survivals of capitalism in the minds of people are the religious superstitions. These superstitions poison up to the present time the mind of a part of our people, [and] hinder their active participation in the building up of Communism."

Consequently it is the basic proposition of the Soviet rulers to combat the religious concept of life as an error and as a potentially inimical force. Atheism and materialism are integral parts of the Communist teaching and are its prospective standards for the popular mentality. To deprive the Churches of the possibility of exercising an influence upon the people, even outside of politics, has been the real tenor of all acts of the Soviet Russian Government. To create conditions for the replacement of religion by atheism has been its real aim.

In pursuit of this aim, the Soviet policies have varied. The years 1922-1923 and 1929-1930 are marked with the most severe suppression of Churches and persecution of high prelates and clergymen. The laws then enacted deprived the Churches of the conditions indispensable to the normal life of a religious community. Churches have been deprived of the right of property, right of teaching religion, exercising charity, of their place in public life and recognized organization over the parishes. This is all laid down in the Law of April 7, 1929 and the Instruction issued on its implementation.[11]

A sharp change took place during World War II. Suddenly, numerous concessions were made to the Russian Orthodox Church, the Church of a majority of the Russian population. The restrictive laws remained unchanged, but the government allowed a Church Council to convene in 1943 and to elect a patriarch for the first time since the death of Patriarch Tichon in 1925. When the elected Patriarch Sergii died on May 15, 1944, another Council was convened in January-February 1945 and elected a new patriarch, Alexii. In the presence of a high government official charged with religious affairs, the same council adopted Rules on the Administration of the Russian Orthodox Church.[12] Some provisions of these Rules imply recognition of the Church hierarchy by the Soviet Government and grant powers to the Church conflicting with the previous highly restrictive laws. The Soviet Government neither repealed nor modified the old laws nor did it extend officially any approval to the Rules. The concessions made are deprived of any authority of law, and may as easily be withdrawn as they were given. Again, they relate only to the Russian Orthodox Church and were coupled with several attacks on the Holy See.

Behind these transformations one can discern some permanent features of the status of the Church under the Soviet regime in Russia. The Church remains expressly prohibited from teaching religion, outside of special courses for training priests. Under the Law of April 1, 1929, Sec. 17, several activities are prohibited to the Churches and it is stated there that Churches "may not organize for children, young people and women, special prayer or other meetings, or, generally, meetings, groups, circles, or departments for biblical or literary study, sewing, working, or the teaching of religion . . . Only books necessary for the purpose of the cult may be kept in the buildings and premises used for worship."

Soviet Statutes of 1918 and 1929 prohibited "the teaching of any form of religious belief in governmental public and private teaching and educational establishments."[13] A Decree of 1921 prohibited also in general the "teaching of religious doctrine to persons under 18 years of age,"[14] and a Decree of 1923 prohibited any private religious instruction of children in groups comprising over three children.[15] Violation of these rules is subject to prosecution in court under Sec. 123 of the RSFSR Criminal Code.

The Law of 1929 states that "religious instruction is permitted exclusively in special theological courses" which may be opened by a special permit by the higher Soviet authorities for the preparation of ministers of religion (Sec. 18). Several such courses were opened after 1945.

A definite task of atheistic education is clearly set in the statutes governing the Soviet schools. For example, the RSFSR Statute on Secondary Schools of 1934[16] reads:

13. The teaching of any form of religious worship, as well as the performance of any rites or rituals of a faith, and any other form of religious influence upon the growing generation shall be prohibited and prosecuted under the criminal law.

The primary schools and secondary schools shall secure an antireligious upbringing of the students and shall build instruction and educational work upon the basis of an active fight against religion and its influence upon the student and adult population.

The more recent statutes, for example, that on teachers' colleges of 1944, refrain from any general statements on the atheistic purpose of education. However, the same purpose is implied in the instructions for teaching the natural sciences. "The study of natural sciences must secure" [not knowledge pure and simple] "the development in the student of a dialectic-materialistic view of nature (origins of life on the earth, origin of animals and men, origin of men)."

Thus, Soviet legislation is designed not only to bar the Church from religious instruction, but also to put an end to the teaching of religious doctrine in general and achieve antireligious education.

It is significant that the early Soviet Constitution of 1918 in declaring the separation of Church and State, stated that "freedom of religious and antireligious propaganda is secured to citizens."[17] In 1929, "freedom of religious propaganda" was officially deleted[18] and it was officially announced that freedom of religious propaganda "exceeds the limits of religious freedom recognized by law."[19] The federal Constitution of 1936, Sec. 124, which is still in force, is even more restrictive. It merely recognizes "freedom of performance of religious cults and freedom of antireligious propaganda." It was officially commented that performance of a religious cult is reduced to "prayer and performance of ceremonies and the like. Activities exceeding the satisfaction of these needs are not permitted."[20] Under the new policy, followed since 1943, the constitutional provisions were not changed and the Church activities remain restricted. Thus the 1947 and 1948 editions of the large Soviet encyclopedia states that:

"The Soviet State proceeds from the proposition that the business of the Church consists only of the performance of the cult. Any kind of activities of a propagandistic, moralizing or educative nature (on the scale extending beyond a definite religious community) should not belong to the Church as a union of believers created and existing only for the performance of the cult."[21]

The first Decree on Separation of Church and State of January 23, 1918, declared all the property of all Churches in Russia public property (Sec. 13), *i.e.,* confiscated it without compensation. By this and later decrees and laws, the Churches were deprived of "the right to own any property" (Sec. 12), in particular church buildings, utensils, vestments and other objects destined for liturgical or any other ceremonial use. It is especially emphasized by laws that churches "shall not enjoy the rights of a corporation (legal entity)," *i.e.,* may not, in their own name, own anything or enter into a contract. Any assumption by a Church of the rights of a corporation or of "administrative, judicial or other functions pertaining to public law" constitutes a criminal offense (Criminal Code of the RSFSR, Sec. 126). Government ownership of any object "necessary for the cult," *i.e.,* indispensable for worship, applies not only to such objects possessed by the Church prior to the revolution, but also to any object "acquired by the believers or given to them for religious purposes" under the Soviet regime. This is the express provision of Sec. 12 of the Decree of 1918 and the Law of 1929.

The only way for Soviet citizens to have a place of worship is to get it from the local soviet under a contract. Each parish, in order to obtain such a contract, even for a place which they formerly owned, had to be organized anew as a "religious association" and register, *i.e.,* obtain a license for their existence which could be granted or denied at the discretion of the local soviet. At least 20 parishioners should sign the contract and assume full personal liability for the upkeep of the place and the objects needed for religious ceremonies. From 1918 to 1930 each parish had to undergo two or three such registrations to survive. On any of these occasions or at any other time, the churches could be withdrawn from the use of the parish and many of them were converted into storehouses, clubs, motion picture theaters and antireligious museums.

The Rules of the Russian Orthodox Church of 1945, Secs. 37-39, and the large Soviet Encyclopedia, 1947 edition, show that in that respect the status of the churches remains unchanged under the present policy of the Soviet government.[21]

No full account of churches withdrawn or destroyed is available. Church edifices of utmost historical and artistic value have been largely withdrawn from religious use and many have been destroyed, *i.e.*, The Cathedral of Our Lord the Savior and many other churches in Moscow, where in 1942 only 17 churches remained in use by the parishioners from a total of over 600 before the revolution.[23] The closing of churches was particularly extensive in 1929-1930. These are the incomplete figures derived from Soviet sources: from 1921-1923 about 722 monasteries were closed in the RSFSR alone;[24] in 1927 some 134 churches;[25] in 1928 nearly 600;[26] but in 1929, 1,450.[27] Some newly created cities have no churches at all, *e.g.*, Magnitogorsk, with 200,000 inhabitants; Karaganda with 120,000; and Stalinsk with 200,000.[28] Valuable articles and artistic paintings were for the most part removed in 1922-1923 (*infra*). In 1930 the Soviet press continually reported the burning of ikons and religious books in small places in such quantities as 12 wagonloads, 8 wagonloads, 4,000 ikons and 1,000 religious books.[29] The opening of reliquaries was made on a large scale on order of the RSFSR Commissariat for Justice of August 25, 1920 which reported 58 instances of opening of reliquaries and insisted on "complete liquidation according to a plan of relics" by placing them in museums where they were exposed to desecration. Thus the same Commissariat reported in 1921, of placing side by side with the relic of a saint, a mummified rat.[30]

Beginning with the Constitution of 1918 and until 1936, "present and former clergymen of all denominations (ministers, deacons, rabbis, *et cetera*), monks and nuns "were deprived of the right to vote. In 1929, 248,000 persons were disfranchised on this ground, and 161,000 in 1931, the decrease being officially explained by the "natural decrease in the number of ministers."[31] The disfranchised constituted a kind of outcast who were officially discriminated against in employment, obtaining rationed food, housing, education of their children, and taxation.[32]

An all-out assault on churches was made in 1922-1923. The preceding year, 1921, was marked by famine in the central, most fertile zones of Russia. The churches were by that time stripped of all their assets, but there remained numerous objects made of or adorned with precious metals, many of which were consecrated.

The Patriarch Tikhon of the Russian Orthodox Church, elected in 1918, issued an appeal for help for the famine-stricken in August 1921. A Russian Church Committee was formed for famine relief and parishes collected food and money. Then the government ordered them to turn the collections over to the government relief organizations.[33] On December 21, 1921, the government again allowed the churches to conduct collections and instructed the central official relief organization *Pomgol* "to reach an agreement with religious societies as to the form of collection of donations and the methods of forwarding of what is collected having in mind the wishes of the donors."[34] It was officially reported that such an agreement had been reached.[35] On February 15, 1922, a message by Patriarch Tikhon was printed in *Izvestiia* calling upon the parishes to donate adornments of ikons and broken pieces of gold and silver.[36] But on February 23 the Soviet Government had instructed "the local soviets to remove within one month's period . . . from church property . . . all precious articles of gold, silver and precious stones, the removal of which does not essentially infringe upon the interest of the cult.[37] It was officially commented "that golden and silver chalices, reliquaries, metal adornments of ikons, vestments and the like" could not be retained.[38] The Patriarch answered by a message to the faithful, in which he restated that he had "allowed, in view of the emergency, the Church to donate objects which were not consecrated and not used in the divine services." But, he also stated that "we cannot approve the removal from the churches of consecrated objects even by voluntary donations, as their use for any purpose other than the church services is prohibited by the canons of the universal Church."[39]

But forcible removal of all valuables from the churches was ordered by the Soviet Government. A total of 1,414 bloody incidents caused by resistance by the faithful was allowed to appear in the Soviet press.[40] Numerous trials took place before the revolutionary tribunals which until June 1, 1922 were not bound by any rules of statutory criminal law or procedure and were at liberty to apply any punishment, including the death penalty.[41] Incomplete figures show that at least 45 executions and over 500 imprisonment terms were pronounced.[42]

During one of the trials of 54 priests and laymen in Moscow in May 1922, which ended with eleven death sentences, Patriarch Tikhon was called to testify as a witness and boldly assumed the responsibility for the defense of consecrated objects. On May 2, 1922, he was indicted and placed under arrest, pending his own trial.[43] A similar trial of the prelates of the Roman Catholic Church also took place. Bishop Jan Cepliak and Mgr. Butkiewicz were sentenced to death and several other Catholic priests to long-term imprisonment.[44] This fact alone disproves the allegations of the Soviets that the prelates of the Russian Church were prosecuted because of their alleged connections with the monarchists.

A group of priests of the Russian Church, headed by the priest, Vvedensky, declared their complete acceptance of social revolution and the Soviet platform, and, as they stated in the petition to the arrested Patriarch they "obtained permission for the opening and functioning of the chancery of the Patriarch" and for visiting him. The Patriarch conceded on May 18, 1922 that they take over the files of the Synod" for the transmission to Metropolitan Agaphangel.[45] But Metropolitan Agaphangel could not come, being under house arrest in Yaroslavl. The Vvedensky group, later called the Living Church, assumed the administration of the Church affairs, setting up a Provisional Administration of Church Affairs. Metropolitan Agaphangel was arrested and exiled to Narym (Siberia). Nevertheless, he issued a message calling on the faithful to remain loyal to the arrested Patriarch and advised the bishops to administer each diocese independently until true Church authority was restored.[46]

At a gathering of the Vvedensky group of 42 persons on July 4, 1922, rules for the Living Church were adopted, the justice of the social revolution was declared, and abolition of the patriarchate and such uncanonical changes as consecration of married priests as bishops were advocated. At another convention in August, consisting of 154 delegates with only three bishops out of 143, it was reported that 60 bishops who were against the new Church administration or were noncommital were forced to retire.[47] The background for these developments is supplied by the fact that throughout these turbulent times six metropolitans, three archbishops and 56 bishops were either arrested or exiled.[48]

The reformist movement soon became split into several groups but a joint Sobor convened on April 29-May 9, 1923. At the Sobor, the Patriarch was neither present (he was still under arrest) nor represented; no evidence against him was produced and yet the Sobor dethroned him and reduced him to layman status on May 2, 1923. The Patriarchate was abolished and various uncanonical changes were confirmed.[49]

The trial of the Patriarch, who had been imprisoned for almost a year, was officially announced in April 23 and then postponed. Lord Curzon threatened to recall the British mission. Then on June 27, the announcement was published that the Supreme Court had set free the Patriarch on his petition of June 16. In the published text of the petition the Patriarch stated that he "was actually hostile to the Soviet power," recognized "the correctness of the court in bringing him to trial" and declared that "henceforth I am not an enemy of the Soviet Power."[50]

Upon his release the Patriarch declared the Sobor of 1923 uncanonical, his dethronement illegal and assumed his office, being enthusiastically greeted by the flock.[51] Not only parishioners but also bishops and priests who joined the Living Church repented and were admitted to the fold. Among the bishops were Sergii and Alexii, the future patriarchs.[52]

Nevertheless, the Living Church, now renamed Renovated, continued to enjoy Soviet recognition and existed apart from the Patriarch in spite of several attempts at reunion.

On March 26, 1925, the Patriarch died. From that time on and until 1943, for eighteen years, no election of a new patriarch was allowed. The late patriarch appointed as a keeper of his office, in the first place, Metropolitan Cyril, but he was placed under arrest, in the second place, Metropolitan Agaphangel, who was in exile and in the third place, Metropolitan Peter, who took the office.[53] In October 1925, a Sobor of the Renovated Church convened, but Metropolitan Peter showed an uncompromising attitude against the Sobor and the revisionist movement in general. He was attacked in the Soviet press.[54] On December 23, 1925, Peter was arrested and in the summer of 1926 exiled to Siberia where he died in 1936.[55] With him ended the unquestionable legitimate succession of authority.

Before his exile, Metropolitan Peter appointed as the deputy keeper of the patriarchal office, Metropolitan Sergii of Nijni Novgorod and three other prelates as alternates.[56] At the same time, a group of bishops of the patriarchal Church headed by Bishop Grigorii was promised by the Soviet government legalization of Church administration. Moreover, Metropolitan Agaphangel was allowed to return from exile and claimed the office under the earlier arrangement of the late patriarch. In this confusion, Metropolitan Peter (*supra*), being under arrest, first gave the authority to Sergii, then in January 1926, agreed to transfer it to Grigorii's group and then in April 1926 to Agaphangel. But Sergii, who was in and out of prison, asserted his own authority, being supported by several bishops. He succeeded in persuading Agaphangel to give up his claim. In brief, out of eleven hierarchs appointed to be keeper of the Patriarchal office, or his deputy, ten were in prison or exile.[57] Metropolitan Sergii, who finally assumed the office of the deputy keeper, was arrested in early 1926 during the crisis, brought to Moscow, then in March sent back to Nijni Novgorod and released. He was again arrested on December 13, 1926 and released in April 1927.[58] During all this time, he negotiated with the Soviet authorities on the conditions of the Church administration. Evidently, a compromise was reached since soon after his last release, Metropolitan Sergii announced the official opening of his administration and on June 29, 1927 pledged in a message not only complete loyalty but also a wholehearted support of the Soviet government.[59] Since then, he has repeatedly done what the government expected him to do, and only in 1943 did the government answer with some concessions. Metropolitan Sergii has shown an uncompromising attitude against the Renovated Church but ordered the prayers for the Soviet Government to be said during the Church service and required pledges of loyalty to the Soviets not only from the clergy in Russia but also from those abroad.[60] Some of the bishops, clergy and parishioners did not accept his submission to the atheist authority and those in Russia went into exile and imprisonment. An underground Church came into being.[61]

In spite of the complete submission of Sergii to the Soviets, the attack on the Church and religion was intensified. The association of militant atheists founded in 1925 became extremely active. Numerous antireligious periodicals and numerous books and pamphlets were printed. Special atheistic courses and publishing offices were organized. In 1929, the Constitution was changed, dropping from its clauses permission for religious propaganda. The Law of 1929 sought to destroy the Church as an organized body of parishes. In 1929-1930, many churches were closed, books and ikons were burned (*supra*). Metropolitan Sergii continued to fulfil his pledge and publicly denied any persecution of the Church in Russia before the Russian and foreign correspondents in 1930.[62]

There was, however, a great disappointment in store for the Soviet leaders. Religion has been regarded by them as a mere "remnant of capitalism" which no longer existed in Soviet Russia. In 1936, Stalin declared that "the victory of the socialist system in all spheres of the national economy is now a fact."[63] However, neither the social transformation of Russia, according to the Communist plan, nor the measures taken to deprive Churches of their influence on the people, achieved the aim of putting an end to religion in Russia. In 1939, the official Communist Party periodical candidly recognized that "it is much more difficult to uproot religion from the minds of the workers than to liberate them from the exploitation of capitalism."[64] The Soviet press carried statements frankly admitting that at least one third of the city population and more than one half, perhaps two thirds, of the rural population still believed in God.[65]

The Church has to be reckoned with as an independent social

force which is not going to disappear in the foreseeable future despite adverse conditions created by the Soviet Government. The Soviet rulers gradually arrived at the idea of attempting to make this force serve the general communist policies. The conduct of Metropolitan Sergii seemed to promise the possibility of such a tactic. With the beginning of World War II Metropolitan Sergii continued to show his Church's complete loyalty to the Soviet Government and identified it with the patriotic devotion to the country. Stalin was hailed "as a divinely anointed leader."[66]

A change in policy was further prompted by the news from German-occuppied territories that there the closed churches were reopened and church life was revived. Both these factors induced concessions to the Russian Orthodox Church which appeared to be willing to go along with Soviet policy. Nicholas, the Metropolitan of Kiev and Galicia, was appointed a member of the government committee to investigate German atrocities.[67] He and the Metropolitan Sergii were officially received by Stalin on September 4, 1943 and a Sobor of 19 bishops (compared with 69 at the Sobor of 1917) convened on September 8 to elect Sergii the Patriarch of Russia.[68] A committee for ecclesiastic affairs of the Russian Church was created and attached to the Council of the People's Commissar (renamed in 1946, Council of Ministers), the supreme executive body.[69] The Journal of the Moscow Patriarchy began to appear. The opening of seminaries for the training of priests was announced. Solemn church services followed each victory of the Soviet troops.

Thus, by the end of the war, when Soviet influence was spread to the satellite countries, it was a new Soviet Church policy, to refrain from direct attacks on religion and aim at making the Church an obedient instrument of government policy, which was carried into these countries. But no concession was made to the Catholic Church in Russia. The attacks on the Holy See were intensified, and attempts were made in the satellite countries to produce a separation of the lower clergy from the episcopate in the fashion of the "Living Church" in Russia (*supra*).

The concessions to the Russian Church in the Soviet Union

were never put in the form of law, nor were the restrictive provisions of old laws abrogated. Concessions today still remain a
matter of policy and not of law. For its recognition as a union
"existing only for the performance of the cult" the Russian
Church pays the price of giving active support to all campaigns
of the Soviet Government in international relations. The Church
had to join the World Congress of supporters of peace, the
Stockholm peace petition and even filed with the United Nations
a protest against its action in Korea, accusing the United States
of aggression.[70]

Thus, the Soviet Russian Government has committed the
Russian Church to a policy of unconditional fealty and blind
support in exchange for precarious recognition—a policy which
was soon to be attempted in the satellite countries.

NOTES TO INTRODUCTION

1. For Hungary see pp. 72-79, for Poland pp. 175-178.
2. *Antireligious Movement in the U.S.S.R. and Abroad* (in Russian, Government Antireligious Publishing Office, 1933) pp. 12, 15, 16
3. Lenin, *Collected Works* (2nd Russian ed. Moscow, 1926), vol. 14, p. 68, this edition is cited throughout the present work.
4. Engels, *Anti-Duering* (English Translation, 1935), p. 311.
5. Lenin, "Two Letters to Gorky" (1913), *Collected Works,* vol. 17, p. 85, see also *ibid.,* vol. 14, p. 71.
6. Lenin, "Socialism and Religion," *Collected Works,* vol. 8, p. 422.
7. Lenin, *Collected Works,* vol. 17, p. 82.
8. Lenin, "The Attitude of the Labor Party towards Religion" (1909), *Collected Works,* vol. 14, p. 74; see also vol. 21, p. 42.
9. *Ibid.* p. 75.
10. Theses adopted at the Party Conference on Antireligious Propaganda and at the Central Committee of the U.S.S.R., April 27-30, 1926, Sec. V. English translation, quoted from Hecker, *Religion and Communism* (1933), p. 279. See also Lukachevsky, *Antireligious Propaganda at the Present Stage* [of the Soviet regime] (in Russian, 1936), pp. 1, 3, 5, 9.
11. *R.S.F.S.R. Laws* (1929) text 353, hereafter cited as Law of 1929. Instruction of the R.S.F.S.R. People's Commissariat of the Interior of October 1, 1929, No. 328 (hereafter cited Instruction 1929); *Bulletin* of the same Commissariat, 1929, No. 30, also Orleansky, *Law Concerning the Religious Associations in the R.S.F.S.R.* (in Russian, 1930), p. 27. This is the semi-official commentary to the law. For detailed analysis of the law see Gsovski, V., "The Legal Status of the Church in Soviet Russia," *Fordham Law Review,* January 1939, No. 1, pp. 8-28.
12. *The Call of the Russian Church, Report of the General Council of the Russian Orthodox Church* (London, n.d.), p. 11.
13. Decree of 1918, Sec. 9; Law of 1929, Sec. 18.
14. Decree of June 13, 1921, Section 3, note; Gidulianov, *Separation of the Church from the State in the U.S.S.R.: Complete Collection of Decrees* (in Russian, 3rd ed., 1929), p. 365.
15. Instruction of the Commissariats for the Interior and for Education, December 22, 1923, *Bulletin of the Commissariat for the Interior* (in Russian) Jan. 22, 1924, No. 3; also Gidulianov, *op. cit. supra* note 14, p. 367.
16. *R.S.F.S.R. Laws* (1934) text 263.

17. R.S.F.S.R. Constitution 1918, Sec. II, *ibid.*, 1925, sec. 4.
18. Law of May 28, 1929, *R.S.F.S.R. Laws* (1929) item 495.
19. *Godless* (in Russian), February 6, 1930.
20. Orleansky, *op. cit. supra* note 11, p. 11.
21. *Bolshaia Sovetskaia Entsiklopediia, Soiuz Sovetskikh Sotisalisticheskikh Respublik,* Moskva, 1947 (1948) columns 1783-1784.
22. Ibid., p. 1786 ff. For translations of sections 37-39 of Rules of 1945 see V. Gsovski, *Soviet Civil Law,* Ann Arbor, vol. II, 1949, pp. 334-335.
23. *Truth on Religion in Russia* (in Russian, n.p. Moskovskaia Patriarkhia, 1942) a luxuriously printed collection of articles, pictures, speeches, and reports designed to show German atrocities towards the Church in contrast to the freedom of religion under the Soviets. From the list of parishes contributing to patriotic purposes in Moscow, pp. 163-190 and passim, it follows that not more than 17 churches in Moscow remained in the use of the faithful. The prerevolutionary number of churches in Moscow is estimated by various sources at from 400 to 675.
24. *The People's Commissariat for Justice. Report to the 9th All-Russian Congress of Soviets* (in Russian, Moscow, 1921), p. 48.
25. *Izvestiia,* December 29, 1936.
26. 445 churches, 59 synagogues, and 38 mosques. *Young Guard* (in Russian, 1930) No. 22; *Izvestiia,* March 22, 1929.
27. In the cities: 550 churches, 111 synagogues, and 96 mosques; in villages: 589 churches, 15 synagogues, and 98 mosques, *Antireligious* (in Russian, 1930) No. 3.
28. *Izvestiia,* December 29, 1936.
29. In Lisichansk and Denisovo, *Godless* (in Russian), March 10 and March 30, 1930. In Tver, *Izvestiia,* January 8, 1930. In Andreevka, *Godless,* (in Russian) 1930, No. 5, p. 4.
30. *Op. cit. supra* note 24, p. 44. The address of the museum given there is Moscow, Petrovka street, no. 14.
31. *Elections to the Soviets and the Compositions of Agencies of the Government* (in Russian, 1931). p. 35.
32. *R.S.F.S.R. Laws* (1921) item 67; Gidulianov, *op. cit. supra* note 14, pp. 294-295; Decree of the R.S.F.S.R. Commissariat for the Interior, July 30, 1929, No. 259; Resolution of R.S.F.S.R. Central Executive Committee, Dec. 27, 1927, sec. 2; Orleansky, *op. cit. supra* note 11, p. 56-58; Standard Charter of Universities, *U.S.S.R. Laws* (1934) text 87 (b) secs. 44, 47 (b); *ibid.,* (1928) text 212, sec. 28; (*ibid.,* 1930) text. 462.
33. Curtis, *The Russian Church and the Soviet State,* Boston, 1953, p. 107.
34. Gidulianov and Krasikov, *Church and State According to Legislation*

of the R.S.F.S.R. (in Russian, 1923) XII, 5, p. 52. Emhardt, *Religion in the Soviet Union,* Milwaukee, 1929, p. 55

35. *Izvestiia,* January 26, 1922.
36. *Ibid.,* February 15, 1922; Stratonov, *The Turmoil of the Russian Church* (1921-1931) (in Russian, Berlin, 1932) pp. 48-52.
37. *Izvestiia,* February 24, 1922; *R.S.F.S.R. Laws* (1922) text 217 sec. 1.
38. *Church and Revolution* (in Russian, 1923) No. 1/2, p. 5.
39. Valentinov, *Black Book, Assault on Heaven* (in Russian, Paris 1925) pp. 253-254.
40. *Pravda,* May 17, 1922, No. 108. Statement by the priest Krasnitsky of the Living Church.
41. *R.S.F.S.R. Laws* (1920) text 115, Secs. 1, 24, 29. "In the jurisdiction of the [revolutionary] tribunals a complete liberty of repression was advocated, while sentencing to death was a matter of everyday practice." In these words Krylenko, the noted prosecutor, especially in cases of the prelates of the church, characterized the activities of the tribunals. Krylenko, *The Judiciary of the R.S.F.S.R.* (in Russian, 1923), p. 206; See Gsovski, *op. cit. supra* note 22, Vol. I (1948), p. 234 ff.
42. A soviet writer hostile to the patriarchal church tabulated for 55 tribunals 33 executions and 585 convictions. Brikchev, *Patriarch Tikhon and His Church* (in Russian, Moscow 1933) p. 19-20, quoted by Curtis who considers these figures incomplete *op. cit. supra* note 33, p. 126, but Hecker, *Religion and Communism* (New York, 1933) p. 209 tabulated 45 executions and 250 long term prison sentences from Soviet sources. These figures do not include executions by the secret police—Cheka and GPU.
43. *Izvestiia,* May 7, 1922.
44. *Izvestiia,* March 27, 1923. See also McCullagh, Francis, *The Bolshevik Persecution of Christianity,* London, 1924, pp. 99-185; Emhardt, *op. cit. supra* note 34, pp. 18-192.
45. *Vestnik* of the Holy Synod of the Renovated Church, 1925, No. 2, p. 18, Emhardt, *op. cit. supra* note 34, p. 59 ff; Polskii, *Canonical Status of the Supreme Ecclesiastical Authority in the U.S.S.R. and Abroad* (in Russian, Jordanivlle, New York, 1948) pp. 8, 10-11; Curtis, *op. cit. supra* note 33, p. 130 ff; Spinka, *The Church and the Russian Revolution,* New York, 1927, p. 201 ff.
46. Message of June 5/18, 1922, Polskii, *op. cit.,* pp. 14-15; Curtis, *op. cit. supra* note 33, p. 134; Spinka, *op. cit. supra* note 45, p. 207; Emhardt, *op. cit. supra* note 34, p. 307.
47. *Izvestiia,* August 10, 15, 1922; Curtis, *op. cit. supra* note 33, p. 138-139. Spinka, *op. cit. supra* note 45, p. 213. ff.
48. Valentinov, *op. cit. supra* note 39, p. 257-259.

49. *Izvestiia,* May 6, 10, and 30, 1923; Spinka, *op. cit. supra* note 45, p. 240 ff.

50. *Izvestiia,* June 27, 1923.

51. *Ibid.,* July 3, 1923; Polskii, *op. cit. supra* note 45, p. 23; Mikhail Sviaschenik (pseudonym of Polskii) *Status of Church in Soviet Russia* (in Russian, Jerusalem, 1931), passim; Spinka, *op. cit. supra* note 45, pp. 255-260.

52. Polskii, *op. cit.,* pp. 97-98; Timasheff, *Church in Soviet Russia,* New York, 1942, p. 33 ff; Curtis, *op. cit. supra* note 33, p. 168; *Tserkovnyia Vedomosti* published by the Supreme Administration of the Russian Church abroad, Sremske Karlovtsi (Yugoslavia), No. 7/8, 1924.

53. The events of the confusing days which followed the Patriarch's death up to the final assumption of the duties of the deputy keeper (*locum tenens*) of the patriarchal office by Metropolitan Sergii are to be found in *Tserkovnyi Vedomosti, op. cit. supra* note 52, Nos. 5/6, 9/10, 11/12, p. 6 ff; Stratonov, *op. cit. supra* note 36, pp. 126-130, 150-155, 174-180; Curtis, *op. cit. supra* note 33, p. 27; Polskii, *op. cit. supra* note 45, pp. 27-41; Emhardt, *op. cit. supra* note 34, pp. 141-150; Spinka, *op. cit. supra* note 45, p. 292 ff.

54. *Izvestiia,* Nov. 15, 1925.

55. Polskii, *op. cit. supra* note 45, pp. 27-28; Curtis, *op. cit. supra* note 33, p. 180; Emhardt, *op. cit. supra* note 34, p. 144; Spinka, *op. cit. supra* note 46, p. 310.

56. The alternates were: Metropolitan Michail, exarch of the Ukraine, and Archbishop Josef of Rostov, later of Leningrad. Polskii, *op. cit. supra* note 45, p. 9. When Metropolitan Sergii was arrested in late 1926, the deputy *locum tenens* became Serafim of Uglich who according to Polskii declined to continue in office under the conditions insisted upon by the G.P.U. *op. cit.* p. 13, 15, 30. Emhardt, *op. cit. supra* note 34, p. 146 and Spinka, *op. cit. supra* note 34, p. 311 mention also that Metropolitan Josef and Archbishops Cornelius and Thaddeus succeeded the arrested Sergii but were later also arrested.

57. Curtis, *op. cit. supra* note 33, p. 183.

58. *Ibid.,* p. 182-183.

59. For full translation in English see Emhardt, *op. cit. supra* note 34, p. 146-150.

60. Curtis, *op. cit. supra* note 33, pp. 187, *Izvestiia,* Aug. 19, 1927.

61. Polskii, *op. cit.* note 45, pp. 44-57; Andreev, *Position of the Orthodox Church in the Soviet Union* (in Russian, Jordanville, 1951) passim Alexeev, Wassilij, *Russian Orthodox Bishops in the Soviet Union, 1941-1953,* Research Program on the U.S.S.R., in Russian, mimeographed, N. Y. C. 1954, pp. 58-62, indicates passages in the

Journal of Moscow Patriarchy which suggest the existence of catacomb churches in the Soviet Union.

62. *Izvestiia*, February 16, 1930, W. H. Chamberlin, *Russia's Iron Age*, London, 1936, pp. 323-324.

63. Stalin, *On the Draft of the Constitution of the U.S.S.R.*, Moscow, 1951, p. 17.

64. *Partiinoe stroitelstvo* (in Russian 1939) No. 11 quoted from Timasheff, *op. cit. supra* note 52, p. 98.

65. Yaroslavsky, *On Religious Propaganda* (in Russian 1937); *Pravda*, May 17, 1937; *The Anti-Religious* (in Russian) 1940, No. 2, p. 23.

66. *New York Times*, November 10, 1942; *op. cit. supra* note 23, pp. 15-27, 83-86, 98-111, 168; Curtis, *op. cit. supra* note 33, p. 290 ff.

67. *Vedomosti*, November 2, 1942, No. 40.

68. *Op. cit. supra* note 33, pp. 292, 293; *Izvestiia*, September 5, 1943; *Zhurnal* of the Moscow Patriarchy (in Russian), No. 1, 1943.

69. In October, 1943. *Op. cit. supra* note 21, p. 1788.

70. *Zhurnal* of the Moscow Patriarchy (in Russian), Special No., 1945; Nos. 2, 5, 11, 1949; Nos. 5 and 6, 1950.

Dr. Alois Böhmer, Dr. Stephan Kočvara, and *Dr. Jindřich Nosek*

CHURCH AND STATE IN CZECHOSLOVAKIA

Vladimir Gsovski, *editor*

CHURCH AND STATE IN CZECHOSLOVAKIA

by Dr. Alois Böhmer, Dr. Stephan Kočvara, and Dr. Jindřich Nosek

ABBREVIATIONS

Coll. Law No.—Sbírka zákonů a nařízení—Collection of Laws and Decrees of Czechoslovakia, usually abbreviated in Czech *Sb. z. a nař.* In the text of the report the number is indicated under which the law or decree was printed (*číslo*), which numbering runs consecutively throughout each year.

Law (Decree) No. followed by Arabic numerals—Austrian or Czechoslovak Law or Decree; the Arabic numerals indicate the number (*No.* or *číslo*) under which the law (decree) was printed in RGB1 or Coll.

Law No. following Roman numerals—Hungarian law, the Roman numeral indicated the number under which the law was printed in the annual volume of Országos Törvénytár—Collection of Hungarian Laws.

RGB1—Reichsgesetzblatt für die im Reichsrate vertretenen Königreiche und Länder—Austrian Law gazette.

I. INTRODUCTION

A. *The Formation of Czechoslovakia*

Czechoslovakia was formed in 1918 from former provinces of Austria (Bohemia, Moravia, and Silesia—called the Czech lands), from former provinces of Hungary (Slovakia and Sub-Carpathian Ruthenia), and from a small area of Germany (Upper Silesia).

Simultaneously with the formation of Czechoslovakia, on October 28, 1918, Law No. 11 of 1918 was enacted, by virtue of which the Austrian and Hungarian laws remained in effect in their respective provinces, subject to subsequent repeal or amendment by Czechoslovak legislation. Application of the most important Austrian laws was later extended to the former German area (Law of January 30, 1920, No. 76, and Decree of March 11, 1920, No. 152).

Thus, in fact two jurisdictions did, and to an extent still do exist in Czechoslovakia: the provinces with the heritage of Austrian laws and those with the heritage of Hungarian laws.

Conditions in Sub-Carpathian Ruthenia are not treated in the present study because under the Treaty of June 29, 1945 (Law of November 22, 1945, No. 2 of 1946 Coll.), it was ceded to the Soviet Union and is not at the present time a part of Czechoslovakia.

B. *Background of Religious Life in Czechoslovakia*

1. *Historical Survey*

The Czechoslovak Republic was formed at a time (1918) when after a prolonged struggle the great ideals of freedom of conscience and freedom of religion had gained wide recognition in the free world and had become essential elements of the legal order of the modern democratic state. At first strong efforts were made in Czechoslovakia to put across new and revolutionary ideas concerning the task of the modern state and its relationship to the Churches. However, after long debate in the National Assembly, many of these ideas were rejected and others were accepted only in a far milder form. The history of religious life in the Czech Lands and in Slovakia is reflected in this parliamentary struggle.

Christianity was first introduced into the Czech Lands and into a portion of Slovakia in the ninth century. In an attempt to counteract Franco-German influences, the Moravian princes invited St. Cyril and St. Methodius, then preaching within the Byzantine Empire, to proselytize in the West. But once having accepted Christianity, the Czech Lands were brought into the orbit of Western culture; they became participants in, and suffered from, Western religious conflicts.

The early years of Czech history were marked by the struggle against German expansion, with the Germans frequently utilizing Catholic churches and Catholic missionaries to further the German aims. At the end of the fourteenth century and during the first half of the fifteenth century, conditions within the Roman Catholic Church provoked attempts for Reformation which in the Czech Lands reached their climax in the teaching of Johannes Hus and the subsequent Hussite struggles. This was the beginning of Protestantism and of the fight for religious freedom in the Czech Lands and in Slovakia. This later period was marked by the struggle against the oppressive Hapsburg dynasty, a powerful protector of the Catholic Church. As could be expected, the people's resentment toward their oppressors was sometimes confounded into resentment toward the Church. In general, the fight for religious freedom coincided with the fight against the Hapsburg dynasty, the protector of Catholicism.

The sixteenth and seventeenth centuries were a period of religious conflicts. The revolt of the Czech estates, provoked by the zealous activities of the Hapsburg against the Reformation, was crushed in the battle of the White Mountain in 1620. Thereafter the strictest counter-reformation was imposed, and Roman Catholicism became the only acknowledged confession in the country, despite the fact that before the battle of the White

Mountain approximately nine-tenths of the Czech population was Protestant. Many Protestants, especially among the gentry, went into exile, and the Protestant preachers, including Comenius, were expelled. The new gentry was entirely Catholic.

In the beginning of the eighteenth century the Counter-Reformation received its first check in Slovakia, where because of the opposition of the Hungarian estates, Protestant Churches were again tolerated. It is for this reason that even today in Czechoslovakia, Protestantism has most of its followers in Slovakia (former Hungarian provinces). In the Czech Lands it was not until October 13, 1781, when Emperor Joseph II issued the Patent of Tolerance, that the Lutherans, the Calvinists, and members of the Greek Orthodox Church were legally permitted to worship. However, only about 2 percent of the Czech population returned into the fold of the Protestant churches. In spite of some anti-Vatican movements—i.e., the *Los von Rom* movement at the end of the nineteenth century—Catholicism was overwhelmingly predominant in the Czech Lands before World War I (according to the census of 1910, in Bohemia 95.67 per cent of the people were Catholics, and in Moravia, 95.42 per cent).

In 1855 the Roman Catholic Church entered into a concordat with the Emperor of Austria and thereby gained a privileged position. However, in 1867, in 1874, and at other times the Austrian Government, against the wishes of the Vatican, unilaterally modified its relationship with the Church and interfered with the internal affairs of the Church.

2. Religious Freedom and the Problem of Separation of Church and State

In the second half of the nineteenth century, at last, freedom of conscience was, in general, recognized by both the Austrian and the Hungarian laws. Both protected the so-called "recognized" Churches and guaranteed to them not only the unfettered exercise of faith but also autonomy in their internal organization and all conditions, both spiritual and material, necessary for the normal existence of the Church organism as required by canon law and the rules of the given denomination. In general, the principle of freedom of conscience and tolerance, and not that of the separation of Church and State, governed the status of the Church. The recognized Churches were bodies of public and not of private law; they were protected and supported by the State, not separated from it. Some traces of the former predominant position of the Roman Catholic Church were, however, evident from its status.

After 1918, people in Czechoslovakia were more inclined than before to change their religious affiliations. About 1,400,000 persons left the Roman Catholic Church, nearly half of whom remained without any denomination. The strongest defection from the Church was in Bohemia; it was considerably weaker in Moravia and Silesia. Slovak Catholics, however, remained completely faithful to the Roman Catholic Church. Whereas in 1910 only 12,981 persons in the Czech Lands and in Slovakia were without denomination, by 1921 the number had increased to 724,507, of whom 658,084 were in Bohemia. Persons without denomination consisted mostly of workers organized in the Social-Democratic and Communist Parties and of a part of the intelligentsia in the towns.

In view of these historical developments, it seemed, in the first years of the new Czechoslovak State, that separation of Church and State would be the basis of a new relationship between the State and Church. Many persons saw in this separation the liberation of the State administration from the influence of the Churches, especially from the Catholic Church.

Separation of Church and State was formally proposed in the Declaration of October 18, 1918, more commonly known as the Washington Declaration, in which the basic ideals for the new Czechoslovak State were presented for the first time. President Thomas G. Masaryk favored separation, for he believed that it would best assure freedom of religion (*cf.* Masaryk's message of October 28, 1919 to the meeting of the Revolutionary National Assembly).[1]

But separation of Church and State was never achieved in Czechoslovakia. An insufficiently clear conception of this new arrangement and how it might be achieved and, especially, a respect for popular opinion and wishes, made it impossible to carry out separation. A desire for a marked change in the status of the Church gave way to acquiescence to more traditional arrangements. Although the original draft of Section 121 of the Czechoslovak Constitution prescribed separation, in the end, under the pressure of political considerations, only a general provision for freedom of conscience and religious creed was incorporated.

The Government solved the problem of Church and State relations step by step in a number of special laws modifying to a limited degree the Austro-Hungarian legal order, which continued in force. The legal status of the Churches of various denominations, including the Roman Catholic Church, continued to be governed in the Czech Lands by the Fundamental Law of December 21, 1867, No. 142, and by laws enacted in its implementation; and in Slovakia by several Hungarian laws (_infra,_ p. 16.) Some of the Czechoslovak laws introduced uniform changes for the whole of Czechoslovakia and others affected only a part of the country. Since there were about 21 Churches and larger denominations in Czechoslovakia before World War II, the religious problem was very complex.

3. _Individual Churches and Their Organization_

In the Czech Lands—Bohemia, Moravia, and Silesia—a distinction was made between religious associations (Churches) recognized by the State according to the still valid Austrian regulations, and denominations which were not so recognized and which were regulated by Sections 121 and 122 of the Constitution. Religious associations in this second category did not come under the State's provisions specifically concerned with worship, but were regulated only by other provisions, e.g., those concerning associations, assemblies, societies, and the like.

Among the Churches recognized by the Austrian regulations were the Roman Catholic Church, the Old Catholic Church, the Evangelical Church, and the Israelite community. Within the newly formed Czechoslovakia the legal organization of the Catholic Church remained the same as under Austrian rule.

After 1918 the Evangelicals, however, founded three Churches, all of which were recognized by the State: the Evangelical Church of Czech Brethren, the German Evangelical Church, and the numerically small Augsburg Church of Evangelicals in East Silesia. A new religious association, the Czechoslovak Church, was also recognized by the State (1920). The Roman Catholic Church and the Evangelical Churches received a subsidy from the State fixed by law, whereas the other recognized Churches were subsidized at the discretion of the Government.

In Slovakia and Sub-Carpathian Ruthenia two groups of denominations were recognized by the State. The older denominations were considered as privileged, inasmuch as their relationship with the State was legally secured and they enjoyed its financial support. The Roman Catholic Church, the Greek Catholic Church, the Evangelical Church of the Augsburg Confession, the Reform Church (Calvinists), the Serbian Orthodox Church and Israelite community were in this group. The Churches of the other group were also recognized by the State, but their organizations were restricted and did not enjoy financial support from the State. Included in this group were the Baptist Church, the Czechoslovak Church (1925), and the Evangelical Church of Czech Brethren (1928).

The organization of the Churches in Czechoslovakia is described below.

(a) *The Roman Catholic Church* was organized into two archbishoprics (Prague and Olomouc) and nine dioceses or bishoprics (České Budějovice, Hradec Králové, Litoměřice, Brno, Nitra, Banská Bystrica, Spiš, Rožňava, and Košice). There were two Catholic seminaries, one in Prague and one in Olomouc. The Czechoslovak Government had the right to participate in the nomination of Church dignitaries, but it was obliged to pay the *Kongrua*[2] and to subsidize Church funds.

(b) *The Greek Catholic Church* (Uniates) was only in Slovakia and Sub-Carpathian Ruthenia. It had two eparchies, one in Prešov and one in Mukačevo. (*See* also pp. 269-270, 285).

(c) *The Evangelical Church* was organized, within the several parts of Czechoslovakia, into the following groups:

In the Czech Lands there were three Churches:

(1) The Evangelical Church of Czech Brethren. This had twelve presbyteries and, in 1925, nearly 250,000 members. Its supreme legislative and administrative body was the synod.

(2) The German Evangelical Church. This Church was divided into seven districts; its legislative body was the church assembly; and in 1925 it had about 110,000 members.

(3 The Evangelical Church of the Augsburg Confession. This had only seven parishes and about 40,000 members.

The State Evangelical Divinity School was located in Prague. All Evangelical Churches in the Czech Lands were subsidized by the Czechoslovak Government.

In Slovakia and Sub-Carpathian Ruthenia there were two Evangelical Churches:

(1) The Evangelical Church of the Augsburg Confession. This was divided into two bishoprics, eastern and western, and had more than 350,000 members. Its legislative body was the General Synod, and it had its academy of divinity in Bratislava.

(2) The Reform Church (Calvinist). With more than 200,000 members, this Church was divided into three districts and its legislative body was called the General Synod.

(d) *The Czechoslovak Church* was formed in 1920. Its members were Czechs who were dissatisfied with the Catholic Church, which in the period immediately following World War I sometimes bore the brunt of resentment against the Hapsburg dynasty. The Czechoslovak Church was recognized by the State in the Czech Lands in 1920 and later, in 1925, in Slovakia and Sub-Carpathian Ruthenia. It was divided into four dioceses, each having a bishop; and the bishop in Prague was made patriarch and head of the Church. In 1925 the Czechoslovak Church had approximately 750,000 members. The State was not under obligation to subsidize it.

All matters concerning public worship in Czechoslovakia came within the jurisdiction of the Ministry of Education and National Culture.

4. Statistics on Religious Denominations in Czechoslovakia (1921 and 1930)

According to the census of 1921 and the census of 1930, the membership of the various religious denominations in Czechoslovakia was as follows:

Census of 1921

Total Population	. . .	13,613,172
Roman Catholics	. . .	10,384,833
Greek Catholics	. . .	535,543
Evangelicals	. . .	990,319
Greek Orthodox	. . .	73,097
Czechoslovak Church	. . .	525,333
Israelites	. . .	354,342
Without Denomination	. .	724,507

Census of 1930

Total Population . . . 14,729,536

Roman Catholics . . . 10,831,696 (73.54 per cent)
(in Moravia and Slovakia: 85.88 ” ”)
Greek Catholics (Uniates) . . 585,041 (3.97 ” ”)
(359,167 in Sub-Carpathian Ruthenia: 49.52 ” ”)
Evangelicals . . . 1,129,758 (7.67 ” ”)
(555,900 in Slovakia: 16.69 ” ”)
Greek Orthodox (Pravoslavni) . . 145,598 (0.99 ” ”)
(112,034 in Sub-Carpathian Ruthenia: 15.44 ” ”)
Czechoslovak Church . . . 793,385 (5.39 ” ”)
(618,305 in Bohemia: 8.70 ” ”)
Israelites . . . 356,830 (2.42 ” ”)
(in Slovakia: 4.11 ” ”)
(in Sub-Carpathian Ruthenia: 14.14 ” ”)
Without Denomination . . 854,638 (5.80 ” ”)
(727,916 in Bohemia: 10.24 ” ”)

C.   Basic Provisions of the Former Austrian and Hungarian Laws

1.   Austrian Laws

Although the Austrian Government entered into a concordat with the Holy See in 1855, several of its provisions were unilaterally denounced by the Austrian Government through a series of laws enacted in 1867 and 1868, and finally it was repealed by the Law of May 7, 1874, No. 50. Thus, on the eve of the formation of Czechoslovakia the following laws were in effect and remained in force until replaced by the laws of the Communist government:

The Austrian Law of December 21, 1867, No. 142, which declared absolute freedom of religion and conscience. Free public exercise of faith was guaranteed to all Churches or religious communities recognized by the State. The law preserved their autonomy in the administration of internal affairs. The Churches continued to be in possession of their institutions, foundations, and funds established for cultural, educational, and charitable purposes, subject only to the general laws to which all associations were subject.

The law also declared freedom of scholarly research and publication. Every citizen who met certain requirements fixed by law was allowed to open schools and educational institutions and to teach in them. The teaching of religion in schools was said to be the duty and privilege of the Churches and religious associations concerned.

The Law of May 25, 1868, No. 47, allowing civil marriage in some instances (see *infra,* p. 32) and establishing the jurisdiction of civil courts in cases involving marital relations.

The Law of May 25, 1868, No. 48, defining the status of the Churches with regard to education. The Churches were entitled to conduct and supervise religious instruction in the public elementary and secondary schools. But any recognized Church was also free to establish and maintain with its own funds schools for the education of youth professing that particular religion. These schools were subject to the general laws on education and to requirements established by law in order to obtain an officially recognized status.

Law No. 49 of 1868 for regulating interdenominational relations, as amended in 1920 by the Czechoslovak Law of April 15, 1920, No. 277, and superseded by the Law of April 23, 1925, No. 96.

The Law of May 7, 1874, No. 51, which regulated the contribution to funds for the support of the Roman Catholic Church.

The Law of May 20, 1874, No. 68, which regulated the requirements which the new denominations should meet to obtain the status of a Church recognized by the government.

2. *Hungarian Laws*

Hungarian laws continued to be in force in Slovakia; a survey of these laws is to be found in the report on Hungary.

II. CZECHOSLOVAK LEGISLATION ON RELIGION, ENACTED BEFORE 1938

A. *Constitutional Provisions*

Czechoslovak legislation carried even further the principles of complete freedom of conscience and tolerance as embodied in the Austrian legislation. With regard to religion, the Constitution provided as follows:

> *Sec. 117* (1) Every person may express his or her opinion by word, in writing, in print, by picture, et cetera, within the limits of the law.
> (2) The same applies to legal entities within the limits of their competence.
> (3) No one shall suffer in the sphere of his work or employment for exercising this right.
> *Sec. 121* Liberty of conscience and religion is guaranteed.
> *Sec. 122* All inhabitants of the Czechoslovak Republic enjoy in the same degree as the citizens of the Republic the right to profess and exercise publicly and privately any creed, religion, or faith

whatsoever, so far as the exercise of the same is not in conflict with public law and order or with morality.

Sec. 123 No one shall be compelled either directly or indirectly to take part in any religious rite or ceremony whatsoever, rights pertaining to paternal or custodial authority being nevertheless respected.

Sec. 124 All religious denominations shall be equal before the law.

Sec. 125 The performance of specific religious rites may be prohibited if they are in conflict with public order or public morals.

B. *Other Laws*

The Law of April 15, 1920, No. 277, superseded by the Law of 1925, No. 96, provided:

Sec. 1 (1) The parents of a child shall have the right to specify its religion within 14 days of its birth, or to leave the child without denomination.

The Law of April 23, 1925, No. 96, concerning the mutual relations of religious denominations states:

Sec. 1 (1) Children who are born in marriage or who enjoy equivalent rights shall follow their parents in denomination when both parents are of the same denomination. In case of a mixed marriage, children of the male sex shall follow the denomination of their fathers; children of the female sex [shall follow the denomination] of their mothers. Parents may, however, determine by agreement that the religion of their children should be in the reverse order, or determine to which denomination their children should belong. The denomination of children born out of wedlock shall be that of their mother. If the parents are unknown, the denomination of a child shall be determined by the person who has the right to bring up the child.

(2) The preceding provisions shall not apply if the persons having the right thereto shall determine another religious denomination for the child within 14 days from its birth. The following persons shall have this right: for children born in wedlock, both parents, when they are in agreement; for those born out of wedlock, the mother; for orphan children, the surviving parent, or the legal guardian of the child, if both parents are dead. This determination shall occur by virute of an announcement of entry in the register of births.

(3) Agreements made with anyone concerning the denomination of children shall be invalid.

Sec. 15 The status "without denomination" shall also be considered as religious denomination within the meaning of the present Law.

Moreover, the Czechoslovak laws declared the right of every

citizen not only to choose a denomination but also to be officially registered as having no religious denomination (*bez vyznání*). During this period several religious denominations obtained the status of a recognized religion as a consequence of this policy.

The only essential change took place with regard to marriage and divorce. In this respect there was a difference between the law of the Czech Lands and that of Slovakia, which difference was eliminated by the Czechoslovak legislation (see *infra* III).

Optional cremation was enacted by the Law of 1919, No. 180.

Certain changes took place with reference to the financial support of ministers of religion by the government, the so-called *Kongrua*. It is more suitable to discuss this in connection with the provisions of Law No. 218 of 1949 (*infra* III).

Thus, in the main, the status of the Church in the Czech Lands continued to be governed by Austrian law and in Slovakia by Hungarian law. Some particulars about these laws are given *infra* under III.

C. *Special Laws for Slovakia*

The situation in Slovakia called for special legislation. A portion of the Roman Catholic clergy in Slovakia met the creation of Czechoslovakia with misgivings and did not display the expected loyalty to the new regime. Moreover, the new frontier severed some dioceses from their seats in Hungary. This situation raised, among other things, the question of the administration of Church property located in Slovakia but subject to the jurisdiction of authorities now situated across the border. These problems, together with some others, were regulated by the Law of December 10, 1918, No. 64. The officials of the central and local government and the officials and dignitaries of the Church were temporarily allowed to continue in their offices provided that they delivered a pledge of loyalty to the Czechoslovak Government. Appeals from the decisions of authorities or courts in Slovakia filed with these officials were to be held up pending further orders if they were subject to decision by the appellate authorities located across the new border.

A Central Board for the management of Church property located in Slovakia was established by the Decree of August 11, 1919, of the Minister for the Administration of Slovakia. These problems were ultimately settled as described below.

D. *The Agreement between the Czechoslovak Government and the Holy See* (Modus Vivendi)

By an agreement of 1928 between the Czechoslovak Government and the Holy See it was determined that no part of Czechoslovakia would be subject to the authority of a bishop abroad. The boundaries of the dioceses were to be established by agreement. The management of the Church properties was assigned to a central board subordinated to the Slovak Episcopate. Any disposition or alienation of such property requiring the approval of the bishop under the existing laws was subject to the approval of the Slovak Episcopate. Homes of monastic orders in Czechoslovakia were not subject to the authority of superiors of the same order residing abroad.

The Holy See agreed to appoint archbishops, diocesan bishops, coadjutors *cum iure successionis,* and army chaplains from among Czechoslovak citizens and to communicate the names of the candidates to the Czechoslovak Government to afford the latter the opportunity of raising objections. The appointed prelates were to take the pledge of loyalty to the Czechoslovak Government. It reads:

> *Juro et promitto sicuti decet Episcopum fidelitatem Reipublicae Cechoslovacae necnon nihil me facturum quod sit contra salutem, securitatem, integritatem Reipublicae.*

The Czechoslovak Government agreed to adjust the existing legal provisions to the *modus vivendi* without delay.

III. COMMUNIST LEGISLATION
REGARDING RELIGION

A. *General Survey*

There is no need to analyze any enactment of the period of subjugation, which extends from September 30, 1938, to May 4, 1945, because after the liberation such enactments were declared not to be an element of the Czechoslovak legal order (Law No. 12 of 1946). Czechoslovakia was to return to its pre-Munich laws. Until the Communists seized power on February 25, 1948, new legislation did not affect the status of the Churches. Furthermore, until October 1949, the Communists refrained from any general enactment defining the status of the Church in their State.

However, by the Law of April 21, 1948, the Churches were deprived of the right to have their own schools (Law No. 95) and by the Law of March 21, 1948, land owned and possessed by them was seized (Law No. 46).

With regard to agricultural land, the local People's Farmer's Committees were authorized to leave not more than 30 *ha* (about 70 acres) for one parish for the upkeep of the parish clergy (but not for the higher clergy) (Section 1, subsection 3, at the end).

It may also be mentioned that under the laws concerning the nationalization of industry (Presidential Decrees Nos. 100 and 101 of 1945 and Laws Nos. 114 and 115 of 1948, etc.) the Church lost practically all its profit-yielding enterprises.

The Government began to interfere with Church affairs, directing its attack primarily against the Roman Catholic Church for the purpose of bringing it under control. This policy did not appear in the form of a law or decree until October 14, 1949. Then several laws were enacted by which a special Government Bureau for Church Affairs was established as a device for controlling the Churches (Law No. 217 and Decree No. 228 of 1949). Clergymen were required to take a loyalty pledge and were placed on the government payroll under the authority of the said Bureau (Law No. 218 and Decrees 219-223 of 1949). The religious marriage ceremony was deprived of any legal effect (Law of December 7, 1949, No. 265) and the keeping of civil status records (vital statistics) was taken away from the Church in the Czech Lands (Law No. 268, *infra* p. 34).

The Roman Catholic Episcopate took steps against the Government's planned interference and against its imposition of control over Church matters by presenting a petition to President Gottwald on October 21, 1949 (see Chapter IV). The Episcopate stated therein its attitude towards the new legislation and courageously pointed out that new laws and decrees violated the religious rights and liberties of the Czechoslovak people. The petition, however, had no success.

Taken as a whole, the provisions of these laws show a far-reaching program of complete abolition of Church autonomy, which was replaced by the authority of an atheistic Communist Government.

B. *Survey of the New Legislation by Topics*

1. *The Banning of Denominational Schools*

The principle announced in the Constitution, Sec. 13, that "all schools shall be State schools" was developed by the Basic Law Concerning the Schools of April 21, 1948, No. 95. Section 4 of the law reads:

(1) The schools shall be educational institutions of the State.
(2) Exceptions from the provisions of Subsection (1) shall be established by law.

The meaning of these provisions is even clearer in the light of the report introducing the law to the National Assembly, which reads:

This stipulation abolishes all present provisions relating to the establishment of private schools and any exceptions [from this rule] are reserved to a future law.

No special law making an exception for schools maintained by the Churches was enacted. Thus, the Churches were deprived of their schools.

2. *The Government Bureau for Church Affairs*

Beginning with October 14, 1949, a series of laws was enacted in order to subject the Churches, the Catholic Church in particular, to the control of the government.

The Law of October 14, 1949, No. 217, provides for the establishment of a Government Bureau for Church Affairs as the central governmental authority for these matters. According to the Law, a member of the Cabinet was to be assigned by the President of the Republic to direct the Bureau. This provision was amended by the Cabinet Decree of January 31, 1953, No. 6 Coll. to the effect that the President should appoint the Chairman of the Bureau from persons outside the Cabinet.

The law defines the purpose of the Bureau in rather general terms, not disclosing its real function. A Cabinet Decree of October 25, 1949, No. 228, implementing this law, however, makes its function clear.

Law No. 217 states that the purpose of the Government Bureau for Church Affairs "shall be to see to it that Church life and religious life develop in accordance with the Constitution and principles of the people's democratic order." (Sec. 2). The provisions of the Constitution of 1948 relating to the Church differ but slightly from those of the Constitution of 1920. However, neither in the Constitution nor in any law is it made clear what the "principles of the people's democratic order" exactly mean, and therefore the Government is at liberty to interpret them at will.

The Cabinet Decree No. 228, Sec. 2, contains a detailed enumeration of the powers conferred upon the Government Bureau for Church Affairs. This enumeration, though only exemplary, shows the broad power of the Bureau to control all religious life, excepting only the Church ritual. The Government Bureau for Church Affairs has complete direction and control of all matters pertaining to Church and religion: Personnel matters and emoluments of clergymen; administrative and economic matters of Churches, religious associations and religious establishments; supervision of Church and property and property rights; teaching of religion; approval of textbooks; evaluation of the ecclesiastical press and publications; charitable activities, and others. (Decree No. 228, Sec. 2).

In Slovakia the activities of the Government Bureau for Church Affairs are performed by the Slovak Bureau for Church Affairs, the chairman of which is appointed by the Cabinet (Cabinet Decree of January 31, 1953, No. 7 Coll.).

In the provinces and counties the Government Bureau for Church Affairs acts through the local People's Committees, which in this field are subordinate to it. Within the Provincial People's Committees special Church Sections were established to carry out this function.

3. Church Sections of the Provincial People's Committees

Of particular importance in this connection is the Proclamation of May 12, 1950, No. 320, Official Gazette (*Úřední list* I) which created Church Sections of the Provincial People's Committees (See Appendix).

The proclamation gave the Church Sections full control of religious life and Church affairs in the provinces. The Church Sections have the right to inspect all activities of Churches and religious associations. Their approval is needed for the creation of new parishes, congregations, religious communities, and the changing of their boundaries (Subsec. 6). They approve the appointment of lower clergy to posts established with the consent of the Government, and handle the removal of those who have become ineligible for such posts (Subsec. 6). They decide all interdenominational matters. Church Sections control all property owned by Churches or religious bodies, congregations or associations, exercise full control over their financial affairs, administer financial affairs of the members of the clergy, and grant salaries and personal emoluments, additional remunerations, rank allowances, efficiency bonuses, and leave to members of the clergy (Subsec. 20).

Particularly wide are the powers of the Church Sections in the teaching of religion and the training of priests. In order to provide proper indoctrination of the clergy Church Sections supervise the activities of theological schools and seminaries, and control the appointment of teachers and technical workers to these institutions (Subsec. 9). Church Sections are charged with censorship of the religious and Church press and radio broadcasts. Even the social and charitable work of Churches and religious associations is subject to supervision and coordination by the Church Sections.

4. Appointment of Clergymen

The Law of October 14, 1949, No. 218, and the decrees issued in its implementation on October 18, 1949, Nos. 219-223, bear a rather harmless title, namely, Decrees to Provide Economic Security to Churches and Religious Associations through the Government. Decree No. 219 deals with the Roman Catholic Church.

While the law and the decrees profess to deal with "economic security," they do so only insofar as they provide for emoluments of the clergy and current expenses connected with the upkeep of Churches. Their real effect, however, is to give the Government complete control over the material conditions necessary for the existence of the Churches and to establish the decisive influence of the Government upon the appointment of clergymen and the system of Church organization.

It is true that clergymen are declared to be employees of the Church and not of the State. However, no clergyman may perform his duties without the consent of the Government (Law No. 218, Sec. 7, Subsec. 1; Decree No. 219, Sec. 16), and governmental consent to every appointment must be obtained in advance (Law No. 218, Sec. 7, Subsec. 2; Decree No. 219, Sec. 17). Furthermore, they must satisfy "all general requirements for employment with the government" (Law No. 218, Sec. 2; Decree No. 219, Sec. 7).

Thus, the consent of the Government is required before any clergyman may exercise his profession. To eliminate any doubt, Decree No. 219 states that this applies to clergymen with or without monastic vows performing strictly religious functions (Sec. 2), to clergymen active in Church administration (in consistories or as members of chapters) (Sec. 3), and to teachers at the theological schools (Sec. 4). Sec. 7 of Law No. 218 expressly stipulates that only those who have obtained the consent of the Government may exercise the activities of a minister of religion in a Church or religious association. Sec. 16 of Decree No. 219 expressly requires that the clergymen must ask for such consent. The consent is given for clergymen of Classes I and II by the provincial People's Committees; for clergymen of Class III, by the Government Bureau for Church Affairs; and for those of Class IV (archbishops, diocesan bishops and apostolic administrators), by the Cabinet.

Furthermore, Government consent to appointments is required. The consent is given by the same authorities which gave consent for the clergyman to exercise his profession (Law No. 218, Sec. 7, Subsec. 2; Decree No. 219, Sec. 17). The appointment may be made only to positions established with the consent of the Government. Positions so established are those which were declared such by the Governmental Bureau for Church Affairs (Sec. 5, Decree No. 219). In doing so, the Bureau shall consult the competent Church authorities, but is not bound to follow their opinion. The consent of the Government is also needed for the establishment of new positions. If the position was filled without the consent of the Government, it is considered vacant and the clergyman appointed does not receive emoluments from the Government (Decree No. 219, Sec. 18). The vacant positions must be filled by the Church authorities within 30 days; otherwise the Government is authorized to take steps "to ensure the performance of the strictly religious functions, Church administration, or theological teaching assigned to the post." In other words, the Government proceeds in such cases as an administrative Church authority. In this connection the provision of Section 30 of Decree No. 219 concerning the exercise of patronage may be noted. There it is expressly stated that the Government exercises patronage by nominating parish priests. The applications for a vacant prebend are to be sent to the consistory, which submits all of them to the Government with a designation of those applicants whom the consistory does not consider as suitable for nomination. The Government nominates its candidate from among the applicants who were not eliminated. The Church authority is, however, bound to appoint the nominee. If it does not do so within the fixed time, it is considered that the office has been conferred upon the nominee. This curious stipulation practically means that the Government may enforce the appointment of its candidate.

Finally, consent may be granted by the Government only to ministers of religion who are Czechoslovak citizens, politically reliable, irreproachable, and otherwise meet the general requirements for employment with the Government. In exceptional cases, however, the requirement of citizenship may be waived (Sec. 2 of Law No. 218 and Sec. 7 of Decree No. 219).

5. *The Loyalty Pledge*

A pledge of loyalty is required from one who is performing religious functions. The pledge reads as follows:

> I promise on my honor and conscience to be faithful to the Czechoslovak Republic and to its people's democratic order, and I shall not undertake anything contrary to its interests, security and integrity. As a citizen of a people's democratic State, I shall conscientiously perform the duties inherent in my office and I shall do everything within my ability to support the efforts at [social] reconstruction for the welfare of the people (Decree No. 219, Sec. 19).

It may be observed that the Czech text of the concluding phrase of the oath which is translated above as "efforts at [social] reconstruction" is rather enigmatic.—*Budovatelské úsilí* literally translated simply means "efforts at construction." However, being frequently used by the Communists, it has acquired a specific, defined meaning. It actually means the Communist effort for the reconstruction of society along the lines of their program. The use of it in the text of oath shows the desire of the legislator to avoid spelling out the requirement of support by the clergy of the Communist efforts by couching it in a veiled wording.

The pledge is given to the chairman of the competent People's Committee. The higher clergymen (dignitaries of chapters, vicars-general, vicars of chapters, suffragans, and abbots) give the pledge to the chairman of the Government Bureau for Church

Affairs, and the archbishops, bishops of dioceses, and apostolic administrators give it to the Prime Minister.

6.   Church Property

The Government supervises the property of the Church (Law No. 218, Sec. 10). It supervises the economic activities of the Church and its approval is required for all important transactions involving Church property (Decree No. 219, Sec. 27).

7.   Patronage

All private or public patronage of Churches, prebends, and other ecclesiastical institutions has passed over to the Government (Law No. 218, Sec. 11). All obligations to contribute to the Church, communities, institutions, foundations, church buildings, prebends, and funds based on patronage, other legal reasons, or on long-standing customs, have ceased.

8.   Emoluments of Clergymen

Law No. 218 states that the Government is to grant emoluments to clergymen who, with its consent, either perform strictly religious functions or are employed in Church administration or establishments for the training of clergymen. However, it authorizes the Government Bureau for Church Affairs, in exceptional cases, to grant emoluments to clergymen who are engaged in other activities (Sec. 1).

Decree No. 219 determines the salaries of clergymen and their allocations. They correspond, on the whole, to the salaries of civil servants. It may be noted, however, that the decree provides for a special reward which may be granted to clergymen for exceptional work, for their public activity and "for their cooperation in the effort at [social] reconstruction of the working people" (Sec. 8, Subsec. 2).

The Government also compensates clergymen for the expense of their official travels. But each journey must be reported in advance to the county People's Committee (Decree No. 219, Sec. 13).

Until November 1949, the Churches and religious associations

paid their ministers of religion from their own funds. These
salaries were supplemented by the Government treasury up to a
sum fixed by Law No. 246 of 1920, Law No. 122 of 1926,
Law No. 116 of 1945, and Law No. 167 of 1946. These subventions, so-called *Kongrua*, were paid only to clergymen who
were Czechoslovak citizens and were holding posts (offices)
established with the consent of the Government. But the laws
concerning the *Kongrua* did not in any way affect the rights of
the Church, particularly the right of administrative autonomy
and property rights. In contrast to this situation, the Churches,
under the laws issued by the Communist Government, have been
deprived of practically all properties helping to defray expenditures for upkeep and personnel, and for education and charity.
Thus, financial support by the State progressed from a supple-
mentary to a main source of revenue. The Government assumed
some obligation to render such support, but at the price of
depriving the Church of all its independent major sources of
revenue and subjecting the administration of the Church to the
Government.

9.   Current Expenses

The Government may defray some expenses of upkeep but
there are several conditions attached thereto. The Government
has undertaken to defray such expenses only insofar as they are
not covered by the Church's own revenues. Moreover, in order
to obtain the appropriation from the Government, each diocesan
consistory must submit a budget of the diocese and its parishes
to the Government Bureau for Church Affairs for approval.
Decree No. 219 describes in detail what is considered as expenses
for upkeep subject to Government defrayal (Decree No. 219,
Secs. 22-26).

10.   Duty to Teach Religion

The clergymen in the ecclesiastical offices must teach religion,
without remuneration, at elementary and secondary schools
where a special teacher of religion is not available.

11. Schools of Theology

The Government also maintains the schools of theology and seminaries (Law No. 218 of 1949, Sec. 12).

The teaching of religion in public schools was first governed by the Law on Schools of April 21, 1948, No. 95, Sec. 19 of which follows:

> Sec. 19 (1) The school must provide for the religious instruction of children in accordance with their religious denomination, with the exception of cases where the parents (persons authorized by law to represent the child) renounce such instruction.
>
> (2) Religious instruction shall be given and its control exercised by Church authorities (religious communities) without prejudice to the right of supreme control and direction, which shall be reserved to the Ministry of Education (Sec. 7).
>
> (3) The syllabus of religious instruction shall be established by the Ministry of Education, on the proposal of the Church authorities (religious communities); this Ministry shall examine the syllabus from the point of view of civil and religious tolerance.
>
> (4) Teachers of religion (Church authorities and religious communities) shall observe the regulations issued by the school authorities according to the statute.
>
> (5) Religious instruction must be in accord with the educational activity of the school.

It should be noted that Subsec's. 2 and 3 of Sec. 19 were superseded by Decree No. 228 of 1949, which considerably tightened governmental control of religious teaching and transferred it from the Ministry of Education to the Government Bureau for Church Affairs. Section 2, Clause "f" of this Decree stipulates that the jurisdiction of the Government Bureau for Church Affairs shall embrace regulations for the teaching of religion, approval of the syllabuses, textbooks, equipment and devices, and general supervision, in agreement with the Ministry of Education, Science and Art, over the teaching of religion and over denominational educational institutions of any kind.

The Cabinet Decree of July 14, 1950, No. 121 goes even further in the governmental effort to control the teaching of religion. It claims to regulate the salaries of lay teachers of religion, but as a matter of fact it does more. Although the teaching of religion by laymen had existed for several years in Czechoslovakia, it was limited to the few places where a clergyman was not available. Lay teachers were chosen exclusively by the respective church authorities and approval by the Government was no more than a formality. This was changed by Cabinet Decree No. 121, which considerably reduced the function of Church authorities in the appointment of lay teachers of religion. Section 3, Subsection 1 reads:

> Teachers of religion shall be appointed within the framework of the approved plan of employment after the Church authority of the respective denomination has been heard.

Thus the appointment of teachers of religion is completely in the hands of the Government Bureau for Church Affairs, which may or may not take into consideration the suggestions of the Church authorities.

As for the qualifications required for a teacher of religion, Section 4, Subsec. 2 contains the following characteristic provision: "Only a teacher who has proved his *higher political ability,* and higher special knowledge, and has had good results in his work, shall be eligible for the higher grade of the basic salary." (Italics supplied). There is no doubt that this provision is another efficient tool in the efforts of the Government to restrain the influence of Churches and, in particular, of the Roman Catholic Church.

Simultaneously with the above quoted Cabinet Decree No. 121 which regulates the financial status of lay teachers of religion, Cabinet Decree No. 112 of July 14, 1950, provided for a substantial reduction and centralization of schools of theology.

The decree provides that Roman Catholic study of theology shall be conducted in only two schools of theology, one in Prague and the other in Bratislava; all other Roman Catholic schools of theology are to be abolished. It is noteworthy that the government gave an identical name to both of these schools: "Cyril and Methodius Roman Catholic School of Theology." The use of the name of these "Apostles of the Slavs" who brought Christianity to Moravia and Bohemia from Constantinople seems to stress that Christianity did not come to Czechs from the West.

Likewise it was stipulated that the study of Evangelical theology should be conducted in three divinity schools: two in Prague, and the third in Bratislava.

A divinity school was to be established in Prague for Greek Orthodox theological teaching.

The schools of theology and the divinity schools are to be headed by the Dean and the Council of the Faculty, members of which shall be representatives of the teaching body of the faculty, of the respective Church, and of the students. The Dean and his deputy are appointed by the Chairman of the Government Bureau for Church Affairs (Sec. 5, Subsec. 2). The Dean is responsible to the chairman for the activities of the family (Sec. 5, Subsec. 3).

Other pertinent provisions of Cabinet Decree No. 112 are as follows:

> Sec. 4—Subsec. 2. The Government shall jointly with the Churches, see to it that the instruction of students of theology is carried out *in the people's democratic spirit* and in accordance with the principles of the Church. (Italics supplied).
>
> Sec. 9 (1) Students shall be accepted by theological faculties according to the abilities of the applicants and with regard to the planned needs of Churches and religious communities.
>
> Sec. 9 (2) Plans of studies and examinations, statutes, syllabi, and rules for admission of students, shall be decreed by the Government Bureau for Church Affairs, which shall take into consideration proposals of the Council of the Faculty and of representatives of the respective Churches.

The provisions concerning the schools of theology and the teaching of religion, quoted above, show a clear tendency:

(a) to restrain the influence of Churches and religious communities in schools of theology and in the teaching of religion;

(b) to tighten the control of the Government, which gradually takes over the rights reserved to the Churches regarding schools of theology and the teaching of religion;

(c) to infiltrate the schools of theology and the teaching of religion with Communist political doctrine.

12. Penal Provisions

The Law No. 218 of 1949 penalizes any act or omission

contrary to the law or to other legal provisions based on it. Offenses are punished by the administrative authorities by a fine not to exceed 100,000 Czechoslovak crowns, and, if the fine is not collectible, by imprisonment not to exceed six months. These provisions seem to be superseded by the new Criminal Code of July 12, 1950 (Law No. 86, Coll. 1950). This code and the new Criminal Code for Administrative Authorities contain the following provisions with regard to the Church:

(a) Criminal Code of 1950.

Sec. 173 (1) Whoever performs pastoral functions in a Church or religious association without governmental consent shall be punished by confinement not to exceed three years.

(2) Whoever performs pastoral functions in a Church or religious association at a post for which he was not appointed with governmental consent shall be punished in like manner.

(3) Whoever, without governmental consent, appoints another for performance of pastoral functions in a Church or religious association, shall be punished by confinement for from one year to five years.

Sec. 174 (1) Whoever intentionally frustrates or obstructs governmental supervision over a Church or religious association shall be punished by confinement for from one year to five years.

(2) Whoever intentionally violates the provisions of laws affording Governmental protection of Churches and religious associations in any other manner shall be punished in like manner.

(b) Criminal Code for Administrative Authorities of 1950.

Sec. 101: Protection of Order in Church Affairs. Whoever does not discharge his duties or violates a prohibition pertinent to the legal relations of Churches or religious associations; in particular, whoever endangers or interferes with the execution of supervision over the property of Churches or religious associations; shall be punished by a fine not to exceed 100,000 crowns or by confinement not to exceed three months.

13. Marriage and Divorce

For a marriage to be valid, the law of the Czech Lands (Austrian General Civil Code, Sec. 75) originally required the celebration of a religious ceremony according to the rules of the religion of the two parties. Law No. 47 of 1868 introduced civil marriage, but it was allowed only in cases where the minister of a recognized religion refused to perform the marriage ceremony for reasons not stated in the Civil Code (Art. II). Civil marriage was also introduced by Law No. 51 of 1870 for persons not belonging to any religion recognized by the State.

In contrast to the restricted role of civil marriage in the Czech Lands, civil marriage was the only marriage with legal effect in Slovakia (Hungarian Law No. XXXI of 1894, Secs. 28 through 40). This difference was removed by the Czechoslovak Law of May 22, 1919, No. 320, according to which a religious or civil marriage ceremony was equally valid throughout Czechoslovakia. Thus, civil marriage was introduced in the Czech Lands and religious marriage in Slovakia as optional forms. Divorce was not allowed to Roman Catholics under the law of the Czech Lands, but it was open to them in Slovakia. Law No. 320 of 1919, Sec. 13, allowed divorce for reasons stated therein to all citizens, regardless of their religion. The procedure was also made more uniform (Law No. 113 of 1924).

The Law on Domestic Relations of December 7, 1949, No. 265, introduced the civil form of marriage uniformly for all Czechoslovakia, beginning on January 1, 1950.

> Law No. 265 of 1949:
> Sec. 1. Marriage shall be contracted by the man's and woman's declaration to enter into marriage made before the local People's Committee. If this declaration of the betrothed that they consent has not been made before the local People's Committee, no marriage shall come into being.
> Sec 7. Religious celebration of marriage shall be allowed; however, it may take place only upon the contracting of the marriage in accordance with the provisions of the present Law.

The same law has also changed the provisions concerning divorce, for which the law uses the term *rozvod,* equivalent to separation in the previous law, and not *rozluka,* hitherto used to designate divorce.

Divorce is granted, not on grounds specified by law as was required by Sec. 13 of Law No. 320 of 1919, but on grounds to be determined according to the discretion of the court. This is evident from the following provisions:

Part Three—Divorce
Sec. 30. (1) If, for serious reasons, a deep and lasting discord has
developed between the spouses, a spouse may petition the court
to terminate the marriage by divorce.

It may also be mentioned that vital statistics were kept by
the local Government only in Slovakia; in the Czech Lands they
were kept primarily by the Churches. The Law of December 7,
1949, No. 268, on Civil Registry Records (Vital Statistics)
changed this situation by requiring that all such records be kept
by the local People's Committees. All records kept by the
Churches became Government property and had to be turned
over to the People's Committees on January 1, 1950.

IV.   THE ROMAN CATHOLIC CLERGY AND THE
NEW LEGISLATION

Before enacting new laws and decrees, beginning with October
14, 1949, the Czechoslovak Government sought to obtain the
consent of the Roman Catholic bishops to its new Church
policy. When the dignitaries of the Church showed their un-
willingness, the government set its whole propaganda machinery
in motion, accusing these dignitaries of subversive acts against
the State and of refusing to enter into an agreement. Thus the
bishops felt compelled to inform the faithful of their point of
view in a pastoral letter (June 15, 1949). Some excerpts from
this letter are quoted below. (See Chapter VI.)

The Cabinet rejected the conditions, as outlined in this pastoral letter, under which the Roman Catholic bishops were willing to come to terms with the Government. On October 14,
1949, it had the National Assembly pass the laws and issued the
decrees (see Chapter V) without regard to the opposition of the
Church representatives.

The Roman Catholic Episcopate made one further attempt

to deflect the Government from its anti-Church policy by presenting the Petition of October 21, 1949, which states:

The new legal status of Churches established by the recently enacted laws on Churches concerning the establishment of the Government Bureau for Church Affairs and economic security for Churches and religious associations introduced by the Government has induced the bishops and the Roman Catholic ordinaries to express their attitude towards the said laws. We, therefore, submit to the Government of the Czechoslovak Republic, pursuant to Article 23 of the Constitution of the Czechoslovak Republic of May 9, 1948, the following Petition:

The new laws and the decrees enforcing them violate directly and indirectly the religious rights and liberties of the Czechoslovak people, which are guaranteed by the Constitution, because they are designed to serve as a basis for justifying and strengthening the measures hitherto taken in order to infringe upon the rights of the Church and to restrict liberty.

1) We state that the maintenance of the organization of the Roman Catholic Church and the fulfillment of her mission are guaranteed neither by the present state of affairs nor by the general provisions of the law dealing with the status of the Church. On the contrary, the legal order in force until now, even though not entirely favorable to the Church, has now been radically changed, so that the Roman Catholic Church in our country has been put outside the law.

The new legal status of the Church constitutes a drastic violation of international rules concerning the affairs of the Church, [rules] which have been in force in our country up to the present time by virtue of agreements concluded between the Church and the State, and which are necessary for good relations between the two.

2) The Church has been deprived of her freedom to ordain, which was based on her constitution and organization; and the Government has usurped for itself the right to interfere in the future with the appointment of clergymen to ecclesiastical posts— and the right to refuse, for ideological and political reasons, its approval of the appointment of a clergyman to an ecclesiastical office. This is contrary to the fundamental provisions of the Constitution of the Czechoslovak Republic concerning freedom of religion because the concept of freedom of religion also includes the freedom of the internal organization of the Church.

3) In spite of the fact that priests will retain the position of Church employees in the future, the Government has unilaterally assumed the right to regulate their conditions of service in accordance with the regulations on Government employees. This is a

violation of the fundamental right of the Church, which has the exclusive power to appoint priests to ecclesiastical offices.

4) The law establishing the Government Bureau for Church Affairs refuses to respect the power of the Church to regulate matters of faith, morals, rite, discipline, religious education, and Church membership in accordance with laws in force. On the contrary, it gives the Bureau the right of unrestricted interference in ecclesiastical and religious matters. The present state of affairs fails to safeguard the freedom to profess religion; on the contrary, the Government authorities have made the act of professing one's own religion, by the very fact of belonging to the Church, in danger of becoming difficult or impossible.

5) The purpose of the laws is to eliminate obsolete remnants of feudalism from ecclesiastical law. We are struck by the fact that simultaneously with these laws, a new feudal institution—State patronage—is introduced. Ecclesiastical law firmly rejects the creation of the new patronage as a medieval relic. It must be mentioned that patronage rights, tolerated and still in force, were based on bilateral contracts executed between the patron and the Church, and their application was conditioned by the adherence of the patron to the Roman Catholic Church.

6) The statement of reasons for the law creating the Government Bureau for Church Affairs recognized this agency's full legislative and executive power in ecclesiastical and religious matters. On the other hand, the Church is not guaranteed the freedom to regulate her more internal spiritual matters autonomously—such as matters of conscience, the sacraments, adherence to the Church, and ecclesiastical discipline. With reason, therefore, we fear that in the future the Church will be restricted, in regulating these internal matters, that her spiritual activity will be judged from the purely political point of view and declared illegal and directed against the Government. Thus, the provisions of both laws as they have been enacted are in opposition to the Constitution of the Roman Catholic Church and to the Constitution of the Czechoslovak Republic of May 9, 1948, as obviously violating rights and liberties guaranteed by Articles 15, 16, and 17 of the Constitution.

In addition, the decree to enforce the above-mentioned laws, which was issued without consulting the representatives of the Church, strengthens the construction of the new laws to a still greater disadvantage to the Church. It seems that it is practically impossible to execute some of its provisions, even with the good will [of the Church]. Therefore we are really afraid that the consequences provided for in Article 172 of the Constitution of the Republic of Czechoslovakia are present.[3]

The Catholic bishops and ordinaries of the Czechoslovak Republic wish to emphasize that the above statements have been made for one reason only—to request (in accordance with the right of petition granted by Article 23 of the Constitution) that the Government conclude an agreement with the Church eliminating the existing difficulties from political and ecclesiastical life; that [the Government] revise the above-mentioned laws and corresponding decrees of enforcement, enact general provisions concerning the status of religion, and thus provide a secure legal status for the Roman Catholic Church and autonomy in her internal affairs.[4]

The fear of the episcopate that political standards would be applied to the spiritual activities of the clergy, which could lead to characterizing their acts as illegal acts directed against the State, was soon proved justified. On October 14, 1949, during the parliamentary debate on the bills, Dr. Čepička, the then Minister of Justice, who was later appointed Chairman of the Government Bureau of Church Affairs, declared: "If the Church hierarchy believes religious freedom means freedom for them to commit subversive and disruptive acts against the State and the Government, they are mistaken and bear full responsibility for such an attitude . . . Crime is crime, even if it is ordered by the Vatican or the bishops." [5]

Hundreds of priests were jailed for their opposition to the new Church legislation. Several trials followed.

On April 5, 1950, the Court (*státní soud*) in Prague found nine high-ranking members of Roman Catholic Orders guilty of attempting to overthrow the people's democratic legal order and imposed upon them sentences varying from nine years' to life imprisonment. The presiding judge, in his opinion, stated that the nine convicted of attempting to overthrow the Government conspired partly among themselves and partly with others; that some entered into direct, others into indirect contact with foreigners and established direct and indirect contact with foreign countries for the purpose of betraying State secrets. He emphasized that this trial involved not only the nine convicted but also whole religious orders and congregations which worked against the Republic and its people. According to the judge, they obeyed the Vatican, which was influenced by the evil designs of American imperialism. Thus, they were trying to disrupt the people's democratic legal order and to restore capitalism in Czechoslovakia.[6]

The first consequence of the trial was a resolution by employees of the national company *Stavobet,* in Prague, demanding confiscation of all monasteries. Following this resolution *ČTK,* the Czechoslovak official news agency, announced on April 18, 1950:

> It has recently been discovered that Catholic monastic orders have become the tools of the foreign foes of the Republic. It was proved at the recent trial [of monastic priests] for anti-State and subversive activities that many monasteries were being used to shelter hostile agents, spies, and even murderers. In some monasteries weapons and secret broadcasting sets were discovered, and many monasteries served as bases for espionage and disruptive activities.
>
> Particularly since the new Church laws were passed which put an end to the hope that the secular clergy could continue to be entrusted with subversive tasks, the reactionary Catholic hierarchy, on instructions from the Vatican, first of all designated the male orders (monastic brotherhoods) as its main aids in accomplishing its subversive aims.
>
> To stop these hostile activities of the Catholic monastic orders, measures have been taken which will return these orders to their original and truly religious mission. It has been established that only a few people lived in their monasteries and that they did not work, but for the most part busied themselves with stirring up the population.
>
> The various orders have, therefore, been assembled in a small number of monasteries, where they will be able to devote themselves to their purely religious activities according to the instructions of their own orders.
>
> Empty monastery buildings will continue to serve the needs of Catholic charities and social and health purposes. Some will be made over into apartments for people living nearby who cannot find any.[7]

Additional steps were taken by the Ministry of Labor and Social Welfare on June 6, 1950.[8] The Ministry authorized the Local People's Committees to apply the measures provided by the Law on the Economical Use of Dwellings[9] to all dwellings and premises used by the Church, including its seminaries and monasteries, etc. These committees were thus authorized, with the consent of the Regional People's Committees, to make alterations on these dwellings and premises and to assign them for housing purposes.

Of the many other political trials of clergymen, let us mention two. On December 2, 1950, the State Court in Prague sentenced Bishop Stanislav Zela to 25 years' confinement and eight high-ranking clergymen to confinement varying from 10 years to life.[10] On Janurary 15, 1951, Bishops Michael Buzalka and Pavel Gojdič were sentenced to life imprisonment by the State Court in Bratislava, and Bishop Jan Vojtaššák was sentenced to 24 years of confinement for attempting to destroy the people's democratic legal, economic, and social order, for contacting a foreign power, for espionage, etc.[11]

At its Prague convention on September 23, 1949, the Union of Czechoslovak Lawyers adopted a resolution classifying the Vatican as a foreign enemy to be resisted.[12] The Union appraised the two trials of the bishops as follows:

> Both these trials served to unmask the ways in which the Vatican espionage service collected its information, delivered it to the Vatican, and from there to the Americans; it was shown anew that the Vatican is an unusually important instrument of the international forces of reaction, those forces craving to unleash a third world war. . . .
>
> The high hierarchy joined the work of the espionage network built by the Vatican, centered in the office of the papal internuncio and directed successively by Msgrs. Ritter, Forni, Verolino, and de Lira. They gathered data on the construction of factories, production, the fulfillment of the two- and five-year plans, economic bottlenecks, labor, foreign trade, reports on security units, and important news of a military and security character, all of which should have been kept secret for the defense of our State. The very character of these reports makes it clear that they were destined to further preparations for any imperialist war against Czechoslovakia and the other socialist countries. . . .[13]

The records of the trials contained in the pamphlets cited above (see footnotes 7, 10 and 11, *supra*) do not quote the opinion of the court relating to each sentence, and therefore it is impossible to ascertain which acts of the accused were considered espionage by the Court (*Státní soud*). The appraisal of the Union of Czechoslovak Lawyers, however, indicates that reports are involved which would be considered innocent in the free world.

So far as the Five-Year Economic Plan is concerned, Law No. 241 of 1948 on this plan states in its first section that "its main goal shall be to raise substantially the standard of living of all classes of the working people in town and country by means of the increased productivity of labor, and by this means to strengthen the ties between the workers, peasants, intelligentsia, and middle classes in the towns and cities." Few in the free world will understand why the fulfillment of this plan, whether successful or unsuccessful, should be concealed. Or has the plan a different goal, which needs to be concealed?

The trials, by accusing Vatican circles and high Church dignitaries of espionage activities, were evidently designed to justify legally and morally the measures taken by the Czechoslovak Communist regime to separate the faithful from the supreme visible head of the Church and to destroy the organization and spiritual unity of the Roman Catholic Church in Czechoslovakia. Evidently the Church was the greatest obstacle to the building of a monolithic totalitarian state claiming the citizen in his entirety, his body and his soul.

V.   TRANSLATIONS OF PRINCIPAL LAWS

A. *Law of October 14, 1949, Establishing the Government Bureau for Church Affairs.*

(Law No. 217 of 1949, promulgated on October 17, 1949.)

The National Assembly of the Czechoslovak Republic has passed the following Law:

Sec. 1 — A Government Bureau for Church Affairs shall be established as the central governmental body; a minister assigned by the President of the Republic shall direct it.

Sec. 2 — The purpose of the Bureau for Church Affairs shall be to see to it that Church life develops in accordance with the Constitution and the principles of the people's democratic order and thus secure to everybody the right of freedom of religion based upon the principles of religious tolerance and equal rights for all denominations as guaranteed by the Constitution.

Sec. 3 — The jurisdiction in all matters of Church and religion which until now has been exercised by other departments shall pass to the Government Bureau for Church Affairs.

Sec. 4 — The minister directing the Government Bureau for Church Affairs shall exercise his jurisdiction in Slovakia as a rule through the Slovak Bureau for Church Affairs, which shall be directed by a commissioner assigned by the Cabinet.

Sec. 5 — Detailed provisions on the jurisdiction and organization of the Government Bureau for Church Affairs and the Slovak Bureau for Church Affairs and on procedure shall be established by a degree of the Cabinet.

Sec. 6 — This law shall take effect on the day of promulgation; it shall be carried out by all members of the Cabinet.

B. *Cabinet Decree of October 25, 1949, on the Jurisdiction and Organization of the Government Bureau for Church Affairs.*

(Cabinet Decree No. 228, promulgated on November 4, 1949)

On the basis of Sec. 5 of the Law of October 14, 1949, No. 217, Coll., establishing the Government Bureau for Church Affairs, the Cabinet of the Czechoslovak Republic decrees as follows:

Sec. 1 — As the central government body the Government Bureau for Church Affairs shall exercise all jurisdiction in matters of Church and religion, and in particular the jurisdiction exercised until now by other Government departments.

Sec. 2 — The jurisdiction of the Government Bureau for Church Affairs shall embrace the following matters:

a. Issuance of general rules and direction and supervision in all matters of Church and religion;

b. Administrative matters of the Churches, religious associations and their branches, communities, institutions, foundations, Church buildings, prebends, funds, monastic orders and monasteries, as well as their economic and financial matters (legal transactions relating to property, matters involving public construction, administration of Church funds and foundations, and the like);

c. Protection of religious monuments;

d. Matters involving the budget, credit, and planning in the ecclesiastical and religious sphere, without prejudice to the jurisdiction of the Government Planning Bureau;

e. Personnel matters and emoluments of clergymen, teachers, and employees of the theological schools of universities, [other] theological schools and seminaries, as well as of teachers of religion;

f. Regulation of the teaching of religion, approval of syllabuses, textbooks, equipment and devices, and general supervision, in agreement with the Ministry of Education, Science, and Art, over the teaching of religion and over denominational educational institutions of any kind;

g. Expert evalution of the ecclesiastical press and publications;

h. Issuance of an official gazette for clergymen and issuance of information bulletins and publications;

i. Matters involving religious associations and organizations, without prejudice to the jurisdiction of the Ministry of the Interior;

j. Matters involving charitable activities of the Churches and religious associations;

k. Taking care of the development of religious life in accordance with the Constitution;

1. Keeping informed on the development of the international relations of the Churches and religions.

Sec. 3 — (1) The work of the Government Bureau for Church Affairs shall be performed in a Section for Religious Affairs, Personnel Section, Information Section, and an Economic and Administrative Section.

(2) For the performance of accounting, clerical, typewriting, messenger service, and similar work, the Government Bureau for Church Affairs shall be provided with its own accounting office, disbursing office, and clerical and supply service.

Sec. 4 — The Slovak Bureau for Church Affairs shall be organized in accordance with the provisions of Section 3.

Sec. 5 — In provinces and countries the jurisdiction in religious and Church matters shall be exercised by competent Provincial and County People's Committees which, in this respect, shall act as subordinates of the Government Bureau for Church Affairs.

Sec. 6 — The present Decree shall take effect on the day of its promulgation; it shall be carried out by the minister charged with the direction of the Government Bureau for Church Affairs, in agreement with the interested members of the Cabinet.

C. *Law of October 14, 1949, to Provide Economic Security for Churches and Religious Associations through the Government.*

(Law No. 218 of 1949, promulgated on October 17, 1949)

The National Assembly of the Czechoslovak Republic has passed the following law:

Emoluments of Clergymen

Sec. 1 — According to the provisions of the present Law stated below, the Government shall grant emoluments to the clergymen of Churches and religious associations who with the consent of the Government either perform strictly religious functions, or are employed in Church administration or in establishments for the training of clergymen. The Government Bureau for Church Affairs may exceptionally in agreement with the Ministry of Finance also grant emoluments to clergymen who are engaged in other activities.

Sec. 5 — Governmental consent may be granted only to ministers of religion who are Czechoslovak citizens, are politically reliable, are irreproachable, and who otherwise meet the general requirements for employment with the Government. The Government Bureau for Church Affairs may waive the requirement of citizenship in cases deserving special consideration.

Sec. 3 — (1) The emoluments of clergymen shall consist of:

    (a) A basic salary;
    (b) Additional pay according to rank; and
    (c) Efficiency bonuses.

(2) The Cabinet shall establish by decree the amount of the basic salary, the rates of increases and the methods of granting them, the requirements for granting additional pay according to rank, and its amount, as well the requirements of granting an efficiency bonus and regulation of the details concerning it.

Sec. 4 — Compensation for travel, moving and other expenses. Clergymen entitled to emoluments shall also be entitled to compensation for travel, moving, and other expenses according to the general provisions.

Sec. 5 — Obligation to Teach Religion. Clergymen performing strictly religious functions are under the obligation to teach religion in schools, without remuneration, unless there is another arrangement for the teaching of religion. The extent of this obligation and its further regulation shall be fixed by the Minister directing the Government Bureau for Church Affairs in agreement with the Minister of Education, Science, and Art.

Sec. 6 — Social Benefits. Social benefits, in particular allocations for dependent children and pension benefits for a clergyman and members of his family shall be granted in accordance with provisions for governmental employees. The details shall be determined by the Cabinet.

Sec. 7 — Activities and Appointment of Clergymen. (1) Only those persons may carry on the activities of a minister of religion (preacher and the like) in a Church or religious association who have obtained the consent of the Government therefor and have taken an oath.

(2) Every employment (by election or appointment) of such persons shall require the consent of the Government, given in advance.

(3) Vacant posts must be filled within 30 days. If this is not done, the Government may take the necessary measures to secure the regular per-

formance of the religious functions, Church administration, or the education of clergymen.

Sec. 8 — Expenses of Upkeep. (1) The Government shall reimburse
Churches and religious associations for regular expenses of upkeep relating to the divine service, to other religious functions, and to the Church
administration in accordance with their budgets, as approved [by the
Government Bureau for Church Affairs].

(2) The Government may grant a special subsidy for extraordinary
expenses of upkeep if they are justified.

Sec. 9 — Budgets. (1) Representatives of Churches and religious associations as well as managers of Church property must prepare budgets
and final accounts and submit them for approval to the Government
Bureau for Church Affairs.

(2) The budgets of current expenses of upkeep shall be set up in conformity with actual needs, in accordance with the rules for the drafting
of the Government budget; the particulars shall be determined by the
Government Bureau for Church Affairs in agreement with the Ministry
of Finance.

Sec. 10 — Property. (1) The Government shall supervise the property
of the Churches and religious associations.

(2) The representatives of Churches and religious associations as well
as managers of Church property shall take an inventory of all personal
property, real property, and property rights of the Churches and religious
associations, their branches, communities, institutions, foundations,
Churches, prebends, and funds, and shall submit them to the Government
Bureau for Church Affairs within three months after the date on which
the present Law takes affect. The details shall be determined by the
Government Bureau for Church Affairs.

(3) Any disposal or encumbering of the property of Churches and
religious associations shall require the consent of the Government administration, given in advance.

Sec. 11 — Termination of Obligations. (1) All private and public
patronage of churches, prebends, and other Church institutions shall pass
over to the Government.

(2) All obligations to contribute to the benefit of Churches and religious
associations, their branches, communities, institutions, foundations,
Church buildings, prebends, and funds based on patronage or other legal
reasons, or on long-standing custom, shall cease to exist, with the exception of the obligations of members of the Churches and religious associations resulting from establishments approved by the Government.

Sec. 12 — Schools for the Education of Clergymen. The Government
shall maintain schools and institutions for education of clergymen.

Sec. 13 — Penal Provisions. Acts or omissions contrary to this law or
other provisions based on it shall be punished, if they are not punishable

by the courts, by the County People's Committees as administrative offenses with a fine not to exceed 100,000 Czechoslovak crowns. According to the gravity of the offense a substitute penalty of imprisonment not to exceed six months, shall simultaneously be determined in cases where the fine cannot be collected.

Sec. 14 — Repeal of Previous Provisions. All provisions of law which govern the legal relations of Churches and religious associations are hereby repealed.

Sec. 15 — The Effect and the Implementation of this Law. The present Law shall take effect on November 1, 1949; it shall be carried out by all members of the Cabinet.

D. *Cabinet Decree of October 18, 1949, to Provide Economic Security to the Roman Catholic Church through the Government.*

(No. 219 of 1949, promulgated on October 26, 1949)

On the basis of the Law of October 14, 1949, No. 218 Coll., to Provide Economic Security to Churches and Religious Associations through the Government, the Cabinet of the Czechoslovak Republic decrees as follows:

Sec. 1 — (1) Clergymen are employees of the Church.

(2) The emoluments of clergymen shall be granted by the Government, provided that with the consent of the Government they perform strictly religious functions or are active in Church administration or in theological schools.

Sec. 2 — (1) A clergyman performing strictly religious functions shall be understood to be a clergyman with or without monastic vows, who with the consent of the Government, independently or as an assistant, performs strictly religious functions within a parish in a position established with the consent of the Government.

(2) Strictly religious functions shall be understood to be the spiritual care of Catholics in a parish, and the performance of ecclesiastical services required for this care.

(3) Assistant clergymen may be appointed if so required by the needs of spiritual care (extent of the parish, number of parishioners, pastorates in public establishments e.g., hospitals and the like).

Sec. 3 — Clergymen active in Church administration shall be understood to be clergymen employed with the consent of the Government, in consistories and members of chapters, provided they hold positions that were established with the consent of the Government.

Sec. 4 — Clergymen active in the theological schools shall be understood to be clergymen who are teaching in theological schools with the consent of the Government, or who are officials in seminaries for the training of priests, provided that they hold positions established with the consent of the Government.

Sec. 5 — (1) Positions established with the consent of the Government shall be understood to be positions which were declared as such by the Government Bureau for Church Affairs upon consulting the competent Church authority.

(2) The consent of the Government Bureau for Church Affairs, given in agreement with the Ministry of Finance, shall be required for the establishment of new posts.

Sec. 6 — The Government Bureau for Church Affairs may, in agreement with the Ministry of Finance, and upon consulting the competent Church authority, grant emoluments to clergymen engaged in activities other than those stated in Section 1, Subsection 2, provided that the clergymen apply for it in writing.

Sec. 7 — (1) Only clergymen who are Czechoslovak citizens, are politically reliable, are irreproachable, and who otherwise meet the general requirements for employment with the Government may be appointed to the posts established with the consent of the Government and may receive the emoluments provided by this decree.

(2) In cases deserving special consideration the Government Bureau for Church Affairs, may, on request of the clergyman or by the competent Church authority, or *ex officio*, grant an exception as to the requirement of Czechoslovak citizenship.

Sec. 8 — (1) Emoluments of the clergymen referred to in Section 1, Subsection 2, shall consist of the basic salary, additional pay according to rank, and the efficiency bonus. These are to be paid in the same way as the emoluments of governmental employees.

(2) Additional pay according to rank may be granted to clergymen who are in charge of an office involving special responsibility. Exceptionally onerous work of a clergyman, his public activity, and his share in the effort of the working people to construct [the new order] may be rewarded by an efficiency bonus.

Sec. 9 — (1) The basic salary shall be 36,000 Czechoslovak crowns per annum, and after every three years of creditable service it shall be increased by 3,600 Czechoslovak crowns per annum, but this increase may be given no more than 12 times.

(2) The time spent in any ecclesiastical function, in public or military service, and in private service shall be deemed creditable service, to the same extent as for government employees.

(3) The basic salary shall be reduced by any other steady income received by the clergyman from public means. This provision shall not affect rewards for undertaking the spiritual care of public institutions, rewards for teaching religion in schools, the salaries of members of the

Cabinet, of the Board of Commissioners, of the National Assembly, and of the Slovak National Council, and the rewards of members of People's Committees.

Sec. 10 — Clergymen shall be entitled to allotments for adopted children and foster children in accordance with provisions for Government employees.

Sec. 11 — (1) In order to determine additional pay according to rank, clergymen are divided, on the basis of their degree of responsibility and the importance of their office, into the following classes:

I. Independent pastors, clergymen in a supervisory function, and officials of consistories;

II. Superiors of seminaries for the training of priests, teachers in schools of theology, chancellors of consistories, secretaries of the consistorial office [executive secretaries of the consistory], and canon residents;

III. Dignitaries of chapters, vicars-general, vicars of chapters, suffragans, and abbots;

IV. Archbishops, bishops of dioceses, and apostolic administrators.

(2) The additional pay according to rank shall be at the following rate per annum:

In class I .... 12,000 Czechoslovak crowns
In class II .... 24,000 ,, ,,
In class III .... 36,000 ,, ,,
In class IV .... 48,000 ,, ,,

(3) Clergymen included in class I and II shall be allocated additional pay according to rank by the Provincial People's Committee; clergymen included in class III and IV, by the Government Bureau for Church Affairs.

Sec. 12—(1) The efficiency bonus may not be higher than 2,000 Czech crowns per month. The total amount of these bonuses may not exceed 15 per cent of the salary and additional pay according to rank.

(2) Decision on the allocation of a bonus and its rate shall be reserved, as far as the clergymen in classes III and IV are concerned, to the Government Bureau for Church Affairs, and as far as other clergymen are concerned to the Provincial People's Committee which must consult the competent Church authority.

Sec. 13—(1) Clergymen are entitled to receive compensation for travel, moving and other expenses for indispensable official travel in accordance with the provisions established for Government employees.

(2) Except in an emergency, the People's Committee of the county where the clergyman's permanent official post is located must be informed in advance of [anticipated] trips.

(3) Travelling expense accounts shall be sent, once a month, to the County People's Committee, which shall verify them and submit them

to the Provincial People's Committee for their decision on the compensation.

Sec. 14—(1) Clergymen performing strictly religious functions are under the obligation to teach religion, without remuneration, in the elementary and secondary schools where a special teacher of religion is not available within the parish.

(2) The obligation to teach without remuneration shall be, for assistant priests, 10 hours weekly; for independent pastors, 8 hours weekly. Clergymen with supervisory functions shall have no such obligation.

(3) If the school is situated at least one and a half kilometers from the clergyman's residence, the time to go to school and back shall be computed in the time of obligatory teaching without remuneration, four kilometers being computed as one teaching hour.

(4) The obligation of the clergyman to teach without remuneration shall be considered as fulfilled even if the total number of teaching hours in a parish is below the number of hours fixed by Subsection 2.

(5) If the teaching exceeds the number of hours of the obligation to teach without remuneration, the excess hours, not including transportation to school, shall be compensated according to the appropriate provisions, and for traveling to school and back the clergyman is entitled to a compensation according to Section 13, Subsection 1.

(6) If, through no fault of his own, the clergyman was unable to fullfill his obligation to teach without remuneration during a week, his remuneration of excess hours in other weeks shall not be reduced because of that.

Sec. 15—(1) Clergymen and their families shall be entitled to pension insurance benefits, in accordance with the provisions established for governmental employees.

(2) The basic pension rate benefit is 75 percent of the last basic salary and additional pay according to rank.

Sec. 16—(1) Any ecclesiastical activity by clergymen with or without monastic vows may be undertaken only with the consent of the Government.

(2) A clergyman shall apply for Government consent to the Provincial People's Committee [with jurisdiction over the place] of his permanent residence, or, as the case may be through its intermediary [the Provincial People's Committee] to the Government Bureau for Church Affairs (clergymen of class III) or to the Cabinet (clergymen of class IV).

Sec. 17—(1) The prior consent of the Government is needed for every appointment of a clergyman to a post established with the consent of the Government.

(2) The competent Church authority shall apply by letter for this consent to the Provincial People's Committee regarding [the appointment of] assistant priests and clergymen of classes I and II and to the Government Bureau for Church Affairs regarding clergymen of class III. The consent

of the Cabinet is needed for the appointment of clergymen of class IV.

Sec. 18—(1) If a clergyman is appointed without the prior consent of the Government, the consequence shall be that he shall receive no emoluments, and the post shall be considered vacant.

(2) If a clergyman becomes disqualified for appointment as required by Section 7, Subsection 1, the authority which is competent according to Section 17, Subsection 2, shall settle the case with the competent Church authority; and if, within 14 days, no remedial action has been taken, it [the civil authority] shall require the competent Church authority to remove the clergyman and shall decide simultaneously whether the payment of his emoluments should cease. If the Church authority does not meet the requirement to remove the clergyman within 14 days, the post shall be considered vacant.

(3) A vacant post must be filled, at the latest, within the 30-day period; after the expiration of this period the government may take the necessary measures to ensure that strictly religious functions, Church administration, or theological teaching will be carried on regularly. The Government Bureau for Church Affairs may, in justifiable cases, as an exception, grant an extension of the period.

Sec. 19—(1) A pledge of loyalty to the Czechoslovak Republic shall be a prerequisite for engaging in ecclesiastical activities.

(2) The pledge reads:

I promise on my honor and conscience to be faithful to the Czechoslovak Republic and to its People's democratic order, and I will not undertake anything contrary to its interests, security, and integrity. As a citizen of a people's democratic State I shall perform conscientiously the duties of my office and I will do evertyhing within my ability to support efforts at [social] reconstruction for the welfare of the people.

(3) This pledge shall be taken before the chairman of a County People's Committee by assistant priests and clergymen of class I; before the chairman of a Provincial People's Committee by clergymen of class II; before the minister in charge of the Government Bureau for Church Affairs by clergymen of class III; and before the Prime Minister by clergymen of class IV.

Sec. 20—(1) The Provincial People's Committee shall keep a record on every clergyman, which shall include personal data pertinent for his service status, for the granting and determining of emoluments, and for the claims of social benefits.

(2) A clergyman shall report these data immediately after his first appointment, and he shall report all changes relating to his service status.

Sec. 21—(1) The emoluments fixed by the present Decree shall replace all permanent emoluments which, until now, clergymen derived from their vocation or in connection with it, from prebends, from patronage and all other obligations, or from governmental funds, or from public funds according to the provisions in force until now, and also replace all individual personal payments, assistance, help, or rewards.

(2) The provision of Subsection 1 shall not affect the payment and rewards referred to in Section 9, Subsection 3, Clause 2.

Sec. 22—(1) The Government shall reimburse the Church for the regular expenses of upkeep, and the expenses for work performed by persons who are not clergymen.

(2) In justified cases the Government shall grant special aid to defray extraordinary expenses of upkeep.

Sec. 23—(1) Expenses of upkeep consist of the expenses for divine service and of administrative expenses.

(2) Expenses for divine service shall be understood to be the expenses for Church buildings, for equipment and objects for divine service, and for the divine services themselves.

(3) Administrative expenses are expenses connected with the carrying on of Church offices.

Sec. 24—(1) Ordinary expenses are those incurred regularly every year. The expenses for current work to preserve the building and furnishings are included in these expenses.

(2) Extraordinary expenses shall be understood to be those for construction and other investments, expensive renovation of furnishings, and similar items.

Sec. 25—(1) The amount of ordinary expenses for upkeep shall be evaluated, within the diocese, on the basis of partial budgets and final accounts of the individual Church units having their seat in the diocese.

(2) The budgets must be set up according to the rules for the establishment of the governmental budget and strict economy shall be observed. Detailed regulations on the establishment of budgets and final accounts shall be issued by the Government Bureau for Church Affairs in agreement with the Ministry of Finance.

(3) From the partial budgets of individual units within its jurisdiction the consistories shall set up a total budget of the diocese for the next year and shall submit it for approval, before the end of March of the current year, to the Government Bureau for Church Affairs, together with the final accounts for the past year worked out in a similar way.

(4) The budget for the year 1950 must be submitted before November 15, 1949.

Sec. 26—(1) On the basis of the submitted budgets and final accounts the Government Bureau for Church Affairs shall appropriate the necessary sums to defray the actual needs of individual dioceses.

(2) The actual need is determined by the difference between the annual expense and income.

(3) Income shall include the yield of all movable and real property of the Church irrespective of whether it served, until now, to defray personal expenses or the expense of upkeep, as well as the yield from all property rights, and also collections, gifts, successions, legacies, and all other revenues, with the exception of stole fees.

(4) In order to find a basis for verification of the income according to the preceding Subsection, the consistories shall take an inventory of all the property and property rights of all Church units in the diocese, including the individual communities, institutions, foundations, Churches, prebends, and funds.

(5) The consistories shall, by January 31, 1950, send the inventories of the property to the Government Bureau for Church Affairs and shall report to it regularly, every year, changes concerning the property which occurred up to December 31 of that year.

Sec. 27—The Government shall supervise the Church property by examining the economic management of the Church and shall reserve for itself the right to approve, in advance, all important legal transactions concerning this property. The Government Bureau for Church Affairs shall determine the manner in which individual authorities shall exercise their jurisdiction.

Sec. 28—(1) To defray the extraordinary expenses of upkeep, the individual Church units shall apply for special help through the consistories, to the Government Bureau for Church Affairs.

(2) The application must include evidence showing that the expenditure is urgently needed, that it will be economical, and that it has been foreseen in the uniform economic plan.

Sec. 29—The patronage of Roman Catholic Churches, prebends, and other Church establishments exercised until now by public funds, foundations, communities, counties, provinces, and other entities of public law, as well as the patronage connected with the ownership of property referred to by the Laws of April 18, 1919, No. 215 Coll. on the Sequestration of the Large Landed Property; of July 11, 1947, No. 142 Coll. on the Revision of the First Land Reform; of March 21, 1948, No. 46 Coll. on the New Land Reform (the permanent regulation of the ownership of agricultural and forest lands); the Presidential Decree of June 21, 1945, No. 12 Coll. on the Confiscation and Accelerated Allotment of Agricultural Property; the Decree of the Slovak National Council of August 23, 1945, No. 104 Coll. of Decrees of the Slovak National Council on Confiscation and Accelerated Allotment of Agricultural Property; and the Presidential Decree of October 25, 1945, No. 108 Coll. on the Confiscation of Enemy Property and Funds of National Reconstruction, as well as other public and private patronage, shall pass over to the Government.

Sec. 30—(1) The Government shall exercise patronage in nominating [and submitting] to the competent dignitary suitable candidates for the vacant prebends.

(2) Invitations to apply for vacant prebends shall be published by the competent consistory in the forthcoming issue of the Gazette of Catholic Clergymen (*Věstník katolického duchovenstva*). The consistory shall submit all the applications to the Government and, in a report accompanying them, shall indicate the applicants whom it does not consider suitable for nomination. The rejection must be properly justified by reasons which are not in contradiction to the laws of the Czechoslovak Republic. From among the applicants who were not duly rejected, the Government shall nominate the clergyman whom it considers most suitable. The competent ordinary is bound to appoint the nominee to the ecclesiastical office within 14 days after his nomination. If he fails to do so within the time limit, it shall be considered that the office has been conferred upon the nominee.

Sec. 31—All obligations to contribute to the benefit of the Church, its units, communities, institutions, foundations, church buildings, prebends, and funds based on patronage or other legal reasons, or on long standing customs, shall cease to exist.

Sec. 32—(1) The theological schools and ecclesiastical seminaries shall be the institutions for the education of clergymen.

(2) The Government shall defray [to the schools] the expenses of the personnel as well expenses for upkeep.

Sec. 33—This decree shall take effect on November 1, 1949; it shall be carried out by the minister charged with the direction of the Governmental Bureau for Church Affairs in agreement with the Minister of Finance.

E. *Proclamation No. 320 of the Government Bureau for Church Affairs of May 12, 1950, concerning the Functions of the General Internal Affairs Divisions of the Provincial People's Committees in Church and Religious Matters and the Establishment of Church Sections.*

This Proclamation, the text of which follows, was a directive implementing Government Decree No. 233 of February 22, 1949, which specified the general jurisdiction of provincial authorities in religious affairs. The Proclamation quotes in distinctive type several subsections of Sec. 2 of the Decree and follows these by instructions which develop them and provide for their enforcement.

Proclamation of the Government Bureau for Church Affairs of May 12, 1950, No. 320, Official Gazette (*Úřední list I*) concerning the Functions of the General Internal Affairs Divisions of the Provincial People's Committees in Church and Religious Matters, and concerning the Establishment of Church Sections.

The Government Bureau for Church Affairs, in agreement with the Ministry of the Interior and other interested central agencies, provides, by virtue of Sections 1 and 3 of Government Decree No. 35 of 1949, on the General Internal Affairs Divisions of the Provincial People's Committees (hereafter referred to as "the Division"), as amended by Government Decree No. 232 of 1949, which modified certain provisions concerning divisions of the Provincial People's Committees (Proclamation No. 233 of 1949 Coll.) as follows:

Part I

Functions of the Division on Church and Religious Affairs.

Within the scope of tasks determined in Section 2 of Proclamation No. 233 of 1949 (reproduced herein in italics) functions of the Division on Church and Religious Affairs shall be determined in detail as follows:

Paragraph 1: The Division shall see to it that Church and religious life in the provinces develops in harmony with the Constitution and the principles of the people's democratic order, and accordingly shall insure to everyone the right of freedom of denomination guaranteed by the Constitution and based on principles of religious tolerance and equal rights for all denominations.

Paragraph 2: Without prejudice to the jurisdiction of other agencies (offices) the Division, in order to fulfill the tasks fixed in paragraph 1 shall in particular take charge of the following activities:

Subs. 6: It shall administer the government of Church and religious affairs and supervise activities of all Churches, religious associations, monastic orders, and monasteries in the provinces.

It [the Division] shall inspect all activities of Churches and religious associations, their agents, branches and institutions.

It shall cooperate in Church and religious matters with the representatives of the agencies of Churches and religious associations.

It shall keep records of and supervise the activities of monasteries and their members; it shall provisionally approve the creation of new houses for religious orders, of social orders and congregations which already have been established in the Czechoslovak Republic.

It shall approve provisionally the creation of new parishes, congregations, communities etc., and of changes of their boundaries.

It shall confirm representatives of Churches and religious associations and their branches.

It shall receive the pledge of loyalty of clergymen of Class II.

It shall install newly appointed Roman Catholic clergymen of Class II.

It shall approve performance of ecclesiastical activities by the auxiliary clergymen and clergymen of Class I and II.

It shall approve the designation (election, appointment) of auxiliary clergymen and clergymen of Classes I and II to positions established with Government approval.

It shall handle cases of removal of auxiliary clergymen and clergymen of Classes I and II who have become ineligible for assignment to posts established with approval of the Government and of the ecclesiastical authorities.

It shall assure orderly performance of religious functions, Church administration, and the education of clergymen to fill a vacancy whenever the post of an auxiliary clergyman or of a clergyman of Class I or II becomes open.

It shall decide appeals in Church and religious matters, especially concerning the use of one Church's facilities by another Church, the use of cemeteries, burials, and interdenominational matters.

Subs. 7: It shall supervise the property of Churches, religious associations, monastic orders and monasteries, examine their management, and approve all legal transactions concerning Church property.

It shall cooperate with the agencies of the Churches and religious associations in preparing the budget of the individual Church branches.

It shall supervise financial affairs of Churches, religious associations, and their branches.

It shall keep records of Church property.

It shall take care of the upkeep of church buildings and other property of Churches and religious associations and their branches.

Subs. 8. It shall protect religious monuments.

It shall keep records of religious monuments and take care of their maintenance.

Subs. 9. It shall supervise the teaching of religion and Church schools.

It shall supervise the teaching of religion in all schools.

It shall determine areas in which teachers of religion shall be authorized to teach.

It shall cooperate in establishing boards of examiners for teachers of religion.

It shall keep records of institutions for the education of clergymen (theological schools, universities and seminaries); it shall supervise the activities of these institutions.

It shall propose the appointment of teachers and other professional workers at institutions for education of clergymen.

Subs. 10. It shall make expert evaluations of the religious and Church press, and shall monitor the provincial press and broadcasts from the religious and ecclesiastical point of view.

It shall monitor, make expert evaluation of, and keep records of the Church press in the provinces from the point of view of Church policy.

It shall collect news on Church and religious life in the provinces.

It shall monitor provincial periodical and non-periodical publications and provincial broadcasts involving the propagation of ecclesiastical regulations.

Subs. 11. It shall observe religious life in the provinces.

It shall observe the activities of religious associations and organizations, pilgrimages, religious assemblies, missions, and other religious meetings from the religious and Church-political point of view.

It shall cooperate with the Catholic Action.

Subs. 12. It shall supervise the charitable activities of Churches and religious associations, Church and religious clubs, foundations and other similar institutions.

It shall keep records of social institutions maintained by Churches, religious associations and their branches, of Church and religious clubs and organizations (for instance, Catholic Charity); it shall coordinate these activities and supervise them.

Subs. 13. It shall take care of Church endowments.

It shall keep records of Church endowments, supervise their establishment and administration of the property.

Subs. 14. It shall participate in other matters under the jurisdiction of other divisions of the Provincial People's Committees whenever Church and religious interests are concerned.

It shall cooperate especially in decisions on the confiscation of Church property, on redemption of agricultural land, and on housing matters.

Subs. 20. In accordance with regulations in force it shall decide and dispose in personnel affairs of clergymen of Churches and religious associations, who are active in ecclesiastical functions, Church administration, or in institutions for the education of clergymen; it shall take care of the organization of the political and professional schooling of these employees.

It shall supervise the personnel affairs of clergymen.

It shall keep personnel records of the clergymen.

It shall supervise the granting of personal emoluments of clergymen.

It shall decide on questions involving length of service in Church positions, in public, military or other services; it shall give decisions pertaining to the time spent as a partisan in the national struggle for liberation.

It shall grant rank allowances to clergymen of Class I and II.

It shall give bonuses for efficiency to auxiliary clergymen and clergymen of Class I and II.

It shall supervise the assignment of education allowances and special increases above the educational allowances.

It shall supervise the granting of personal emoluments with regard to reactivation of clergymen.

It shall fix overtime compensation for teaching lessons.

It shall award payment to teachers who in addition teach subjects outside their field of specialization.

It shall decide on compensation for travel, moving and other expenses of clergymen; it shall supervise the granting of additional allowances in cases where a clergyman must live separately from his family.

It shall grant leave to clergymen.

It shall deal with personnel and financial matters of teachers of religion.

Part II
Establishment of a Church Section

For the establishment of tasks enumerated in Part I, there shall be established within the Division a new (fifth) Church Section, so that the Division for General Internal Affairs shall now have a total of five Sections.

Part III
Relationship to Regulations in force

This proclamation supplements the Proclamation of the Ministry of the Interior, No. 770 of 1949, the Official Gazette (*Úřední list I*) and the Commissioners Department of the Interior, No. 942 of 1949, Official Gazette (*Úradný vestník*) relating to the functions of Divisions of General Internal Affairs of the Provincial People's Committees and to their partition into sections.

Minister
Fierlinger

VI. TEXT OF CZECH BISHOPS' PASTORAL LETTER ON STATE-CHURCH FIGHT

(From the *New York Times,* June 27, 1949)

Dear Faithful:

In these overwhelmingly serious times of our religious and national life we turn to you with this letter of the right-teaching church.

Love for the nation and for the people of Czechoslovakia leads us to speak in these decisive days, in which we have become witnesses to attacks on the unity and leadership of the Catholic Church here. To know where the truth and right and your place in the church and nation are, hear the voice of your pastors who, being conscious of responsibility before God and the conscience of the whole world, after deliberate consideration cannot remain quiet.

We have all been witnesses lately to a widely based action, the aim of which is to force the Czechoslovak Bishops to come to an agreement with the state. As is our public, we also are of the opinion that relations between church and state are discordant and painful. This situation is surely unnatural, for both societies would complement each other and the present situation does not contribute to general public peace nor the internal peace of the faithful. * * *

To these humanitarian and commonly recognized rights of man belong not only the freedom of privately held religious convictions and the freedom to execute religious rites, but also the free realization of the principles of this faith as the norm of life of individuals and society— and this without fear of losing personal freedom, civic equality and the endangering of the rights of existence.

For the realization and ensuring of this religious freedom for Catholics it is the church's conception, by the ordinance of God, that these further conditions are necessary prerequisites: The recognition of the authority of the Holy Father as the highest visible head of the church and recognition for the authority of his Bishops.

The non-recognition of this fundamental principle means that the Catholic Church as Christ wanted it is not recognized and that every action taken apart and against the will of the Bishops, connected with the Roman Pope, disturbs the church's basic structure, disrupts its unity and necessarily leads to its destruction.

Further basic conditions for the recognition of the rights and freedom of the church, stemming from natural law, are:

1. Respect for the sovereign right of parents over the education of their children. That means education in school and outside school.

2. Recognition of the family as a sacred tie, and the rights and duties stemming from this.

3. The right of the faithful to free assembly in congregations and organizations.

Freedom For Faith to Exist

To these belong also the conditions of free religious life, which otherwise would be unattainable for the Communist or the individual. These conditions include the necessary number of church schools, educational and social and charitable institutions, cultural and philanthropic institutions, sufficient facilities for printing periodicals and books and free unlimited access to all possibilities of social and cultural life.

Finally, financial means and material security for these institutions and establishments are also necessary as without them it would not be possible for the church successfully to develop this activity for the welfare of our people and to save church buildings from deterioration and destruction.

All this we once had to the necessary extent and all this we have been deprived of lately. * * *

It [the Church] stands here today—robbed, deprived of the majority of its freedoms and rights, dishonored, soiled, persecuted secretly and openly.

Only observe how the church is faring in Czechoslovakia at the present time. A concerted campaign is waged against it on the radio and in public proclamations, especially against the Holy Father and the bishops, who are its God-ordained heads. The sacred character of the family and the sovereign rights of parents to the education of their children are wilfully undermined.

All the ecclesiastical press, with a few completely insignificant exceptions, has been stopped. Even the official gazettes of the Bishops, which informed priests also of important state directives, have been stopped. Instead, the Ministry of Education, Science and Art has published the so-called Gazette of the Catholic Clergy, which has no church endorsement and is edited against the will of the hierarchy. Although this so-called gazette is intended for Catholic priests, it is directed by non-Catholics in an anti-church spirit and attempts to govern directly by state organs affairs that are wholly ecclesiastical and thereby attempts to exclude the Bishops from practicing their rights.

Every Catholic book that is to be published—even prayer books—is subjected to preliminary state censorship.

State plenipotentiaries are planted in Catholic publishing houses. An interdiction of assembly and schooling of Catholics outside churches was edited under the threat of prosecution.

Even the fate of church buildings, as was demonstrated by the forced inventory of ritual objects and sacred vessels, is, it seems, insecure.

The church is deprived of the last remnants of its property. Not even the minimum laid down by the law is respected.

Church schools practically no longer exist and the fate of the few remaining is painfully insecure, which causes suffering to pupils and parents. Pressure was even brought to bear upon the parents to take their children out of church schools, and this under a direct threat of consequences.

Teachers of religion are tested ideologically and are given directives on how to teach religion in the materialistic spirit.

All religious education of youth in societies, eucharistic circles, etc., was in many places forbidden under punitive threats and is consistently made impossible by the fact that the state has taken a monopoly on materialist schools and extracurricular education, so that education in the Christian spirit is made impossible and considered as practically illegal.

In this respect, we have come so far that even in theological schools lectures of so-called social science were instituted whose aim it is to bring it about that even theological students should be educated in the materialistic ideology.

An inventory of all church property, even church collections, was ordered, quite illegally. With direct inspection, such inventories were carried out in many cases. They were anti-constitutional searches.

Consistent attempts are made to deprive church buildings of their religious missions, especially by the taking over of monasteries and institutions for the education of clerical and monastic youth.

Especially in Slovakia some monastic houses were forcibly cleared out and the priests taken away in trucks.

The Ministry of Interior gave instructions to the regional command of the state security [police] on how to deal with the church and its members.

In some places even the practicing of religious rites has already been forbidden. In many places religious processions were made impossible or were misused for irreligious purposes.

The conference of Bishops in Dolní Smokovec, which was to have taken a stand on the demands of the Government, was broken up when listening devices were discovered in the conference room. The Ministry of Interior was asked to make an inquiry but up to now no satisfactory answer has been forthcoming.

The latest conference of Bishops in Prague was disturbed by security organs.

At the same time the Prague consistory was occupied by state officers and the Archbishop's residence put under secret police surveillance, so that the freedom of the chairman of the Bishops' conference was totally restricted. These restrictions represent extreme breaches of constitutional freedoms and many of the still-existent laws.

On the whole it can be said that outside the church any religious activity is impossible and many fear to visit churches lest they be accused of reaction and fear the loss of their means of existence. * * *

After all, the whole affair of an agreement between church and state would actually have been a rather simple matter if it had not been for the fact that the state first harmed the church and deprives it of the majority of its rights.

All this organized calling for an agreement would have been quite superfluous if Government personages, on their own initiative, had not interfered before the start of negotiations in church freedoms and rights and formed, by this one-sided action, a painful situation in which the church was deprived beforehand of that which was supposed to have been the subject of the agreement.

So in reality the church was deprived of all possibilities of successful negotiations and given this choice: submission to dictatorship or persecution. * * *

We declare that we were always loyal to the republic. We have stressed this many times and it can be deduced from the oath we undertook when we assumed office. A loyal attitude toward the republic is therefore, a matter of course for us and we are sure to remain faithful to our oath. Therefore we have always demanded from our clergy that they refrain from any political activity, especially from any illegal and anti-state activity.

But we cannot remain quiet when the rights of the Holy Church are violated and when political power is being misused against it.

Most painful is the fact that we have no way of defending ourselves against these gross and untrue attacks. All manner of attempts are being made to force us out of our pastoral offices and the conduct of the church is being taken over by unbelieving persons, persons who have broken away from the church and those who have no right, no competence and no church missions. * * *

In this spirit the Czechoslovak dignitaries at the Bishops' conference of June 7, 1949, in Olomouc, laid down the basic conditions on which agreement would be possible and which should be accepted and guaranteed by the Government beforehand. These conditions are:

1. The Christian world viewpoint (philosophy) will be recognized and respected in public life and education, in word and deed.

2. The Government recognizes the spiritual authority of the Roman Pope as the supreme head of the church in matters religious and ecclesiastical, which, according to valid authority, does not touch the sovereignty of the state but is a natural consequence of recognized basic human rights, and especially the freedom of religion.

3. Before the beginning of negotiations, all measures restricting and threatening religious freedom of Catholics in the Czechoslovak Republic, especially the religious freedom and education of youth, be repealed.

In addition to this:

a. The Gazette of the Catholic Clergy, published by the Ministry of Education, Arts and Sciences, will be published immediately, and that the publishing of all official dignitaries' gazettes will be permitted.

b. The decree of the Ministry of Education, Arts and Sciences of May 23, 1949, about vacant church offices and accompanying stipends, as well as the decree of the Ministry of Interior of May 5, 1949, restricting the freedom of assembly and congregation, and also the decree for regional and district command of the state security police on the procedure against the Catholic Church, must be revoked. * * *

JOSEF [BERAN], *Archbishop of Prague.*
JOSEF CHARLES, *Archbishop of Olomouc.*
JAN, *Bishop of Spišská Nová Ves.*
JOSEF, *Titular Bishop of Thagora, Apostolic Administrator in Košice.*
PAUL, *Bishop of Prešov.*
MAURICE, *Bishop of Hradec Králové.*
ANDREW, *Bishop of Banská Bystrica.*
CHARLES, Bishop of Brno.
JOSEF, *Bishop of České Budějovice.*

STEFAN, *Bishop of Litoměřice.*
EDVARD, *Titular Bishop of Velicia, Apostolic Administrator of Nitra.*
FRANTIŠEK ONDEREK, *Apostolic Administrator of the Czech portion of Wroclaw Archdiocese.*
AMBROSIUS LAZIK, *Apostolic Administrator of Trnava.*
ROBERT POBOŽNÝ, *Capitular Vicar of Rožňava.*

Prague, June 15, 1949.

This pastoral letter is to be read in all parish churches and chapels at public services on Sunday, June 26, 1949. Let the reverend priests not be intimidated from reading this letter by any threats in these so difficult and decisive times. They are bound by their consciences to inform their faithful of the real state of affairs. Willful and intentional neglect of this duty will be prosecuted with ecclesiastical punishment.

NOTES

1. *Národní Shromáždění Republiky Československé v prvém desítiletí 1918-1928.* Prague, 1928, p. 919.

2. Page 28 of this study.

3. Section 172, Subsec. 2: Laws passed after the date established in Section 170 [June 9, 1948] shall, in so far as they are inconsistent with the Constitution or with constitutional laws, be void.

4. *Osservatore Romano* of November 16, 1949, Issue No. 266, page 3, column 6.

5. The New York Times, October 15, 1949.

6. *Rudé Právo* (Red Law), April 6, 1950, Prague.

7. Jindřich Neuls and Miroslav Dvořák, *Co se skrývalo za zdmi klášterů* (What was hidden behind the monastery walls). Published by the Ministry of Information and Culture, Prague, 1950.

8. Proclamation of the Ministry of Labor and Social Welfare of June 6, 1950, No. 362, Official Gazette (Úřední list I), Prague.

9. Law of April 28, 1948, No. 138 Coll.

10. *Trial of Vatican Agents in Czechoslovakia.* Published by the Ministry of Information and Public Culture, Orbis, Prague, 1951.

11. *The Trial of the Treasonable Slovak Bishops Ján Vojtaššák, Michal Buzalka and Pavol Gojdič.* Published by the Ministry of Information and Public Culture. Orbis, Prague, 1951.

12. *Právník* (Lawyer). Published by the Association of Czechoslovak Lawyers, Prague, 1949, Issue No. 9 of 1949.

13. *Bulletin de Droit Tchécoslovaque* (Bulletin of Czechoslovak Law). Published by the Association of Czechoslovak Lawyers, Prague, Issue Nos. 1 - 2, year IX, 1951.

TABLE OF STATUTES

BIBLIOGRAPHY

Beneš, Eduard. *Boj o mír a bezpečnost státu.* Prague: Orbis, 1934.

Bušek, Vratislav *et al. Československé církevní zákony.* 2 vols., Prague: Čsl. Kompas, 1931.

Československá vlastivěda. 10 vosl., Prague: Sfinx, 1929-36, pp. 246-361.

Statistická ročenka republiky československé. Vydal Státní úřad statistický. (In Czech, German, and French.) Prague, published annually.

Denis, Ernest. *La Bohème depuis la Montagne-Blanche.* 2 vols., Paris: E. Leroux, 1903.

Deset let Československé Republiky. Prague, 1928.

Lützow, Franz, Count von. *Bohemia. An Historical Sketch.* London: J. M. Dent & Sons, 1910.

Masarykův slovník naučný. Article "Československo." Prague, 1925-33, pp. 1014-1131.

Národní Shromáždění Republiky Československé v prvém desítiletí. Article "Věci církevní." Vydalo Předsed. Posl. sněmovny a Předsed. senátu. Prague, 1928, pp. 919-934.

Palacký, František. *Dějiny národu českého v Čechách a na Morave.* Prague: B. Kočí, 1908.

——*Geschichte von Böhmen.* 5 vols., Prague: Kronberger und Weber, 1836-67.

Pelzel, Franz Martin. *Geschichte der Böhmen.* 2 vols., Prague, 1817.

Seton-Watson, R.W. *A History of the Czechs and Slovaks.* London/ New York: Hutchinson & Co., Ltd., 1943.

Slovník veřejného práva československého. Article "Církve." Brno, 1929-1948, I, 184-8, 537-58; II, 141-74; III, 535-43, 917; IV, 609-11.

Srbik, Heinrich von. *Die Beziehungen von Staat und Kirche in Österreich.* Leipzig: K. F. Koehlers, 1938.

Thomson, Samuel Harrison. *Czechoslovakia in European History.* Princeton, 1943.

Dr. Alexander Bedö, Hugó Kálnoky, Dr. Leslie LeNard,
Dr. George Torzsay-Biber

CHURCH AND STATE IN HUNGARY

Vladimir Gsovski, *editor*

CHURCH AND STATE IN HUNGARY

by Dr. Alexander Bedő, Hugó Kálnoky, Dr. Leslie LeNard,
Dr. George Torzsay-Biber

ABBREVIATIONS

Abbreviations for the authorities issuing decrees:

Bk.M.—*Belkereskedelmi Miniszter* (Minister of Domestic Trade)

Eln.V.K.M.—notice issued by the Minister of Religion and Public Education and prepared by his Personnel Division

H.M.—*Honvédelmi Miniszter* (Minister of Defense)

Korm.—*Kormány* (Government)

M.E.—*Miniszterelnök* (Prime Minister)

M.T.—*Minisztertanács* (Cabinet)

Mt.h.—*Minisztertanácsi határozat* (Resolution of the Cabinet)

V.K.M.—*Vallás- és Kőzoktátasűgyi Miniszter* (Minister of religion and Public Education)

Hungarian laws are cited by the number in Roman numerals and year of issuance (e.g., Law No. X of 1937). Edicts (decrees with the Force of Law) are cited by the number in Arabic numerals and year of issuance (e.g., Edict No. 5 of 1949); decrees, by the number in Arabic numerals, the year of issuance, and the initials of the authority issuing the decree (e.g., Decree No. 5620 of 1950 V.K.M.).

Decrees were published in the *Budapesti Kőzlőny, Hivatalos Lap* (Budapest Journal, Official Gazette); laws were published in the supplement to this, the *Országos Tőrvénytár* (National Collection of Laws).

At the end of 1944 the *Budapesti Kőzlőny* ceased to exist. On and after January 4, 1945 laws were published in the *Országos Tőrvénytár,* and all other statutes in the newly established official gazette, *Magyar Kőzlőny.* Beginning with the May 1, 1949 issue, the *Országos Tőrvénytár* merged with the *Magyar Kőzlőny,* which then became the sole publication for all laws and legal regulations.

I. STATUS OF THE CHURCHES
PRIOR TO WORLD WAR II

The Constitution of the Hungarian People's Republic of 1949 declared the separation of Church and State. However, the separation of Church and State in present-day Hungary has a meaning different from the American concept. The declaration of separation of Church and State was used in Hungary to dissolve legal ties of a thousand years, to deprive the Church of all its privileges and to subjugate it to a rigid government control.

Prior to the end of World War II the relationship of Church and State was based upon three principles: first, religious freedom, second, equal status and reciprocity of all recognized and accepted denominations, and third, state patronage for the churches.

A. *State Patronage for Churches*

The oldest of these principles is that of patronage, which up to the end of World War II was the very foundation of the material existence of the churches.

Patronage is an institution of canon law which gained a position of its own in the Hungarian legal system as early as the 11th century. Initially the sole patron was the king, whose patronage *(jus supremae patronatus)* consisted of rights to fill benefices of prelates (bishops, archbishops), and rights over the supervision and management of the property of the Roman Catholic Church on the one hand, and on the other hand of duties to furnish her material support. Thus Church and State entered in a legal relationship.

In order to fulfill these duties the king established dioceses, donated estates to the Church, built churches, abbeys, monasteries, and schools, and supported them continuously.

This close relationship between Church and State resulted in a privileged position of the Roman Catholic Church in public affairs. Until the end of World War II only a Roman Catholic could be crowned as king,[1] and the ceremonies of the coronation were to be performed by the Roman Catholic Church. Furthermore, the Roman Catholic Archbishop of Esztergom as primate of Hungary was the supreme chancellor of the kingdom[2] and bore the title of prince primate.

The *jus patronatus* of private persons, which existed until the end of World War II, came into being when the king transferred the support of local churches, parishes, and schools to worthy laymen, usually in the form of donation. Thus the individual estate owner was the patron of the church, parish, and school established in his estate. This *jus patronatus* derived from the king's *jus supremae patronatus* and was therefore related more to Hungarian public law than to canon law. Patronage quite soon lost its canonic personal character and became an encumbrance on the estate, under which every owner of the estate was obliged to fulfill the duties of the patron, and usually was entitled to exercise patronal rights.

The historical development of patronage was rather complex and does not fall within the limits of this study. We shall confine ourselves to its status as of the end of World War II.

In Hungary patronage was a covenant running with the land, which means that the owner was responsible for the fulfillment of the duties included in patronage. These duties, such as maintenance of the church, parish, and school buildings and payment of the salaries of the priest and school teachers or contribution to their maintenance, varied greatly and were fixed in the *canonicae visitationes* for every church under patronage.

Although patronage usually appeared in the form of an encumbrance on the land, it was not a relationship at private law between the priest *(parochus ordinarius)* and patron, but definitely a relationship at public law.

The duties patronage imposed upon the king—later actually fulfilled by the Government—as well as upon private persons existed unchanged until the end of World War II. The exercise of the rights of *patronatus* after World War I was regulated as follows:

Hungary remained a kingdom after World War I, following the overthrow of the short-lived Dictatorship of the Proletariat proclaimed by some Communists in 1919. But since the throne was vacant, the issue as to who was to exercise the right of supreme patronage remained to be settled. The restitution of constitutional[3] order involved the creation of the office of Regent. With certain exceptions the Regent was entitled "to exercise the rights inherent in the royal power under the constitution." But he "may not exercise the right of supreme patronage." In 1927 an agreement was concluded between the Hungarian Government and the Holy See[4] which provided that in case a benefice of a bishop, an archbishop, or the Abbot of Panonhalma is vacant, the Hungarian Government should submit the names of its candidates to the Holy See within two months after the vacancy occurs. In case the Holy See wants to appoint somebody else, it shall inquire of the Government whether it has any political objection against the candidate. A similar procedure was to be followed in connection with the appointment of superiors of the four teaching orders (Benedictine, Cistercian, Premonstratensian of Csorna and Jászó, and Piarist).

The rights of the supreme patron to appoint canons, abbots, and provosts passed over to the bishops or to the Holy See, but the bishop should ask the government's consent prior to any such appointment.[5]

This situation suffered three lethal blows from the regimes in power after World War II. The first was the so-called land reform, dealt with elsewhere in this study, which made the patrons landless and therefore unable to live up to their duties. The second was the cancellation by law of all encumbrances on lands socialized or confiscated during the land reform, and the third the separation of church and state, which meant the abolition of all state support to the churches.

B. *Recognized and Admitted Denominations*

After the Reformation religions in Hungary were classified

according to two categories: recognized religions and admitted religions. We meet the term "recognized religion" (*recepta religio*) in the laws of Hungary as early as 1571, when the National Assembly of Marosvásárhely (Transylvania) enacted that the four *receptae religiones: "Evangelica reformata (vulgo Calviniana), Lutherana sive Augustana, Romano Catholica, Unitaria vel Antitrinitaria"* may exercise their rites freely. In the course of centuries the circle of the recognized denominations (*receptae religiones*) was extended to include the Serbian and Romanian Eastern Orthodox Churches and the Jewish religion.

The legal consequences following upon the recognition of a religion consisted in equal public status with all other religions, the full right to acquire property, and access to financial assistance by the State.

The Protestant Churches first gained recognition in the Principality of Transylvania namely the Evangelical Church in the National Assembly in Torda, 1557, the Reformed Church in Torda, 1564, and the Unitarian Church in Marosvásárhely, 1571.

A special type of organization which developed in Transylvania in the 16th century and existed up to recent years must be mentioned as closely connected with the historical development of the Catholic Church of Latin rite in Hungary. At that period, when other parts of Hungary were occupied by the Turks, Transylvania, almost isolated from the West, managed to a considerable extent to maintain its independence within the Turkish orbit as a principality of its own. In 1557, the Diet of this principality passed the first Bill of Tolerance on the continent. Subsequently, the Catholic Church which up to then had a predominant position, became de jure one among the *receptae religiones*. De facto, because of the spread of the Reformation, its clerical organization deteriorated to such a degree that from 1601 to 1716, the diocese of Transylvania which had been founded by Saint Stephen, the first king of Hungary (997-1038), was without a permanently residing bishop, and practically without clergy. During this period the laymen organized parochial councils and a central council called the *Status Romano-Catholicus Transylvaniensis* the purpose of which was to take care of Church affairs and to administer the Church property. Originally the Status consisted of the Catholic members of the Diet including high Government officials and members of the Supreme Court of Justice. After 1681, when Transylvania by virtue of the Hungarian Crown came under the rule of the Habsburg dynasty, the Status was acknowledged and confirmed by a number of royal diplomas, beginning with the Diploma Leopoldinum of 1690, and the last issued in 1867. When a bishop was readmitted to his See and the clergy reinstated, the bishop, presiding alternatively with a lay-chairman elected for lifetime, became the "natural chairman" of the Status Assembly, and members of the clergy were included in the Status membership. Under the constitutional legislation of 1867, the separate administration of Transylvania was abolished and merged with the rest of Hungary. New statutes of the Status were set up in 1873. Accordingly, its membership was organized as follows:

Clergy: The bishop of Transylvania, the members of the Chapter, other high-ranking clergy and delegates of the Catholic educational institutions, superiors of religious orders, and one delegate of each deanery.

Laymen: High-ranking Government officials, members of the Court of Appeal, mayors of municipalities, members of the faculty of the Kolozsvár university, patrons, and two representatives of each deanery. These representatives were elected by the members of the church councils in the individual communities, who in turn were elected by the heads of the Catholic families. When in 1920, by the Treaty of Trianon, Transylvania was turned over to Romania, the Status continued to function, and the Roman Catholic members of the Bucharest parliament who were from Transylvania became members of the Status Assembly, too. On May 30, 1932, a Protocol was signed by the Holy See and the Romanian Government (Monitorul Oficial Nr 180, August 3, 1932), ratified as late as eight years later by Decree-Law Nr 659 (Monitorul Oficial Nr 52, March 2, 1940), which settled the legal situation of the *Status Romano-Catholicus Transylvaniensis* in Romania. (See also Romanian report.)

In Hungary proper the Diet enacted various laws[6] which recognized the religious freedom. Finally in 1848 all Christian denominations active in Hungary obtained equal status.[7]

The Privilege Diploma issued by King Leopold I on August 21, 1690 safeguarded the freedom of the members of the Orthodox Church of the Serbian mother-tongue. Until 1770, when the independent *(autokephalos)* Orthodox Church in Hungary was established, they were under the jurisdiction of the Patriarch of Ipek (Peć, Serbia). Several royal decrees issued by Maria Theresa (1740-1780) and by Joseph II (1780-1790) provided for the organization of this Church under the Patriarchate of Karlovci (Croatia). In 1791 freedom of religion was enacted for this Church.[8] The Diet of 1792 seated its archbishop and bishops in the House of Magnates[9] while the dignitaries of the Protestant Churches obtained seats in the House of Magnates only in 1885.[10] In 1864 an Orthodox National Congress was convoked which divided the Orthodox Church in Hungary into a Serbian and a Romanian province. The resolutions of the Congress were given the effect of law[11] and an independent Romanian Orthodox Metropolitanate was created in Hungary. This Metropolitanate was detached to Romania by the Peace Treaty of Trianon after World War I and only the bishopric in Buda remained for the Serbian Orthodox Church province of Hungary.

The first bishopric of the Greek-Catholic Church was established in Fogaras, Transylvania in 1721 by the papal bull "Ratione congruit." (*See also* pp. 270, 285).

This bishopric was elevated to the rank of a Metropolis with three suffragan bishops by Law No. XXXIX of 1868, and conducted its liturgy from the very beginning in the Romanian language. While two other bishoprics, that of Eperjes (at present Czechoslovakia) and Munkács (at present U.S.S.R.) followed the Church Slavonic language, no diocese was established until 1912 with a liturgy in the Hungarian language.

The Royal rescript of 1912 enacted by Law No. XXXV of 1913 and the papal bull "Christi Fideles" established the Catholic Bishopric of the Greek Rite of Hajdudorog. Since the end of World War I this has been the only Greek-Catholic diocese in Hungary, the others being transferred to the successor states.

The bishop is a full member of the Bench of the Catholic Bishops of Hungary and the diocese shares the fate of the Hungarian Catholic church.

The Greek-Catholic churches in the other captive countries were merged with the national Orthodox churches. The Greek-Catholic bishopric of Hajdudorog of Hungary up to this day has successfully escaped annexation to the Moscow-dominated Orthodox church.

Between World Wars I and II, 17 dignitaries of the Roman Catholic Church and 14 dignitaries of other Churches and denominations (6 Calvinists, 4 Lutherans, 1 Unitarian, 1 Orthodox and 2 Jewish) were members of the Hungarian Upper House.

The "absolute equality" of all "legally recognized denominations" [12] and freedom of religion and worship were restated in Law No. XLIII of 1895 as follows:

> 6. Laws and statutes concerning the Roman-, Greek-, and Armenian-Catholic, the Reformed and the Evangelical, the Serbian- and Romanian Orthodox, and the Unitarian denominations and their followers, as well as the Jews, shall be kept unchanged.[13]

This provision refers to the equality of the Christian Churches enacted in 1868.[14]

Law No. XLIII of 1895, which conferred equality under public law upon all religions practiced in Hungary, also provided for the admittance of other denominations not yet practicing in Hungary, and thereby created a new category of "admitted" religions. The status of these denominations differed somewhat from that of the recognized denominations. The capacity of the admitted religions to acquire property was limited, and they were unable to collect church dues through the machinery of tax collection. On the basis of this law the Baptist[15] and Mohammedan[16] denominations were admitted.

From the above it may be noted that the development in the legal status of the various churches in Hungary differed from that in some other mid-European countries. Until the Reformation the position of the Roman Catholic Church in Hungary resembled that of an official State religion, although no such institution existed *de jure*.

The denominational schools had equal rights with the public schools. The curricula, admission and graduation requirements, and teachers' qualifications were standardized by the Minister of Religion and Public Education, whose approval of textbooks was required by law. The schools owned and operated by the churches were subject to the control of ecclesiastical authorities under the supreme supervision of the Ministry of Religion and Public Education. Religious instruction was compulsory in every grammar and high school.

With regard to marriage, Law No. XXXI of 1894 put an end to the reign of the different ecclesiastical laws and established a uniform law for all citizens, regardless of religion, in the form of compulsory civil marriage.

The law does not prevent the parties from complying with the rules of their churches. The civil officer is even under obligation to call the parties' attention to the fact that the civil marriage entered into before him does not fulfill their obligations towards their church.

Law No. XXXII of 1894 (amended by Sections 26-30 of Law No. XLIII of 1895) recognized the right of the parents to covenant on the religion of their future children. In the absence of such covenant, the rule "sex follows sex" prevailed.

This problem has been affected by two recent regulations. First the Constitution of the Hungarian People's Republic (Law No. XX of 1949) declared the separation of Church and State in such matters; secondly, the registration of religion in the register of civil status was abolished (Edict No. 19 of 1952).

Law No. XXXIII of 1894 established the civil register and transferred the matter of registration from the Churches to State jurisdiction.

C.   *Religious Freedom*

The relationship between Church and State is closely related to the question of religious freedom. As in every country where the Reformation had a great influence on the development of religious affairs, the struggle for religious freedom lasted for a long time in Hungary. But this struggle ended in 1895 when the unchangeability of laws guaranteeing religious freedom was enacted (Law No. XLIII of 1895). Since Law No. XX of 1848 provided for the religious freedom of all recognized and accepted denominations there was no further question about religious freedom in Hungary. When World War II ended religious freedom again came into the focus of attention.

II. CHANGES IN THE STATUS OF CHURCHES AFTER WORLD WAR II

A. *General Survey*

Apart from the constitutional provision[17] separating Church and State, no comprehensive law defining the status of the Church in Hungary has been enacted thus far. The change of status may be revealed only by an analysis of a series of individual laws and steps taken by the Hungarian Government: agreements made with the individual Churches and a series of statutes which, contrary to the principle of separation of Church and State, provided for an increasing interference of the State in Church affairs and finally for submission of the Churches to the State.

1. The land reform laws[18] provided for nationalization of all landed properties of the churches exceeding 100 holds (141 acres). Although the law promised a compensation "in accordance with the capacity of the State," no such compensation has ever been effectuated. To what extent this measure deprived the Churches of their main sources of temporal existence may be seen from the following figures: According to the official statistics for 1935, 1,006,311 cadastral holds from a total of 16,081,844 cadastral holds of agricultural area including forests,[19] covering the entire country, were owned by the churches and/or denominational schools and institutions.

2. The privilege of clergymen to serve in the ranks in the military service was abolished.

3. The Jewish denominational organizations were deprived of their autonomy when their officers, previously elective, were made subject to appointment by the Government. At the same time two of the Jewish denominational organizations were merged by decree. (*See* Chapter *IV*)

4. Subsequently, individual Churches were induced to sign separate agreements with the Government. According to the provisions of these agreements, the State would grant some financial support to the Churches, while the Churches on their part would fulfil certain obligations to the State. The events which led to the conclusion of these agreements, as well as their individual provisions, are dealt with in Chapter III of this study. It suffices here to mention that they also contained binding pledges on the part of the Government to safeguard freedom of religion and Church activities and the acknowledgment of such freedom on the part of the Churches.

The trial of Cardinal Mindszenty was initiated as a means of pressure to force the Catholic bishops into an agreement with the Government. Criminal prosecution was brought against Archbishop Grősz of Kalocsa after he had signed this agreement.

5. At the same time these agreements were signed and also subsequently, several laws and decrees were issued which deprived the Churches of their schools and progressively restricted religious instruction in schools until it was all but abolished. After denominational schools had been nationalized religious instruction in schools was declared optional. This was done less than one year after the Government, in agreements with the Reformed (Calvinist) and Unitarian Churches, stipulated that such teaching was to be compulsory. Finally, in September of 1950 the optional teaching of religion was regulated in a manner tantamount to its elimination.

By this time the three law schools maintained by the various Churches had been closed. Later divinity schools were detached from the universities and left to the care of the Churches. In this connection it must be mentioned that in November 1951 the Synod of the Hungarian Reformed Church, obviously yielding to government pressure, discontinued two of its four divinity schools, in Pápa and Sárospatak. At the present time the only denominational schools, except for divinity schools, are the few left to the churches in accordance with agreements signed by their representatives with the State. The following table indicates to what extent the number of denominational schools was restricted by the agreements:

	in 1938	in 1952
Catholic	2981	8
Reformed	1117	5
Evangelical	406	2

Even the remaining schools have only a nominal existence as denominational schools since they are under rigid Government control.

6. A large number of national and local charitable, cultural, and economic associations under religious auspices were dissolved by the Minister of Interior. In 1946, 124 Catholic organizations, in 1949 alone, 320 religious organizations and 1300 other associations, clubs, etc., organized by various denominations, were dissolved.

7. Many ecclesiastical holidays were declared regular workdays. St. Stephen's Day (August 20), celebrated since the year 1222 as a national holiday in commemoration of the first king of Hungary, was declared as the Day of the Constitution of the Hungarian People's Republic. On this very day in 1949, the Constitution of the Hungarian People's Republic was promulgated, which provided for freedom of religious worship and separation of the Church from the State.[20] Later developments, however, proved that this separation actually meant a gradually increasing state interference in church affairs, which finally resulted in an almost total control of the churches by the state. The following events represent some highlights in this development.

8. On October 22, 1949, only two months after the principle of separation of Church and State was enacted in the Constitu-

tion, the clergy were forced to take an oath of loyalty to the Government. Subsequently the church communities of the Hungarian Greek Orthodox Church were transferred from the jurisdiction of an independent ecclesiastical administrator residing in Budapest to the jurisdiction of the Orthodox Patriarch of Moscow, who delegated a special administrator for Hungary.

9. The activities of the Roman Catholic religious orders were prohibited and their monasteries confiscated.

10. The Government Bureau for Church Affairs was established in order to "prepare statutes relating to churches," to "put into effect the measures undertaken by the Cabinet in church affairs, and to control their execution."

11. The appointment of bishops and prelates was made subject to Government approval with retroactive effect.

12. A Fund for Church Affairs under the administration of the Government Bureau was established, in part from the "equivalent of lands voluntarily offered [to the State] by the individual churches."

B.   *Statutes Changing the Status of the Churches*

1.   *Separation of Church from State*

The Constitution of the Hungarian People's Republic reads:

> The Hungarian People's Republic shall secure the liberty of conscience of its citizens and the freedom of religious worship.
> In order to protect liberty of conscience, the Hungarian People's Republic separates the Church from the State.[21]

2.   *Abolition of Exemption of Clergymen and Seminarians from Military Service.*

Under law[22] and according to various previous statutes on home defense, clergymen and divinity students had the privilege of serving their military duties in the so-called Alternative Reserve with an abridged term. Similarly, *they could serve in the Medical Corps in the time of mobilization and war.* Members of religious orders were required only for such service as was in conformity with their vocation.

After World War II several provisions of law concerning this question were repealed,[23] and at the present there is no legal provision in Hungary for any special treatment of clergymen in this matter.

3. Dissolution of Associations and Foundations.

(a)   The names of religious associations dissolved were officially published.[24]

> The Minister of the Interior ordered every association to make a report relative to their activities beginning from January 1, 1939; particularly from the [following] point of view: did political considerations prevail in their activities or not; did [the association] take a stand in the issue of war [and peace] and if so, what stand? The names of officers, etc. After the report is received the Minister of the Interior shall decide upon further continuance of the association. If the Minister of the Interior refuses to permit it to continue the association shall be considered dissolved.[25]

(b)   Simultaneously with the nationalization of denominational schools (see *infra*) the remaining assets of the Religious and Educational Fund were taken into State ownership. This fund originated from the assets of monasteries and convents destroyed during the sixteenth century. It further increased when Joseph II ordered the property of the dissolved monastic orders to be assigned for the promotion of the aims of the Roman Catholic Church. The fund was administered from the beginning by government agencies, first by the Chancery and later by the Minister of Religion and Public Education. Its main function was to support schools, parishes, and other institutions of the Roman Catholic Church.

Since the assets of the fund consisted of landed property, it was practically dissolved after the land reform of 1945. Certain assets remaining after the land reform were nationalized by simple orders which were never made public.

The nationalization or confiscation of the funds administered by the Church required a different treatment. Edict No. 2 of 1949 authorized the government to dissolve a foundation: (1) if its existence would endanger public interest; (2) if it becomes impossible for the foundation to carry out its goal; (3) if its purpose could be reasonably achieved only by the government or by municipal or community administration; (4) if the goals of the foundation do not conform to the new situation. The particular minister with supreme supervision over the foundation concerned had exclusive jurisdiction over such dissolution of the foundation.

Under this edict numerous hospitals, orphanages, children's homes, and other institutions were confiscated.

Two months after the publication of Edict No. 2 of 1949 on Foundations, Edict No. 13 of 1949 authorized the Minister of Religion and Public Education to demand a detailed report and description of every collection or individual piece of works of art of permanent and public interest from their owners or custodians, including private persons, churches, denominations, religious corporations, or congregations. The minister is authorized to control or even to expropriate such collections or such works of art. In case of expropriation the Minister of Religion and Public Education shall determine the amount of compensation. No judicial remedy is allowed.

Similar regulations were issued a year later concerning archives (Edict No. 29 of 1950; Decree No. 1610-26 of 1950 (VIII.8 V.K.M).

Thus the effect of earlier decrees confiscating monasteries together with their collections and archives was completed.

The following statistical table shows the losses of schools and institutions suffered by the Roman Catholic Church.

I. Schools and Institutions	Status in 1945	Status in 1952	Percentage of losses
Asylums, homes	191	–	100,0
Elementary schools, 6 grades	1.216	–	100,0
General schools, 8 grades	1.669	–	100,0
Higher elementary schools	20	–	100,0
Highschools	86	–	100,0
Gymnasiums	49	8	83,5
Kindergarten teachers' schools	3	–	100,0
Teacher training schools	32	–	100,0
Professional highschools	22	–	100,0

Professional schools for workers	27	–	100,0
Nursing schools	1	–	100,0
Home economics schools	1	–	100,0
Commercial schools for girls	1	–	100,0
Apprentice schools	3	–	100,0
Commercial highschools	2	–	100,0
Divinity schools	1	–	100,0
Law schools	1	–	100,0
Teachers' colleges	4	–	100,0
Seminaries	22	6	73,0
Preparatory seminaries	8	–	100,0
Boarding schools	167	8	95,1
II. Monasteries and Convents			
Male	187	6	96,8
Female	456	2	99,6
III. Catholic hospitals	9	1	90,0
IV. Houses of Catholic associations	200	–	100,0
Newspaper and publishing offices	50	3	94,0

(Matthias Annabring, *Die katholische Kirche im kommunistischen Ungarn*, Südost-Stimmen, Vol. III, No. 8, December 1953, p. 20.)

4.   Abolition of Certain Church Holidays.

(a) It was declared that Candlemas, February 2; Annunciation day, March 25; and the Nativity of the Blessed Virgin, September 8,[26] the day of the Assumption of Mary, August 15,[27] the Corpus Christi Day, and the Whitmonday[28] shall be common working days.

(b)   St. Stephen's Day was abolished and replaced by the Day of the People's Republic.

The Decree[29] which proclaimed August 20 as the Day of the People's Republic deserves special attention. St. Stephen's day was mentioned for the first time in Hungarian legislation in 1222[30] when the Golden Bull issued by King Andrew II contained the following provision:

> We decree that we shall celebrate the feast of Saint King Stephen each year * * *.

For almost a thousand years this day was celebrated in Hungary in commemoration of her first king as both an ecclesiastical and national holiday. Thus the oldest national holiday was transformed into the holiday of the People's Republic.

5. *Nationalization of Denominational Schools.*

(a)   Denominational and private schools were nationalized.[31] The message accompanying the bill contains the following passages:

With the liberation of our country our economic and social life began to develop along a new line. The churches in their changed economic situation[32] were even less able to support their schools than before the liberation. Therefore the economic burden resulting from the right to maintain schools devolved almost entirely upon the public. At the same time the churches retained the right due to them as independent sponsors of schools, to mention merely the most important among these rights, the right to an autonomous school administration and the right to publish textbooks.[33]

The lack of an orderly relationship between church and state and [the nature] of the educational principles of the church schools, which have been substantially retained from the past and which have not even approximately kept pace with the course of the transformation of our economic and social life, have increased the chaos in our public education up to the present time, to a degree which in the eyes of every soberminded observer will appear as a grave impediment to the further sound development of our public education.

* * * Education, however, can be of true value for the individual only if it enables him to adjust himself without difficulty to the life of the community and to undertake to pursue its aims. In other words, the new aims resulting from the planned organization of our economic and social life present an increasing number of new tasks to the educational system.

These tasks can be accomplished only by a uniform plan and direction. Experience has already shown that the autonomous bodies which have concerned themselves with our educational problems (churches, communities, associations, etc.) are not qualified to achieve these tasks. Their lack of qualification is due not only to their inability to secure the necessary financial means, but also to the fact that the economic and philosophical aspects of modern education cannot be separated from similar manifestations of the life of the State. In other words, an effort to separate them would relegate education to a vacuum and also endanger its economic maintenance. * * *

It is certainly regrettable that the educational principles of many denominational schools are contrary to the democratic aims of the [newly established] general schools. This was proved in a way clearer than the sun by the following circumstance: The state had prepared new textbooks which conformed with our new educational system and which were inexpensive, were of a high level, and had earned undivided recognition. These textbooks were not introduced in the denominational schools but instead instruction was carried out there either without any textbooks at all or, at best, with textbooks which could compete with the State textbooks neither in price nor in level and by their contents only furthered the disintegration of our national education. Besides, the mere fact that in the last school year some hundred thousand school children were without textbooks indicates that the individual autonomous ecclesiastical bodies have neither the necessary means nor the adequate organization to provide their schools with the necessary books.[34]* * *

I must stress that this bill by no means affects the present system of compulsory instruction in religion and morals in our schools but is exclusively aimed at establishing uniformity in public education. Under the conditions prevailing at the present time only the state is capable of establishing this uniformity which is indispensable to the future of our public education. Only the state has the adequate means to educate the children of our people to love their fellow men, to respect their neighbors and to become familiar with labor * * *.

According to this law, all schools of any kind, kindergartens, and student homes connected with the school, were taken over by the government with the exception of schools which served church purposes exclusively, such as divinity schools, deacons' and deaconess' training schools, etc. The entire personnel of the schools taken over by the government was transferred to government service. In fixing the salaries of these teachers the years spent in teaching in denominational schools were considered as government service. All buildings, premises, and any other property and benefits accruing to the school were also transferred to the state. In the future a non-state school could be opened or maintained only by special permission of the cabinet.[35]

The significance of the nationalization of denominational schools may be seen from the following table of the total number of public and denominational schools in Hungary in 1938.

Secondary and Elementary Schools*

	Secondary Schools	Burgher Schools- equal to Junior High Schools	Elementary Schools	Kinder- garten
Public Schools				
Government	67	160	1282	404
Village and City Schools	11	101	827	476
Total	78	261	2109	880
Denominational Schools				
Roman Catholic	45	80	2856	174
Reformed	24	14	1079	6
Evangelical	11	1	395	2
Jewish, Greek Orthodox etc.	15	41	460	78
Total	95	136	4790	260
Grand Total	173	397	6899	1140

*Statistical Yearbook, 1938 (In Hungarian); pp. 276, 286.

The antecedents of the nationalization of the denominational schools may be found in Chapter III.

(b) All the debts of the schools were taken over by the government and cancelled, and the creditors were not reimbursed.[36]

(c) The ancient law schools in Eger (Roman Catholic), Kecskemét (Reformed) and Miskolc (Evangelical) were closed on August 30, 1949.[37] These law schools had been maintained by the churches.[38]

(d) The theological schools of the Universities of Budapest, Debrecen, and Pécs were separated from the universities at the end of the school year 1949/50 and transferred to the respective churches.[39]

6. Religious Instruction in the Schools

(a) Religious instruction no longer compulsory.

The message accompanying the Bill on Nationalization of the Non-State Schools[40] emphasized that "this Bill by no means affects the present system of compulsory religious education in the schools." Furthermore, in the agreements concluded with the Reformed and Evangelical Churches on October 7, 1948, the government had explicitly acknowledged that "compulsory teaching of religion in the schools is within the free sphere of church activities."[41]

On September 6, 1949, however, the Presidium of the Hungarian People's Republic issued an edict[42] which reads:

> According to the provisions of Article 54, Law No. XX of 1949 (Constitution) relating to the separation of the Church from the State, religious instruction in the schools will not be compulsory.

Detailed regulations enforcing the law were issued by the Minister of Religion and Public Education.

It was ordered[43] that beginning with the school year of 1949-1950, religious instruction should no longer be compulsory. Parents who desired religious instruction for their children were required to report this to the school before September 15, 1949.

This decree indicates that normally no religious instruction will be given unless the parents expressly ask for it. But the decree was dated September 6 and the deadline for the request was September 15, so that only a week's time was left to the parents to register their intention. Apart from the obvious difficulties of reporting such intention in due time owing to geographical causes—in the case of schools in the Plain far away from the parents' residence—another circumstance should be considered. The obligation of the parents to request religious instruction for their children individually offered a welcome opportunity for the Communist authorities to discover individuals who continued to adhere to their religion.[44]

(b) Restricting Optional Religious Instruction.

After religious instruction in schools had been made optional the next step, announced in advance by Mr. Révay, Minister of People's Education, in a speech delivered on June 5, 1950, was to issue a decree[45] which made the appointment of teachers of religion in schools subject to the arbitrary decision of the Executive Committees of the Local (Municipal, District) Councils (Soviets) dominated by the Communist Party. Moreover, this provision made the position of the teachers of religion dependent upon their individual attitude toward "the People's Democracy and its orders." A religion instructor who was discharged because he was considered as "hostile" could not be reemployed elsewhere. The decree contains provisions further restricting the activities of the teachers of religion to the point of forbidding him to stay in the school building after the time of his classes, or to assemble his pupils outside of the school, as, for example, for worship in church. These provisions also deprive the teachers of religion all disciplinary power over the student. In addition, the supervision of religious instruction was transferred from the churches to Government authorities. Thus, contrary to the separation of State and Church proclaimed by the Constitution, the state authorities were empowered to control religious instruction or to suppress it at their pleasure.

7.   *Oath Required from the Priests.*

A decree[46] established the oath to be taken by civil servants, members of the armed forces, and persons who are not civil servants but who receive contributions from the State Treasury in addition to their income. This rule refers to priests, who thus became obliged to take the oath of loyalty.

Up to 1918, only bishops appointed by the Apostolic King in the exercise of his right of supreme patronage had to take an oath of loyalty to the king. Parochial priests were not considered civil servants and consequently were not required to take an oath, although most of them received a contribution from the State Treasury.

The decree of October 22, 1949 provides that those who fail to take the oath within the prescribed time must forfeit State contributions. In addition to the moral binding force of the oath, it could be an aggravating fact if the priest were accused of a crime against the State, against the people, or against the Law on the Protection of State and Official Secrets.

The oath reads as follows: "I . . . swear loyalty to the Hungarian People's Republic, its people, and its constitution; I shall keep official state secrets; in exercising my duties I shall act in the interest of the people and see to it with all my endeavor that my activities promote the strengthening and development of the Hungarian People's Republic."

The decree on the oath met with strong resistance on the part of the clergy, who were not prepared to take an oath of allegiance to the Communist government. The priests, however, were threatened with deprivation of their salaries if they did not take the oath. Thus the Bench of Bishops issued a circular in which they gave permission for the priests to take the oath, while the bishops declared that they would do the same after having received special permission from the Holy See.

It was only as late as July 21, 1951, after Archbishop Grösz, who presided over the Bench of Bishops for the imprisoned Cardinal Mindszenty, had likewise been sentenced, and after the position of the bishops itself had been threatened by the retroactive decree requiring government approval for the appointment of bishops, that the remaining Roman Catholic prelates saw themselves forced to take the oath. Their reason for taking this step was explained in an article signed by Bishop Bertalan Badarik, and published in the Budapest daily MAGYAR NEMZET and in the subsequently prohibited Roman Catholic periodical AZ EMBER. This article, entitled "After Taking the Oath" contains the following passage:

> St. Paul, the apostle of the nations, who preached the Gospel in a world empire utterly opposed to Christianity, admonished the believers of the Church community with the following words: 'Let everybody be subject to the higher authorities, for there is no authority except from God, and those who exist have been appointed by God.' (Rom. 13:1)

8. *Hungarian Orthodox Church Communities placed under the jurisdiction of Moscow.*

Besides the Serbian and Romanian Orthodox Church provinces, there are also church communities belonging to the so-called Hungarian Greek Orthodox Church. The congregations of this denomination had, however, no joint ecclesiastical authority.[47] The legal provision[48] on the Greek Orthodox Churches merely was:

> The followers of the Greek Orthodox Religion of other than the
> Serbian or Romanian mother tongue may also henceforth maintain
> all the rights which they have exercised in the past related to set-
> tling the matters of their church communities and schools independ-
> ently, using their liturgical language freely, and managing the
> property and the funds of their church communities.

As late as 1941 the congregations of the Hungarian Greek
Orthodox Church were partly placed under the jurisdiction of a
special ecclesiastical administrator appointed by the Regent.[49]
In 1950 these congregations were placed under the jurisdiction
of the Orthodox Patriarch of Moscow by a notice of the Minister
of Religion and Public Education.[50]

9.   Dissolution of Religious Orders.

Some of the religious orders were brought to the country by
Hungarian kings in the 11th century and some later by the prelates of the Church. Religious orders were mentioned in Hungarian statutes as early as 1092.[51] Later, law[52] required the permission of the king for admittance of new religious orders into
the country and for the foundation of new monasteries. Joseph
II (1780-1790) abolished most of the religious orders. Since he
was not a crowned king of Hungary and no Diet was convoked
under his reign, his decrees, most of which he repealed himself
before his death, were never acknowledged as laws in Hungary.
Under his successors all of the abolished orders were gradually
restored.

Both Roman Catholic and Protestant religious orders, besides
maintaining hospitals and homes for the crippled and mentally
ill, and performing pastoral work, operated a large number of
elementary and secondary schools which were of a very high
standard and were therefore attended by a great number of
pupils of various denominations including the Jewish.

The dispossession of the religious orders began in the Spring
of 1950 and is discussed infra III.

A decree was issued under the date of September 3, 1950,
supplying the legal ground for the dissolution of religious orders
in Hungary.

10. The establishment of a Government Bureau for Church Affairs.

The establishment of a Government Bureau for Church Affairs, less than two years after the principle of separation of Church and State was enacted in the new Constitution, represents the decisive step taken by the Communist Government in its campaign to assume full control over all church activities.

The purpose of this Bureau is clearly revealed in the decree[53] which established it. According to these provisions the jurisdiction of the Bureau extends to "preparing statutes relating to Churches and securing the enforcement of these statutes" and "carrying out the measures undertaken by the Cabinet in church affairs and controlling their fulfillment."

These provisions actually give the Bureau full power to interfere in church affairs at will, as was amply illustrated by subsequent developments.

Mr. István Kossa, Secretary General of the Council of the Trade Unions and a leading member of the Communist Party, was appointed first President of the Bureau.[54] There are also subordinate agencies, since the District Local Councils (Soviets) must include a comparatively high-ranking official for handling church affairs.[55]

11. Appointment of Prelates Subjected to Government Approval.

On July 4, 1951, an edict[56] made the appointment of bishops and other prelates subject to government approval. This decree was made retroactive to January 1, 1946, or, in other words, for six and a half years. According to another provision it was to remain in force until a "bilateral agreement" could be reached on filling these church posts. Although the Holy See is not expressly mentioned in the text, it seems obvious that it was intended to make the Holy See conclude an agreement with the present Hungarian Government similar to that concluded in 1927.

12. Establishment of a Fund for Church Affairs.

In 1951, a special Fund for Church Affairs was established by decree,[57] to consist partly of the equivalent of "lands voluntarily offered by the individual churches [to the State]." The degree of spontaneity of such "voluntary" offers may be seen from the figures mentioned earlier,[58] indicating to what extent the churches had already been affected by the land reform. The administration of this Fund was assigned to the Bureau. In effect, therefore, the president of the Bureau has financial control over the clergy and what real property assets are still left to the churches.

13. Priests Appointed and Paid by the Government.

On April 27, 1951, the Cabinet empowered the Minister for Religion and Public Education to raise, in agreement with the Minister of Finance, the stipends paid to the lower clergy.[59] The wording of the official press-release on the Cabinet-meeting reveals that it is up to the discretion of the Minister for Religion and Public Education whether or not he grants the pay raise in an individual case. Moreover, old-age contribution is payable from the day when the individual priest took his oath of loyalty to the Government. A pamphlet published by the Legation of the Hungarian People's Republic in Washington D.C.[60] discloses that "the Government appoints the religious administrative personnel as well as the low clergy." With this measure, the Government gained full control over the clergy.

14. Compulsory Health Insurance for Clergymen.

A decree of Dec. 21, 1951[61] amends previous provisions relating to compulsory health insurance for clergymen. It grants power to the president of the Bureau to declare whether a clergyman or a given church is eligible for health insurance. The wording of the decree is not quite clear as to whether such a decision may affect an individual clergyman or a church. But the president's right to decide at his own discretion is clearly stated.

15. *Regulation on the Production and Reproduction of Art Objects.*

The decree[62] made the commercial production and reproduction, industrially or manually, of any objects of art, and trade involving such objects, subject to special permission of the Minister for People's Education. Since pictures and statues of religious devotion are also under this provision, the production and reproduction of such objects of art are likewise subject to a special permit of the Government.

III. AGREEMENTS BETWEEN THE INDIVIDUAL CHURCHES AND THE GOVERNMENT

A. *General Survey*

Prior to the Communist regime in Hungary the status of religious denominations generally was regulated by laws. The agreements concluded between the Government of Hungary and the various churches (beginning in 1948) thus represent a new means of regulating the status of religious denominations.[63]

On May 15, 1948 Gyula Ortutay, Minister of Religion and Public Education, requested in a press conference that representatives of the Roman Catholic, Reformed, Evangelical, and Unitarian Churches open negotiations for the settlement of the differences with the Government.[64] These negotiations actually took place with the representatives of the Catholic Church abstaining.

On September 2, 1948, Mr. János Kardos was elected as Head Curator of the Reformed Ecclesiastical District of Budapest as a successor of Mr. Andor Lázár by a margin of 387:244 votes against Mr. Roland Kiss, Under Secretary of Home Defense, who enjoyed the Government's support. However, Mr. Kardos was arrested by the Poltical Police and forced to resign.[65] After the agreement was signed[66] Mr. Kardos was reelected in the elections of November 18, 1948. The elections were thereupon annulled and Mr. Roland Kiss, the Government's candidate, became Head Curator.[67]

1. On October 7, 1948, the Government announced the conclusion of two such agreements, with the Unitarian and with the Reformed Churches.

Although the freedom of the Reformed Church was explicitly recognized in the agreement, its press was stopped and its youth organizations were dissolved.[68]

The Reformed Church, however, did not surrender without a struggle. Bishop László Ravasz had taken his stand together with Cardinal Mindszenty and Lajos Ordas, Bishop of the most important district of the Evangelical Church, against government measures restricting the rights of the churches. Mátyás Rákosi, Secretary General of the Hungarian Communist Party and Deputy Prime Minister, had personally threatened Bishop Ravasz that the salaries of all Reformed teachers would be cut off and the educational work of the Church stopped if he [Ravasz] did not resign.[69]

On April 28, 1948, Bishop Ravasz, Chairman of the Ecumenical Council and of the National Synod, was forced to retire. At the same time Mr. Andor Lázár, Head Curator of the Reformed Ecclesiastical District of Budapest, was arrested by the Political Police [70] and forced to resign.[71]

2. The Unitarian Church, with only a small number of adherents in Hungary proper,[72] followed the Reformed Church in signing a similar agreement with the Government on the same day,[73] without attempting resistance.

3. On December 16, 1948, the agreement between the Government and the Evangelical Church was concluded[74] after Bishop Lajos Ordas and Baron Albert Radvánszky, Supervisor General of the Evangelical Church, had been arrested.[75] Both were sentenced under the pretense of black marketing on October 1, 1948.[76]

The three agreements mentioned above still retain the appearance of having been concluded between equal partners. They include unusual phrases of mutual esteem and recognition; the Churches declare that they enjoy religious freedom to an even greater extent than ever before. In these agreements the Government expressly recognized compulsory religious instruction in schools as "belonging within the free sphere of church activities" and the principle of a "Free Church in a Free State." Nevertheless, compulsory religious instruction in schools was subsequently abolished.

The Churches, on the other hand, are obliged to have prayers said for the Republic, the President, and the Government, and to conduct services on national holidays. Furthermore, the Government, which emphatically recognized the merits of these Churches in the field of public education, left only 5 secondary schools to the Reformed Church, which had previously owned 11.

4. (a) On August 30, 1950, almost two years later, an agreement was concluded with the Roman Catholic Bench of Bishops. In comparison with the other agreements its much more severe provisions and the late date of its conclusion clearly reflect the hard struggle preceding its conclusion and the progress made in the meantime in the Communist Government's antireligious policy in Hungary.

Since the facts leading to this agreement are widely known, only the highlights will be mentioned here.

On May 9, 1948, Gyula Ortutay, Minister of Religion and Public Education, sent a letter to the Roman Catholic Bench of Bishops inviting them to negotiate.[77] On May 15, he informed the press of this invitation and at the same time disclosed the governmental plan to nationalize the denominational schools.[78] On May 19, Cardinal Mindszenty, in answer to Ortutay's letter, agreed in principle to negotiate under the following conditions:[79]

    (1)   That the plan to nationalize the denominational schools be revoked by the Government;

    (2)   that the dissolved Catholic Associations[80] be reestablished and their confiscated property restored;

(3)   that permission be granted to start a Catholic non-party newspaper.

Without referring to these points Mr. Ortutay in a letter of
June 14, 1948, suggested that Cardinal Mindszenty might treat
the school problem as a question of detail on the agenda of
the negotiations.[81] On June 15, Cardinal Mindszenty refused to
negotiate under the prevailing conditions, especially since the
Roman Catholic schools were "being closed by the authorities
and occupied by the police force even before the question had
been brought before the Parliament." "After all this"—Cardinal
Mindszenty's letter reads—"it is senseless to continue to talk of
further pourparlers [since] this question of nationalization would
have been one of the most essential items of the negotiations." [82]
Finally he asked Mr. Ortutay "in the interest of general rap-
prochement, to issue a declaration stating that the question of
nationalization of denominational schools has been taken off
the agenda of Parliament." [83] On the same day the bill on nationalization of denominational schools was submitted to the
Parliament.[84] The next day it was passed in the Parliament[85] by
a margin of 293 votes of the Communist-ruled coalition to 63
votes[86] of the Popular Democratic Party with 71 abstentions.[87]
On July 23, 1948, a number of Catholic leaders and priests,
among them Msgr. Zsigmond Mihalovics, were sentenced by the
People's Court in Budapest for "inciting against democracy."
(Msgr. Mihalovics was tried *in absentia*.)

(b)   On November 17, 1948 the circulation of MAGYAR
KURIR, the official weekly journal of the Roman Catholic
Church in Hungary, was forbidden by the government.[88] The last
pastoral letter of Cardinal Mindszenty, that of November 18,
1948, was to have been published in the next issue of the MAG-
YAR KURIR.[89] This pastoral letter contained the following
passages:

> The country is condemned to silence, and public opinion has
> been made a mere frivolous jest. Democratic freedom in this coun-
> try means that any opinion that differs from the official one is
> silenced. If a man dares to raise his voice in contradiction, he is
> dismissed from his post because of his criticism of democracy, as

many examples show, or he is punished in other ways. I feel the deepest sympathy for the sufferings of these people, and compassion for every man who has fallen victim to these measures. With regard to the fact that between Church and State—or perhaps we should say 'parties'—no agreement has yet been reached, it is well known that*** when the Church was at last invited to negotiate, the main point—the problem of the schools—had already been settled by the State, and the Church had to play the role of scapegoat. Of my predecessors in office, two were killed in action; two were robbed of all their possessions; one was taken prisoner and deported; one was exiled and one died after visiting and nursing victims of an epidemic. However, such a systematic and purposeful propaganda of lies, time and again disproved and time and again repeated, has never been organized against the seventy-eight predecessors in my office. I stand for God, for Church and for Hungary. This duty was imposed on me by the fate of my nation which stands alone, an orphan in the whole world. If I am compelled to speak out and to state the facts as they are, it is only the misery of my people which forces me to do so and the urge for truth.[99] Here I stand, waiting to see what is going to happen to me.[91]

On November 19, 1948, Dr. András Zakar, Cardinal Mindszenty's secretary, was arrested under the charge of "activities against the Nation." [92]

(c)   On November 27, 1948 Mátyás Rákosi, Secretary General of the Communist Party and Deputy Prime Minister, discussing the problem of an agreement with the Roman Catholic Church before the Central Committee of the Hungarian Workers Party [i.e. Communist Party] said:

> If we cannot establish order by mutual agreement, then we shall do so as demanded by the people by exercising the power of the State. We shall put an end to the policy of treating traitors with more indulgence * * * when dressed in robes of priests or cardinals. And there will be an end to the practice that the law hits only the criminals belonging to the minor clergy, but does not touch the higher ranks.

On December 14, 1948, István Dobi, who became Prime Minister December 10, 1948,[93] declared in his program speech in the National Assembly:[94]

> Mindszenty and his clique who head the Catholic Church do not want and do not care for an agreement with the People's Demo-

cracy's State power. Mindszenty wants to make Hungary a colony of the western imperialists. We wish to establish an atmosphere of the kind that both friend and foe will understand: he who opposes the People's Democracy runs his head against the wall.

On December 16, 1948, the Roman Catholic Bench of Bishops, after a special meeting presided over by Cardinal Mindszenty, announced that they were prepared to settle their differences with the State "in a manner corresponding with the dogma, laws and rights of the Church." [95] On December 26, 1948, Árpád Szakasits, President of the Hungarian People's Republic, declared that "the great mass of the people demands the liquidation of the anti-democratic reactionaries of Cardinal Mindszenty's clique." [96] On the same day, December 26, Cardinal Mindszenty was arrested.[97] During his detention he pleaded guilty and declared in a letter allegedly written by him to the Minister of Justice that he was ready to refrain for a time from exercising his office. Half an hour before his arrest he had written the following statement:[98] "(1) I have not taken part in a conspiracy; (2) I shall never resign; (3) I refuse to give evidence; (4) Should anyone hear or read that I have made a confession or resigned, then even if there were evidence proved by my own signature, this must be regarded as a sign of human weakness and frailty and I declare it herewith null and void."

Four days after Cardinal Mindszenty had been arrested, on December 30, 1948, Prime Minister István Dobi invited the members of the Catholic Bench of Bishops for negotiation.[99]

On January 2, 1949, the Vatican announced that it had rejected the Hungarian Government's request for an understanding "independent of the personal case of the Prince Primate of Hungary." [100] On January 12, 1949, the Bench of Bishops in a letter to Prime Minister Dobi refused to continue the negotiations with the Government, which had begun on January 4, 1949. Only one meeting had been held.[101]

Though the trial of Cardinal Mindszenty formed the climax of the Government's campaign against the Roman Catholic Church, this campaign was by no means discontinued and reached another climax with the sentencing of Archbishop Grösz. Even before Mindszenty's trial only one monthly and two weekly papers remained out of 16 Catholic daily papers and a number of periodicals. Priests were arrested for reading pastoral letters, which were frequently suppressed by the Government.[102] The Bench of Bishops on February 27, 1950 and the superiors of the religious orders in Hungary on April 17, 1950, protested to the Government against the illegal steps taken by authorities against the members of religious orders.[103] The letters of the superiors of the religious orders specified such steps[104] as forcing the monks and nuns to leave their convents, taking away parts of the convent buildings, gardens, furniture, houses, cultural institutions and printing shops, hindering members of religious orders in the performance of their pastoral or nursing work, taking away novice training houses and divinity schools.

(d) After a vehemently anti-Catholic and anti-religious speech of the Minister of Public Education,[105] which was followed by the internment of many monks and nuns,[106] the Bench of Bishops and its acting head, Archbishop József Grösz, requested the government to negotiate over the religious orders. These negotiations started on June 28, 1950.[107] The Archbishop informed the Minister of Religion and Public Education in a letter on August 28, 1950 that the Episcopate had authorized him to sign an agreement with the Government. The letter closed:

> The Bench of Bishops did this in the hope that the difficulties which have arisen in the relations between state and church may be settled in a spirit of mutual understanding and that this understanding will be shown in the handling of the question of members of religious orders in a more humane manner. At the same time the Bench of Bishops wishes to stress the fact that by concluding this agreement it intended by no means to affect the rights of the Holy See with regard to the determination of the relations between church and state.

Archbishop Grösz signed this agreement on August 30, 1950.[108]

The agreement differs substantially in several points from the agreements previously concluded by the Government with the various Protestant churches. Whereas in these agreements the rights of the churches "belonging to the free sphere of church activities" were mentioned in detail, the agreement with the representatives of the Roman Catholic Church merely states in general terms that "the Government guarantees full religious freedom to the Catholic believers and freedom of activity for the Catholic Church." The Government further promises to restore 8 secondary schools to the Catholic Church. In addition, the Government agrees that only as many members of religious teaching orders may work in the Catholic denominational schools as are required for teaching. Whereas in the agreements concluded with the Protestant Churches the Government had fixed in detail the extent of the support promised to the churches on the basis of the support previously enjoyed by them and regulated by law, the agreement with the Catholic Church contains only a phrase promising support "in the spirit" of the other agreements and avoids promising support equal to that granted to the Protestant Churches. Moreover, the promise of securing an adequate minimum subsistence for clergymen performing pastoral work implies a discretional right of the Government to fix the amount of this support arbitrarily.

In return, the representatives of the Roman Catholic Church in Hungary, again unlike the Protestant Churches, had to pledge explicitly to support the political order and Constitution of the People's Republic and to take appropriate steps against clergymen opposing the Government and its work; to condemn all activities against the State; to urge the Catholic believers to take part in carrying out the Five-Year Plan; to call upon the clergy not to oppose agricultural cooperatives (*kolkhozes*); to support the Peace Movement, and to condemn warmongering and the use of atomic weapons.

A week later, on September 7, 1950, the Presidium of the Hungarian People's Republic issued an edict[109] by which the religious orders in Hungary were dissolved.[110] On September 10, 1950, the Bench of Bishops, in a pastoral letter signed by Archbishop Grösz, emphatically protested against the total dissolution of the religious orders.[111]

Barely ten months after he had signed the agreement, Archbishop József Grösz, the highest dignitary of the Roman Catholic Church in Hungary after Cardinal Mindszenty, was arrested and sentenced to 15 years imprisonment. What happened subsequently shows clearly the extent of the program to liquidate religion itself. Moreover, the speed with which the Government abolished the rights expressly guaranteed in agreements with the Protestant Churches as "belonging to the sphere of free Church activities" leaves no doubt whatsoever as to the reliability of the promises given by the Government in its agreement with the Catholic Bench of Bishops. Like the Soviet Union, the Hungarian People's Democracy "assures the right of free performance of religious rites and ceremonies"[112] but neither of these States implies more in the concept of "religious freedom."

IV. THE JEWISH DENOMINATION

The history and development of the Jewish denomination in Hungary was entirely different from that of the Christian Churches. Although Jews were mentioned in Hungarian statutes as far back as 1092[113] their oppressed status, somewhat similar to their contemporary situation in other countries, was not significantly improved until the Imperial Rescript of Emperor Joseph II.[114] Before his death, however, the Emperor revoked all his decrees and rescripts and the next Hungarian Diet of 1790-1791 enacted an Article, which declared[115] that Jews shall enjoy the same status they enjoyed on January 1, 1790.

The Diet of 1840 improved the status of the Jews further, enacting:[116]

> 1. Jews born in this country or in the parts thereof as well as those who have obtained legal permission to reside here, may reside freely everywhere in the country and in parts thereof, with the sole exception of the Mining Cities mentioned in Law No. XXXVIII of

1791, and such places from which they are presently excluded by old legal custom regarding mines and mining institutions.

2. According to existing conditions Jews may also establish factories and may pursue trade and handicraft, either alone or with the help of apprentices of the same religion; they may train their sons for these trades and henceforth they may practice the sciences and honest trades which they have previously been practicing.

They shall be compelled to use permanent first and last names and to enter their births in the registers kept by their own rabbis.

Furthermore they are compelled:

4. To prepare all their documents and agreements in any living language used in this country and in parts thereof.

5. In cities where Jews are entitled to acquire city lots the continuance of this practice shall be guaranteed for the future.

6. Any law, custom, resolution, and decision contrary to the present law shall be repealed.

One of the last acts of the Revolutionary National Assembly of 1848-1849 was the law adopted on July 28, 1849 on the "Emancipation of Members of the Jewish Faith." Due to the collapse of the Revolution this law did not become effective.

During the Period of Absolutism (1849-1866) several imperial decrees dealt with conditions concerning Jews, but none with the Jewish religion itself.

The parliament (1867) which dealt with the restitution of the constitution also proclaimed the "Emancipation of the Jews Concerning Civil and Constitutional Rights," [117] enacting:

* * * that the Jewish residents of the country shall be entitled to exercise civil and political rights equal to those of the Christians.

In 1895, status equal to the Christian churches was enacted for the Jewish denomination, proclaiming:[118]

The Jewish religion shall be a legally recognized religion.

After the outbreak of World War II, and following a number of discriminatory statutes, the parliament under the influence of the Nazis repealed the progressive legislation adopted in 1895.[119] The Jewish religion became an "admitted" instead of a "recognized" religion. Thus it lost its status of equality with other leading denominations in Hungary. The law abolished appro-

priations for the support of Jewish schools and institutions and
provided that such institutions would henceforth be supported
exclusively by funds raised by the Jewish community of Hungary. The conversion of a Hungarian citizen to the Jewish religion was deemed void unless it involved persons belonging to
the Jewish race. Earlier, the Jewish religion had been deprived
of its representation in the Upper House.[120]

By the Armistice agreement concluded in Moscow on January
20, 1945, Hungary accepted the obligation to:

> release all persons held in confinement in connection with their
> sympathies with the United Nation's cause, or for racial or religious
> reasons, regardless of their citizenship or nationality, and repeal all
> discriminatory legislation and disabilities therefrom.

As a result of this obligation the Provisional Hungarian Government decreed the repeal of all anti-Jewish legislation.[121]

Until 1871, the Jewish denomination had no national organization; all congregations were entirely independent.

After the enactment of the Emancipation of the Jews the necessity was felt for a Supreme Ecclesiastical Authority for the Jewish community of Hungary. In 1868, a Royal Rescript[122] convoked the Jewish national Congress of Hungary, which set up
rules and a central organization, but did not succeed in unifying
the various Jewish congregations. After 1871 they were divided
into three different groups:[123]

> 1. "Congressional" or simply "Jewish Congregations" organized
> according to the "Congressional Statutes" established by the above-
> mentioned progressive-minded National Jewish Congress and given
> royal sanction.[124] The National Bureau of Hungarian Jews was
> established as the central organization for these congregations.
>
> 2. "Autonomous Orthodox Jewish Congregations," which did not
> accept the above-mentioned "Congressional Statutes," but were
> organized according to the more conservative "Organizational Ar-
> ticles for the Autonomous Orthodox Jewish Denomination in Hun-
> gary and Transylvania." On the basis of royal authorization these
> Articles were promulgated by an Order of the Minister of Religion
> and Public Education.[125] The central organization of the Orthodox
> Jewish denomination was the Orthodox Central Bureau.
>
> 3. "Status-quo-ante" Jewish congregations were those which did
> not readjust their organization according to either of the above-

mentioned statutes but retained the status they had before the Congress was held. They had no central organization until 1928, when they established the "National Association of Hungarian Status-quo-ante Jewish Congregations." The Minister of Religion and Public Education promulgated their by-laws.[126]

A great number of Jews were deported and exterminated during the German occupation of 1944. Outside of Budapest the life of the Jewish congregations was destroyed entirely.

After the Russians occupied Hungary attempts were made to re-establish and reorganize Jewish religious institutions.

Government interference with the autonomy of "Congressional Jews," was felt at first by the establishment of an Executive Committee[127] composed of members appointed by the government. Two years later, in 1947, the Minister of Religion and Public Education changed the organization of this Executive Committee, seemingly re-establishing autonomy.[128]

Due to the fact that the "Orthodox Jewish" congregations of the capital city of Budapest were insignificant in the early postwar period and that in other cities and rural districts of Hungary, the orthodox Jewry had hardly begun its religious life, they did not experience government interference until the middle of 1948. During this period a fairly large number of orthodox Jews moved from the countryside into Budapest, thereby increasing the responsibility of the Orthodox Central Bureau. Therefore the government established the "Temporary National Committee to represent the autonomous orthodox Jews in Hungary until the representation can be newly organized upon by-laws adapted to the changed conditions."[129]

On December 7, 1948, an agreement was concluded between "the Government of the Hungarian Republic, the National Bureau of Hungarian Jews, and the Orthodox Central Bureau as the legal representatives of the Jewish congregations." [130]

This agreement is an almost verbatim repetition of those concluded with the Reformed and the Unitarian churches, containing the same guarantees and privileges. But in contrast to the treatment accorded the Protestant leaders and the representatives of the Catholic Church, it was not until very recently (February

1953) that the Jewish leader and co-signer of the agreement, Lajos Stoeckler, was imprisoned.

After the Communist party gained full control of the government in Hungary it took steps to unify all Jewish congregations under a single authority. On January 12, 1950 an Announcement of the Minister of Religion and Public Education was published in the Official Gazette a part of which reads:

> The Executive Committee of the National Bureau of the Hungarian Jews, representing the Congressional Congregations of Hungary and the Jewish Denominational Communities Status-quo-ante, as well as the Orthodox Central Bureau which is entitled to represent the Autonomous Orthodox Jewish Denomination of Hungary, have by mutual agreement resolved to merge in a uniform national organization corresponding to the changed conditions, and for this purpose to convoke a national meeting.

With this announcement the Election Rules for the Jewish National Congress signed by the Central Bureau of the Autonomous Orthodox Jewish Denomination of Hungary and of the Executive Committee of the National Bureau of Hungarian Jews were also published. The announcement ended with a clause whereby the Minister of Religion and Public Education approved the election procedure,

> provided that the by-laws of the organization to be established by the National Congress should be submitted to him for the purpose of exercising the right of government supervision.

Later in 1950 a National Congress of Jewish Congregations was convoked and the By-laws on the Uniform Organization of the Jewish Denomination were adopted and published.

V. THE TRIALS OF CARDINAL MINDSZENTY AND ARCHBISHOP GRÖSZ.[131]

The relation between Church and State entered a new stage when Cardinal Mindszenty was arrested and brought before a court on various charges of a political and economic character.

Until December 26, 1948, when the Cardinal was arrested, the Government dealt with the Churches in a comparatively open manner, i.e. primarily by laws, decrees and agreements. But with Cardinal Mindszenty's arrest criminal law was applied by the Government in its fight not only against Church leaders but against the Church herself. After the Cardinal was sentenced his successor in the leadership of the Hungarian Catholics, Archbishop Grösz, was arrested, tried, and sentenced, together with another group of Catholic leaders.

Cardinal Mindszenty was sentenced on February 5, 1949 and Archbishop Grösz was arrested in spring and sentenced on June 26, 1951.

In discussing these two trials facts which could be gathered from the official publications of the Hungarian Government are presented first (A-D) followed by a legal analysis of the proceedings.

Since this study is confined to the official Hungarian sources only, it does not claim to be conclusive. Too many facts remain concealed behind the Iron Curtain. It is hoped however that it will throw some light on these trials and help to evaluate their true nature.

A. *Courts*

Understanding of present-day Hungarian criminal procedure requires a knowledge of the postwar organization of the criminal courts. While Cardinal Mindszenty was tried and sentenced by the "Special Bench of the Budapest People's Court," Archbishop Grösz's trial was before the "Criminal Bench of the Budapest District Court." It is significant that the same person, Dr. Vilmos Olti, presided over both trials.

While Archbishop Grösz was tried by a regular court under Criminal Law, the People's Court—which tried Cardinal Mindszenty—was a special court created by the Provisional Government at the beginning of the Russian occupation in 1945, with the purpose

that those who caused the catastrophe which afflicted the Hungarian people and/or were participants thereof, shall be punished as soon as possible.[132]

The Bench in the Mindszenty case in accordance with the statutes consisted of a professional judge appointed by special order of the Minister of Justice and four lay judges delegated by the four political parties (Smallholders, Communist, National Peasant and Social Democrat) which under the name of Hungarian Independent Popular Front formed the Government.

For political crimes "a five man special bench . . . with the People's Court at the seat of each Court of Appeals shall be competent for trial." [133] According to Mr. Riesz, Minister of Justice, this provision was dictated by the fact that in such an organization "the democratic parties had a better opportunity of choosing the judges.[134]

Later all the criminal courts were reorganized[135] after the pattern of People's Courts. The only difference is in the number of lay members of the trial bench: the bench in the district courts consists of the professional judge and only three lay members, while the People's Court has four lay members: The goal of the new courts is clearly set forth in the Preamble of the Law:

> In order to ensure the full enforcement of the ideological beliefs of the toiling people in the administration of criminal justice, in addition to legal knowledge, the people shall participate in the courts * * * through their lay representatives who shall sit side by side with the professional judge.

The enforcing decree ordered that:[136] (1) the Hungarian Independent Popular Front shall prepare the list of the lay judges, (2) only members of said Front shall be registered on the list, (3) judges, attorneys and persons with degrees in law are excluded and (4) members of political parties and other democratic organizations shall have adequate representation. The president of the court has the authority to decide upon the tour of duty of the lay judges.

The Constitution of the Hungarian People's Republic[137] defines the duties of the courts:

> 41.   The courts . . . shall punish the enemies of the toiling people, protect and safeguard the State, the social and economic order, the

institutions of the People's Democracy, and the rights of the workers, and educate the toiling people in observance of the rules governing the life of a socialist commonwealth.

The composition of the courts and the individual assignment
of the professional judge guarantees that the application of law
always follows the party line. Thus both cases were tried by an
intentionally partisan court.

B.   *Charges*[138]

1. Sedition

The charges of sedition against the two prelates were based
on the Law on the Protection of the Democratic Political Order
and the Republic by Means of Criminal Law which reads in part:

> 1. Whoever commits an act with the aim of overthrowing the
> democratic political order or the Democratic Republic established
> by Law No. I of 1946, [or] initiates, leads or aids substantially and
> materially a movement or organization [having the same aim] shall
> be punished for a crime.[139]

The great difference between this new formulation of sedition
and the prewar definition is that now commission of an act
merely "aiming at the overthrow" of the government constitutes
a crime, while the prewar regulation required the presence of
the element of "force" in committing or attempting to commit
the act.[140] The fact that the Law[141] does not mention "force" or
"violence" as an element of the crime implies that any act or
attempt aiming at the government or any other institution or
situation protected by law may qualify as sedition.

The official interpretation given by Mr. Riesz, Minister of
Justice,[142] reads:

> Only those who think in a democratic way may claim democratic
> rights.

This not only confirms that *any act* may qualify as sedition
under the present Law but also implies that those who are not
loyal followers of the existing "People's democratic order" are,
partially at least, deprived of their rights.

The new concept of sedition together with the new concept

of criminal law is explained by the Minister of Justice himself as follows:

> The principal aim of the present Law is to guarantee the rights of political freedom arising from the democratic views, viz. equality under law, the liberty to criticize public officials, freedom of speech, and the opportunity to render effective protection to the Democratic Hungarian Republic. Nobody shall be subject to prosecution for criticizing the form of government in an objective political manner, or in a scholarly opinion, or for representing a conservative position in rejecting one or another principle of democracy. But at the same time any assault which aims at the overthrow of the democratic political order, or the change of the republican form of government by illegal means, shall be severely punished.
>
> . . . The goal is to punish any organized reactionary activity striving at the overthrow of the democratic political order and to afford strong protection by means of criminal law not only against direct assault upon the democratic political order and direct attacks against its basic foundations, but also against spiritual infections which endanger the public interest by undermining democracy.
>
> . . . The freedom of assembly for the purpose of introducing a form of government other than republican within the limits of the law, will continue to exist. It is, however, prohibited not only to attack the democratic political order, which is the foundation of life and society of the Hungarian people, by illegal means and violence, but also by any other means, since such activity is always illegal from the point of view of the proposed law.
>
> It is necessary to protect the democratic political order of the Republic not only against overt acts or direct violence but also against those spiritual influences upon smaller or larger groups of citizens which are apt to create an inclination and psychic disporition in the people's minds to overthrow or disturb the democratic political order or to incite hatred against the fundamental institutions and ideas of the democratic political order or against its loyal followers.
>
> The democratic system itself is not so frequently the object of incitements to hatred, since because of its abstract character it is (a less suitable target.) More frequently there will be incitements against fundamental institutions constituting the democracy. It shall be left to the courts to decide what these fundamental institutions are since their exact enumeration is impossible.
>
> Summing up briefly: Democracy is the foundation of our political system and therefore deserves absolute protection by means of criminal law, while the Republic, as a constitutional institution, does not deserve protection to such an extent. Consequently any attempt

to overthrow or disturb the democratic political order is a crime, while only unlawful activity (i.e. coupled with violence) designed to change the republican form of government is prohibited.[143]

The Message shows clearly that the intention of the Government was to control any activity at its pleasure. The essential point in the above quotation is the last sentence stating that "any attempt to overthrow or disturb the democratic political order is a crime." Because "democratic political order" in practice equals the rule of the Communist Party and no definition of the "democratic political order" is given, the Law gives an unlimited power to the Government to eliminate anyone on the charge of sedition. This was the case against the Cardinal.

2. *Treason*

Cardinal Mindszenty's indictment for treason was based on a law enacted in 1930. The sentence was based on the same. The Relevant Sections of the Law read:

> 58. Whoever associates or enters into contact with the government of a foreign power or with a foreign organization in order to induce it to commit hostile acts against Hungary, and also whoever attempts to induce a foreign power to wage war or to use force against Hungary, shall be guilty of the crime of treason and shall be punished by penal servitude for from ten to fifteen years. If a declaration of war has taken place, if the war has broken out, or if force was used, the penalty shall be penal servitude for life.
>
> 60. [The following] shall be guilty of the crime of treason and shall be punished by imprisonment not to exceed five years:
> (1) whoever spies out or illegally obtains a military secret or any other secret affecting other important interests of the Hungarian State, particularly its international or economic situation;
> (2) whoever makes public or communicates to an unauthorized person a secret which has come into his possession or to his knowledge as a consequence of his official position, his official commission, or his relationship or service or contact with a public authority;
> (3) whoever publishes or communicates to an unauthorized person * * * a secret which came to his knowledge or possession, if such act endangers the interest of the State.[144]

Two other statutes were referred to by the prosecution and

the court and both were enacted between the two World Wars under conditions substantially differing from those of the present time.[145] The legal basis on which the courts must adjust the interpretation of the prewar statutes to the ideas of "People's Democracy" is given in a decree[146] which orders the Supreme Court of the Hungarian People's Republic to revise the decisions of the former Royal Hungarian Curia (Supreme Court) "if they do not correspond in spirit to the aims of the Hungarian People's Democracy." Thus Cardinal Mindszenty had to face charges based upon a statute which, enacted under totally different circumstances, was to be interpreted in a new and loose manner.

3. *Foreign Currency Offenses*

Both of the prelates were charged with illegal speculation with foreign currency obtained from American Catholic circles as gifts.

Two statutes were invoked by the Prosecution, one of which was enacted before World War II[147] regulating financial transactions with foreign currency and the other,[148] which replaced the former, upholding a regulation of 1946, by which the transfer of the smallest amount of foreign currency without official authorization was a punishable act.

Under the principles of the present government of Hungary, the punishment for the violation of currency and exchange laws must be construed as a part of political policy rather than as the regular administration of justice.

C. *Facts of the Mindszenty Case as Established by the People's Court.*

The People's Court from other sources has official knowledge of the fact—which, incidentally, is generally known in Hungary—that the main defendant, Jozsef Mindszenty, for years has used his clerical activities (sermons, pastoral letters) to make open or covert attacks against the democratic order and the Republic, and thereby to divert his flock from the democratic reconstruction of the country, and to increase the Postwar economic difficulties of the democratic government. The People's Court withheld from including these inciting and instigating sermons and pastoral letters in the charges.[149]

Notwithstanding this declaration, the People's Court failed to show where this "official knowledge" had been obtained. Nobody can deny that Cardinal Mindszenty's opposition to the regime gradually increased because of the government's more frequent attacks upon the institutions of the Churches.

> The People's Court emphasizes that it was József Mindszenty himself who wanted to turn the Catholic Church and the faithful against the State in order to weaken the democratic State. In the course of his religious activities, he spared no effort to make the democratic order and the Republic repugnant to his followers.[150]

There can be no doubt whatsoever that the Cardinal fought with all his strength against the methods of the Hungarian government.

> Therefore he tried to smear the democratic government in order to influence a significant number of Hungarian Catholics to act against the People's Democracy and to use and organize the dissatisfied to serve his own royalist aims.[151]

Mindszenty was certainly opposed to the acts of the government, he did everything in his power to prevent the subjugation of the Church to the State, but it is nowhere proved that he endeavored to "use and organize" his "followers."

> . . . because of his high position, Mindszenty's activities could (sic) be considered differently from the activities of other individuals . . . Nevertheless, the People's Court declared that when judging the activities of the main defendant, it judged them as activities of József Mindszenty, Hungarian citizen, and not of József Mindszenty, Prince Primate of Hungary, Archbishop of Esztergom.[152]

This declaration of the Court seems, however, to be an empty phrase. The legitimacy of his opposition to the regime was the object of the proceedings of the Court. In other words, Mindszenty was prosecuted because his position, his attitude, and his actions attracted public attention.

"Hapsburg rule and democracy cannot exist side by side." This declaration of the People's Court is directly contrary to the law, which does not prohibit monarchist propaganda, permissible even according to the ministerial report.

Mindszenty's aims were perfectly in accordance with the intentions of the United States of America in connection with Hungary and the People's Democracies in general. The U.S. today supports reactionary forces all over the world. It intends to carry out its aim—the subjugation of the world—by extirpating all forces of progress. Thus to achieve his own aim, Mindszenty needed the help of the U.S.A. and the U.S.A. needed József Mindszenty, head of the Catholic Church in Hungary, to be the propagator of their plans connected with Otto Hapsburg. This is the angle from which the close relationship between Mindszenty and the various American factors must be judged.[153]

This statement of the Court uncovers the background of the trial and shows one of its purposes: to alienate the Hungarian people from the U.S.A.

József Mindszenty and his accomplices found a third war to be the most suitable form of foreign intervention.[154]

Although it is a fact beyond any doubt that Cardinal Mindszenty, with the majority of Hungarians at that time, considered the possibility of a war between Russia and the Western Powers, in the course of the trial no proof was brought before the court that he had done anything to bring it about.

A particularly noteworthy part of this speculation was that the gathering and passing on of information by the accused Mindszenty and his accomplices sent the exponents of imperialist foreign policy untrue information about Hungary, which gave a distorted picture of Hungarian Democracy. Their aim was to support hereby the aggressive purposes of the imperialists. They depicted the country in such a way as to make believe that the people were opposed to the democratic government, that the economic situation was distressing, and that the people could hardly wait for a change, even at the price of war.[155]

As far back as January 19, 1946, Cardinal Mindszenty compared the existing situation with that of 1241, when the country was devastated by the invading Tartars. His opinion was well known everywhere; his connection with the American Minister was not hidden. It may be of interest to notice that no attempt was made by the prosecutor to identify the information supposedly transmitted.

D.   *Facts of the Case of Archbishop Grösz,*
as Established by the Court.

Following Mindszenty's arrest, József Grösz continued Mindszenty's policy against the people.[156]

It is without doubt that Archbishop Grösz, as the highest dignitary of the Roman Catholic Church after the Prince-Primate, could not deviate from the policies of the Catholic Church, which were not "against the people" but against the Church policy of the Government.

The conspirators established close contact with the United States legation in Budapest.

The conspiracy intended to overthrow the people's democratic order of the State (sic) with armed violence, demolition, and assassinations—by means of the bloody terror well known from 1919—and to restore the monarchy with Otto Hapsburg as king. For the realization of their aims they relied partly upon the armed Hungarian fascist troops stationed in Tito's Yugoslavia and in the West,

and partly on armed assistance from the Americans and Tito.[157]

None of these allegations was proved during the trial. The purpose of these allegations was only to create hatred against the West, against the United States, and also against the Holy See, as the court

regarded it as an extenuating circumstance that the guidance of the Vatican has had an extraordinary influence upon the intentions of József Grösz and the other accused.[158]

E.   *Legal Analysis*

1.   *Confessions*

Before venturing a final conclusion a short excursion into Hungarian criminal law is indispensable. The organization of the courts has already been described. But certain questions of criminal law, substantive as well as adjective, deserve attention.

An examination of the publications of the Hungarian Government on Cardinal Mindszenty's and Archbishop Grösz's cases reveals two remarkable circumstances:

First, the full confession of all the defendants that the charges were true, and

Second, the very poor evidence offered by the prosecution and the complete lack of evidence on the part of the defense.

All sixteen defendants but one pleaded guilty, and all sixteen confessed in full to the charges.

In the American jurisdiction the plea of guilty is a well established institution with a definite meaning, but in the continental European jurisdiction the concept has an entirely different and rather vague content.

In American criminal law

> The plea of guilty is an admission of the facts alleged in the indictment, and has the same effect as conviction, 74 Mich 478, 42 N.W. 70.[159]

Thus the plea of guilty automatically precludes presentation of evidence authorizing the judge to proceed with determination of penalty in a sentence. In continental Europe the plea, whether guilty or not guilty, has no essential effect whatsoever, and in fact is not even a "plea" in the procedural meaning, for if the defendant states that he is guilty, this statement is considered only as a sign of repentance on his part, and its only effect is that of a possible mitigating circumstance. Otherwise the trial and the judgment is not influenced by such a plea of the defendant.

It may be stated in general that in Hungarian criminal law the confession of the defendant is not evidence in the sense of American terminology.

With respect to the defendant's position and interrogation during the trial, the provisions of the Hungarian Criminal Procedure (Law No. XXXIII of 1896, in force until May, 1951) read:

> 304 . . . The presiding judge shall interrogate the defendant, and if there is more [than one defendant] then each of them separately, in the absence of the witnesses and other defendants.
>
> The presiding judge shall inquire whether the defendant understands the charges. In case of a negative answer he shall explain the charges to the defendant and afterwards shall inquire whether the defendant acknowledges his guilt or not.
>
> If the defendant denies [his guilt] the presiding judge shall call his attention to the fact that he is entitled to tell the facts contrary to those of the prosecution, that he is entitled to make remarks about the evidence during the trial, that he is entitled to repeat his

overruled motions relative to changing the evidence given by him during the preceding procedure, and that he is entitled to move for a new presentation of evidence. Nobody shall ask the defendant any questions except the presiding judge.

The Hungarian Criminal Procedure guided by the desire to abolish all the self-accusatory elements in criminal law even dealt with the interrogation (which is not considered testimony) of the defendant by the court in a separate chapter and not in that of Evidence. This is quite natural since under the continental European legal concept, on the one hand, it is impossible to have the defendant testify under oath, and on the other hand, the defendant is not compelled to tell the truth.

The Hungarian Government seems to have abandoned this principle by using the defendants' confessions as the principal evidence for theeir conviction. This happened in Cardinal Mindszenty's case when all seven defendants were convicted on their own confession. The prosecution's strongest evidence was the testimony of the various defendants against each other. In the Mindszenty case there was no testimony beside the defendants', or if there was the Government did not find it necessary to publish it in its official publication, the so-called "Black Book" on the Mindszenty case.

In Archbishop Grösz's case there were some witnesses, but what they testified to was pure hearsay. The documents and other instruments introduced by the prosecution were identified without exception only by the defendants. The prosecution did not bother to put the U.S.A. minister to Hungary on the stand and have him identify the letters allegedly written by him. This shows also that the principle which governed the conviction was the confession of the defendants, i.e., the well known principle of self-accusation. Prior to these trials, this was unknown to the Hungarian administration of justice.

A shadow of mystery impenetrable by legal analysis lies over these self-accusations. It seems strange that all the defendants confessed in full and that none among them tried to defend himself or even to find an excuse for the acts with which he was charged. The charges were grave, and the foundation of the charges as presented by the prosecution was exceptionally poor.

2. *Defense*

This fact brings up the question of the defense. The presiding judge announced at the beginning of the trials that in both cases all of the defendants but one had a defense counsel of his own choice. (The Rev. Andrew Zakar, Cardinal Mindszenty's secretary, did not employ a lawyer but had one appointed by the court, according to the same source.)

Now, none of the counsels offered evidence of any kind, the counsels directed questions to the witnesses (who usually were his client's fellow defendants). Naturally, after the defendants confessed to the charges it would be very difficult for the defense counsels to deny the acts. But none of the counsels examined the backgroud of the confessions, nor did they raise any legal issue, although there were plenty of legal questions to be presented to the court.

The first of these questions was the charge of "sedition." The prosecution made its charge on the theory that anything aiming at the restoration of monarchy is a crime. This was amply shown above under the title "Sedition" and it seems sufficient to point out here the contrast between the Law as it is written and as it was applied by the court.

The law itself specifies "overthrow," and the Message emphasizes that the text of the Law aims to assure the rights of the citizen to change the form of government "within the limits of the law."

The court did not judge the activity in the interest of the restoration of the monarchy as a part of the right mentioned in the Message, but declared by accepting the views of the prosecution:

"Hapsburg rule and democracy cannot exist side by side." The prosecutor never tried to prove this view, nor did the defense even attempt to challenge it.

From a legal point of view it is absurd to bring the question of the Holy Crown under this charge. But the prosecution did. The construction of the charge was that the Cardinal did everything to keep the Holy Crown out of the hands of the Hungarian

Government, because it was needed for the restoration of the monarchy. The logic of the prosecution and of the court assumes that because the restoration or any attempt thereof is sedition, any act to keep the Holy Crown abroad is a part of the crime of sedition also, for the Holy Crown is needed for the restoration. This absurd view was taken for granted by the defense and no legal issue was made thereof.

The defense gave the treason charge the same superficial consideration. No comparison was made between the position of the U.S.A. and that of the U.S.S.R. Nobody mentioned that the U.S.A. was a signatory power to the armistice agreement and should be entitled equally with the U.S.S.R., to have an interest in the future development of Hungary.

The "treason" charge extended to such acts as communication with Hungarian priests abroad and especially to the Cardinal's contacts with his fellow cardinals. The defense again neglected to challenge the qualification of these acts as treason and nobody pointed out that the prosecution proved nothing as to the "spying" activities of Cardinal Mindszenty. The record of the trial published by the Government does not show that the Cardinal ever transmitted any classified secret or anything which could hurt his country.

Similarly, no defense whatsoever was offered against the charge of "currency offenses." None of the counsels suggested, and none of the defendants attempted to defend themselves by calling upon the Hungarian National Bank for a statement of the official policy, which could have been that it was permissible to deal with foreign currency sent from abroad to churches or charitable organizations on an open market.[160]

Two suppositions are possible about the defense: that the counsels were willing accomplices of the prosecution or that they were intimidated. In either case, there was no defense. Without defense there is no fair trial.

3. *Conclusion*

Both trials give the impression that the question involved was not one of law but of politics. The defendants were either priests or laymen involved in church affairs. The imprisonment of Cardinal Mindszenty and Archbishop Grösz was intended to deprive the Roman Catholic Church in Hungary of her leadership and prepare for her final subjugation to the State.

Before the arrest of Cardinal Mindszenty the main issue was the socialization of denominational schools. The so-called agreement had to be signed and Cardinal Mindszenty stood strongly against the secularizing forces. His leadership was not only effective but also quite annoying in the eyes of the Government. Masses of the people followed him and observed their religious duties more strictly and devoutly than ever before.

The following characteristic of the situation in the U.S.S.R. as described by Dr. Vladimir Gsovski, is also true of Hungary.

> Observance of the ecclesiastic tradition runs counter to the loyalty to the government which aims to eradicate religion. Therefore, a religious man is suspected in Soviet Russia of being inimical to the government and any accusation of the violation of the "Separation of the State and Church" almost automatically involves accusation of counter revolution.[161]

Although the accusation in these trials is not counter revolution but sedition and treason, the Soviet principle, that all available and necessary means must be employed against the survival of the Church remains unchanged. Thus, these two trials represent the application of the Bolshevik formula to the relations of Church and State.

The official interpretation of the laws, together with the organization of the Hungarian courts on a pure party-political line, the weakness of the facts presented by the prosecution, the loose legal construction of the charges, the absence of defense, and the incredible confession in full of all defendants made both of these cases political trials *par excellence*.

The statement of the former Secretary of State Dean Acheson on the Mindszenty trial seems to be fully justified by the legal analysis.

> In their conduct of the case of Cardinal Mindszenty, the Hungarian authorities do not appear to have omitted any of the usual methods practiced by a police state. Such a proceeding constitutes not the administration of justice, but wanton prosecution.[162]

VI. TRANSLATIONS

A. *Translations of Laws*

1. Decree No. 200 of 1945 M.E. Repealing the Anti-Jewish Laws and Statutes.

(1) All statutes discriminating against the Jews shall be repealed, and their application prohibited; especially Law No. XV of 1938; Law No. IV of 1939; Sections 12, 40 and 41 of Law No. IV of 1940; Subsection 1 of Section 4 of Law No. XXXIX of 1940; Sections 9, 10, 14, 15, and 16 of Law No. XV of 1941; Law No. VIII of 1942.

(2) All laws and statutes shall be entirely repealed which set into force, regulated, modified, or supplemented the laws mentioned in Section (1). All provisions of other laws and statutes which violate the principle of equal civil rights shall be repealed.

2. Law No. XLVIII of 1948 Amending Criminal Laws.

Sec. 19. Whoever uses an abusive expression or commits an abusive act against the Hungarian nation, against the democratic political order, against the Republic or its fundamental institutions, against a national minority living within the country, or against a denomination, shall be punished by imprisonment not to exceed one year, and if the crime is committed through the press or otherwise publicly, by imprisonment not to exceed two years.

3. Edict No. 1 of 1950 on Proclaiming August 20 as the Day of the People's Republic.

The Constitution of the Hungarian People's Republic entered into effect on August 20, 1949.

The Constitution expresses and establishes the results of the basic economic and social changes which our country has experienced since her liberation by the armed forces of the great Soviet Union, and the Constitution also determines the trend of our further progress on the road leading to Socialism. Thence, August 20 represents a turning point of historical importance in the life of the toiling people of Hungary. Therefore, The Presidium of the People's Republic decrees [as follows]:

1. August 20 shall be a national holiday: The Holiday of the Constitution of the Hungarian People's Republic.

2. The Cabinet of the Hungarian People's Republic shall be charged with enforcing the present edict.

4. Edict No. 34 of 1950, on the Authorization of the Religious Orders to Operate.

1. The authorization of religious orders to operate within the territory of the Hungarian People's Republic shall come to an end on the day the

present Edict goes into effect. The present provision shall not apply [to the authorization to operate] of religious orders for men and women engaged in teaching, but [they shall be authorized] only to the extent to which they are required for [the maintenance of] Catholic denominational schools.

2. All religious orders whose authorization becomes inoperative under Section 1 must cease their activities within the territory of the Hungarian People's Republic on the day when the present Edict goes into effect.

3. The Minister of the Interior in agreement with the Minister of Religion and Public Education shall determine which religious orders among those engaged in teaching may continue their activities.

4. This Edict goes into effect on the day of its promulgation; the Minister of the Interior in agreement with the Minister of Religion and Public Education shall provide for its enforcement and see to it that the members of orders whose authorization comes to an end under the present Decree leave the former monasteries within three months.

5. Decree No. 1, 101-11-1 of 1950 (IX. 15) V.K.M. regulating certain Questions of Religious Instruction.

The Minister of Religion and Public Education issues the following order on the basis of the powers given him by Section 2 of the Edict No. 5 of 1949.

Sec. 1. Religious instruction in schools shall be given by full-time and part-time teachers of religion.

Sec. 2. (1) In towns (villages) or schools in which religious instruction is given for a number of weekly hours equal to the number of hours prescribed for the teachers of the school concerned, a full time teacher of religion shall give religious instruction.

(2) The full-time teacher of religion shall teach religion as a principal occupation, and may not have any other occupation (employment) besides this affording him a permanent livelihood by annual payment or benefice.

(3) Full-time teachers of religion shall receive fees and family allowances according to Table No. 4, attached to the Decree of the Cabinet No. 8250 of 1948 (VIII. 1.) Korm, concerning social security and leave; they shall be entitled to the same treatment as civil servants.

(4) The Executive Committees of the District Councils (City Council of the Capital) must report to the Minister of Religion and Public Education in detail by September 15 of each year the number of pupils volunteering for religious instruction in each town (community) and school, as well as their denomination.

Sec. 3. (1) In those cities (villages) or schools in which no full-time teacher of religion functions, religious instruction shall be given by a part-time teacher of religion.

(2) The part-time teacher of religion shall be paid per each hour [of instruction) given by him; his hourly pay shall be equal to that currently

established for teachers functioning in the school concerned. Ecclesiastical employees who receive pay [from the State] for performance of their pastoral duties [lelkészi jövedelem kiegészites] shall be paid for giving religious instruction only in excess of eight hours a week.

Sec. 4. (1) The Executive Committee of the District Council (Municipal Council of the Capital of Budapest) shall appoint full-time and part-time teachers of religion on the basis of proposals made by the competent ecclesiastical authority.

(2) A full-time or part-time appointment for teachers of religion shall be granted only to persons who have the required special qualification. The Minister of Religion and Public Education shall be competent to decide a dispute as to qualification.

(3) The Executive Committee of the District Council shall refuse the appointment of a full or part-time teacher of religion, or shall at any time revoke the appointment of a teacher of religion who takes a hostile stand against the People's Democracy or towards its orders. A person who has been deprived of his appointment to teach religion shall not be appointed to teach religion in any other school.

Sec. 5. (1) The teacher of religion shall prepare a curriculum and time schedule on the basis of the teaching plan and textbooks approved by the Minister of Religion and Public Education, and shall carry out his teaching work accordingly.

(2) The teacher of religion shall not be entrusted with any educational work (substituting for other teachers, supervising during excursions or during the intermissions between lessons, etc.) other than teaching religion. The teacher of religion shall not take part in the conferences of the educational staff and shall stay in the school building only during the time of religious instruction.

Sec. 6. (1) The classes for religious instruction shall be held after the last teaching hour. The classes for religious instruction shall be held exclusively within the school building. The religious instructor shall not assemble the pupils for any other activities outside the school.

(2) Pupils who have volunteered for religious instruction shall form groups corresponding in size to the average number of pupils of the various grades of the school. Religious instruction shall be given within this framework, but following the system applied in schools where one class consists of all the grades (ungraded schools) or of several grades (partly-graded schools).

(3) Pupils shall not receive credits in religious instruction. No disciplinary measures may be taken against pupils because of neglect of their duties in connection with religion lessons.

(4) The educational authorities shall supervise the educational work, the curriculum, and the time schedule of the teacher of religion in accordance with the rules established for the supervision of other instructors.

The principal shall be responsible for the supervision and may employ the general supervisor of studies, the teacher in charge of the grade, the President of the Parents' Labor Community, and the Commissioner of the Trade Union of Pedagogues in carrying out this task.

Sec. 7. The provisions of the present Decree shall apply to the school term of 1950/51. Provisions of former laws inconsistent with the present Decree shall be ineffective.

6. No. 1, 161-1 K-4 of 1950 Eln. No. 6. Notice of the Minister of Religion and Public Education on the Provisional Supreme Authority of the Hungarian Greek Orthodox Church Communities.

The Greek Orthodox Patriarch of Moscow accepted the Hungarian Greek Orthodox Church Communities which lacked a Supreme ecclesiastical authority under his provisional jurisdiction and delegated the Greek Orthodox Dean János [John] Kopolovics as an administrator in order to settle their questions or to resolve their problems.

The Cabinet took cognizance of the appointment of Dean János Kopolovics as an administrator and approved his assumption of activities.

7. Law No. I of 1951, on the Establishment of a Government Bureau for Church Affairs.

Sec. 1. (1) A Government Bureau for Church Affairs shall be established for the purpose of settling matters between the State and the religious denominations, especially for the purpose of carrying out the agreements and settlements concluded with the various religious denominations and of State support of religious denominations.

(2) The Government Bureau for Church Affairs shall be placed under the supreme supervision of the Cabinet. The Cabinet shall exercise its right of supreme control through one of its members.

Sec. 2. (1) The Cabinet shall establish by a Decree the provisions on the organization, jurisdiction, and activity of the State Office for Church Affairs.

(2) The appropriation for expenditures for personnel and supplies connected with the organization and activity of the Government Bureau for Church Affairs shall be provided under a special title in the budget of the State.

Sec. 3. As a result of the establishment of the Government Bureau for Church Affairs, the jurisdiction of the Ministry for Religion and Public Education on Church Affairs shall be discontinued and consequently reference to religion [Church Affairs] shall be omitted in the name of the ministry.

Sec. 4. The Cabinet shall be in charge of enforcing the present Law.

8. Edict No. 20 of 1951 on Filling Certain Church Positions.

Sec. 1. Archbishops, suffragan archbishops, bishops, suffragan bishops, abbots, and provincials of religious orders within the territory of Hungary, may be appointed only with the preliminary approval of the Presidium of the People's Republic.

Sec. 2. The provisions of Section 1 shall be applied for all appointments which have been made since January 1, 1946, to the positions of the Catholic Church enumerated above.

Sec. 3. The present Edict shall become effective on the day of its publication, and its provisions shall remain in force until an adequate new settlement shall be reached, by way of a bilateral agreement, concerning the filling of the Church positions mentioned above.

9. Decree No. 110 of 1951 M.T. Enforcing Law No. I of 1951.

Sec. 1. (1) The jurisdiction of the Government Bureau for Church Affairs (henceforth to be referred to as Bureau) established by Law No. I of 1951, [shall extend to the following matters]:

a) carrying out agreements and settlements concluded with the Churches and religious denominations;

b) administering personnel and business affairs connected with State contributions to the Churches and religious denominations;

c) remitting contributions for personnel and business affairs for the purpose of maintaining the general high schools of Churches and religious denominations exempted [from nationalization];

d) granting appropriations for religious instruction in schools;

e) administering ecclesiastical funds and other matters related to ecclesiastical property rights;

f) preparing statutes related to Churches and securing the enforcement of these statutes;

g) administering matters connected with securing the liberty of conscience and free exercise of religion and securing the undisturbed exercise of religious functions;

h) performing all other activities pertaining to the jurisdiction of Church administration of which the Minister of Religion and Public Education was in charge before Law No. I of 1951 had become effective;

i) carrying out measures undertaken by the Cabinet in Church affairs and controlling their administration.

(2) The Minister of Public Instruction shall exercise supreme State control over denominational (general) high schools operating on the basis of the agreements concluded with the various Churches and religious denominations (Edict No. 14 of 1951, Section 5, subsection 2). It shall likewise be the responsibility of the Minister of Public Instruction and of the [administrative] organs of Public Instruction to supervise the religious instruction in school.

Sec. 2. (1) The Bureau shall be headed by a president to be appointed by the Presidium of the People's Republic upon the proposal of the Cabinet.

(2) In fulfilling his duties, the president shall be supported by a deputy president to be appointed by the Cabinet upon the proposal of the Prime Minister.

(3) The president shall appoint the personnel of the Bureau or assign them to their service.

Sec. 3. The president shall assign the personnel their work and shall establish the administration of business and schedule of activities of the Bureau according to the provisions of the rules for public administration. In its proceedings, the office shall be in immediate contact with the ministries and other State agencies.

10. Decree No. 170 of 1951 M.T. on the Establishment of a Fund for Church Affairs.

The Cabinet of the Hungarian People's Republic in agreements concluded with the various churches determined the contribution of a considerable part of the expenses connected with the activity of the churches. Consequently, it raised the stipends of the pastoral clergy and included the clergy in compulsory health insurance.

Sec. 1. (1) The Cabinet of the Hungarian People's Republic establishes the Fund for Church Affairs (henceforth to be referred to as Fund) in order to secure the financial means necessary for fulfilling the tasks of the churches.

(2) The Fund shall cover the business and personnel expenses of the churches.

Sec. 2. (1) The Fund income consists of the State contribution for the churches provided for in the budget, of the equivalent of land voluntarily offered [to the State] by the individual churches, and of other income from various sources.

(2) Equivalents of the lands offered by the individual churches shall be administered within the Fund for each church separately.

Sec. 3. (1) The Government Bureau for Church Affairs is bound to report annually to the Cabinet on the administration of the Fund.

Sec. 4. (1) The Fund shall be exempt from all taxes and duties.

(2) The Prime Minister's Office shall provide in its budget for the contribution of the State to the Fund.

Sec. 5. The President of the Government Bureau for Church Affairs, in agreement with the Minister of Finance, shall enforce the present decree.

11. Excerpt from Decree No. 214 of 1951 M.T., on Modification and Amendment of Certain Statutes on Compulsory Health Insurance and Social Security.

Part I

Sec. 12. Compulsory health insurance shall be extended to the following persons assigned by the President of the Government Bureau for Church Affairs:

a) clergymen in actual service of the Churches, or receiving old-age pensions; assistant clergymen; full-time teachers of religion, as well as their widows and orphans, enjoying social security payments;

b) other persons filling ecclesiastical posts or former holders of these posts now receiving old age pensions, and their widows and orphans enjoying social security payments.

B. *Translations of the Individual Agreements*

1. Hungarian Reformed Church

Magyar Kőzlőny, No. 227 Oct. 9,

1948

Agreement

The committees appointed by the Government of the Hungarian Republic and by the Synodical Council of the Hungarian Reformed Church to settle the relationship between the State and the Church in a peaceful and proper manner as desired by both parties, have concluded the following agreement:

1. In order to arrive at a new regulation of the status of the church in the Hungarian Republic the government of the Hungarian Republic and the Hungarian Reformed Church appoint a permanent joint committee for drafting new laws concerning religious matters among which first of all a bill concerning the religion of children should be prepared. The legislative body of the church will amend its ecclesiastical laws in accordance with the new national legislation on religion.

2. The government of the Hungarian Republic declares on this occasion too that it shall recognize and guarantee, with all possible and necessary means, the full enjoyment of religious freedom. The Hungarian Reformed Church again recognizes the fact on this occasion that the legislature and the Government of the Hungarian Republic have ensured and protected the enjoyment of religious freedom up to the present time and have even extended it considerably by enacting Law No. XXXIII of 1947 and by granting subventions for personnel and administrative expenses, and have made it possible to maintain church activities at the same level as before.

3. The Government of the Hungarian Republic in accordance with the laws in force deems that the following activities belong to the free

sphere of church activities: the performance of worship in churches, suitable public buildings, private homes and open places; the teaching of the Bible in churches, schools, private homes and congregational houses; missionary work through denominational newspapers and other publications; disseminating the Bible and Holy Scriptures; holding congregational and national ecclesiastical conferences and meetings for evangelization, the compulsory teaching of religion in the schools, and the performance of charitable work. For this purpose the Hungarian Government permits the church to use, where needed, without charge (by agreement to be concluded with the school authorities and carrying with it the obligation of compensation for any damages which might occur) the classrooms or other suitable rooms of the public schools for worship, Sunday schools, Bible lectures, choir and other religious and ecclesiastical meetings and conventions at any time except during the regular periods of teaching until the congregations have secured other buildings for their purposes.

The Government of the Hungarian Republic furthermore deems that the autonomous activities of the church *(iurisdictio)* fall likewise within the sphere of free ecclesiastical life provided that they are within the limits and in a manner set up by ecclesiastical laws approved by the head of the State.

4. The Government of the Hungarian Republic recognizes, respects and shall make others respect those duties of the Church which concern inspiring its members to perform good deeds and especially to take care of the poor, the abandoned, the aged and orphans, which duties are imposed upon her according to the command of Christ and the Church. For this purpose the State will protect the right of the Church to maintain and expand charitable institutions and to collect charitable donations within the limits of the existing laws.

5. The Government of the Hungarian Republic recognizes the manifest endeavor of the Reformed Church to realize the principle: "A Free Church in a Free State."

The Government of the Hungarian Republic declares its willingness to grant subventions temporarily to the Reformed Church as stated below until its financial condition improves.

(a) The Hungarian Republic secures the subvention to the personnel in the amount equal to the salaries of public servants from June 30, 1948 to December 31, 1948, and thereafter for the following five years. The amount of subsidy for personnel shall be reduced by 25 per cent beginning with January 1, 1954, and the government shall continue to furnish the remaining 75 per cent until December 31, 1958. During the period from January 1, 1959, to December 31, 1963, 50 per cent of the present government subsidy shall be paid, while during the period from January 1, 1964 to December 31, 1968, 25 per cent shall be paid. All government subsidies shall cease on December 31, 1968.

(b) The Government shall provide for extraordinary expenses 10 per cent of the annual government subsidies of personnel expenses.

(c) The Government of the Hungarian Republic continues to pay a subsidy for the construction, reconstruction, and equipment of buildings of the Hungarian Reformed Church in the amount equivalent to the yearly rate of the subsidy paid for the same purpose during the time from August 1, 1946 until July 1, 1948, provided that this subsidy will be used exclusively for the construction, reconstruction, maintenance and equipment of ecclesiastical buildings, i.e., churches, congregational houses and manses. This subsidy shall be reduced every five years in a manner similar to the reduction of the subsidy for personnel and the subsidy shall cease on December 31, 1968.

(d) Any other subsidies paid until now shall be paid in the amount reduced according to the above scale.

(e) The Government shall pay the pensions of the Reformed ministers and the widows and children of members of the National Pension Fund in accordance with the rules governing the pensions of public servants; furthermore, the Government shall assume the payment of pensions of those who will retire before December 31, 1953.

6. The Hungarian Reformed Church, in accordance with the clear commandment of the Holy Scripture, shall incorporate prayers for the Hungarian Republic, for the head of the State, for the Government and for the well-being and peace of the Hungarian people in its "Order of Worship," and shall conduct worship conforming with the gospel and the confession of the faith of the church on national holidays. It [the Reformed Church] declares that the new hymn book to be published in the near future contains hymns suitable for such occasions.

7. The Hungarian Reformed Church takes notice of the decision of the Government of the Hungarian Republic that all schools other than the public schools together with the boarding houses connected with them will be socialized by legislative action. The enforcement of the nationalization of Calvinist schools shall be guided by the following arrangement.

(a) The government shall take over into the civil service as of July 1, 1948, the entire former teaching and other personnel of the nationalized schools and the boarding houses organically connected with them, [under the terms] according to the length of service [of each person].

(b) The buildings of the nationalized schools, the boarding houses organically connected with them, and their lands used by the employees shall pass into government ownership with all of their encumbrances incurred before May 15, 1948, and proved beyond doubt either by recording in the Land Register or otherwise. Controversies arising in this respect shall be decided by the Minister of Religion and Public Education after hearing the committee to be established according to Section 1.

(c) The government agrees that those members of the teaching personnel who have acted as cantors may perform their duties under the same conditions as they did before for two years following the conclusion of this agreement. The land which is the benefice of the cantor for his work as such shall remain in church ownership.

(d) Nationalization shall not apply to institutions which are exclusively ecclesiastical in nature and are not institutions of public education, i.e., theological academies, ministers' training institutes, deacons' and deaconess' training schools, and training schools for missionaries or other church workers.

The present legal relationship between the theological faculty of Debrecen and the Ministry of Religion and Public Education shall remain unchanged.

(e) The Government of the Hungarian Republic, partly in appreciation of the merits of the Reformed Church in the field of Hungarian public education, partly as a means of ensuring preparatory training for the new generation of ministers, agrees that the Reformed colleges of strongest historical tradition mentioned below shall remain ecclesiastical schools, not to exceed their present size, viz., the secondary school (*gymnasium*), girls' preparatory school (*lyceum*), and teachers' training school belonging to the Reformed College at Sárospatak;

the secondary school *(gymnasium),* girls preparatory school belonging to the Reformed College at Debrecen, as well as the girls' secondary school *(gymnasium),* girls' preparatory school, and teachers' training school of the Dóczy girls' training institute;

the secondary school *(gymnasium)* belonging to the Reformed College of Pápa;

the Reformed secondary school (*gymnasium*) of Budapest's IX district, Lónyai Street, and as its organic part, the Baár Madas Reformed secondary school *(gymnasium)* for girls.

The permanent committee to be established under Section 1 shall be competent to give suggestions to the government concerning the occasional expansion of the existing framework.

The maintenance of the said institutions shall be supplied by the government of the Hungarian Peoples' Republic for the duration of government subsidy in the same manner as the subvention for personnel provided under Section 5, subsection (a); after the expiration of the period of government subvention their maintenance shall be assumed exclusively by the Church.

(f) The Government of the Hungarian Republic recognizes and secures [as a matter of] right of the Reformed Church that mandatory religious instruction must also henceforth be held at schools of a public character in complete freedom. The question of religious instruction is to be settled anew in one way or another by the new law concerning religious matters, with special consideration to the followers of the free churches and to those who are not affiliated with any religion.

(g) The Government shall take over, grant the proper status in the [civil] service and appoint the teachers of the schools to be closed (schools on the junior high school level (*polgári iskolák*), teachers' training schools for men and women) in the same way as that provided for the other teachers taken over into the civil service.

(h) In case the Law school at Kecskemét should be closed, the State shall arrange for appointments of the professors corresponding to their present positions.

(i) The Government of the Hungarian Republic shall take measures if requested by parents, that in those schools where the mother tongue of the students is not Hungarian (Romanian, Serbian, Ruthenian, Slovak, German) the language of instruction shall be the mother tongue of the students.

At the same time the government of the Hungarian Republic shall make efforts to have similar provisions enacted on a reciprocal basis in neighboring States for students whose mother tongue is Hungarian.

8. The church shall change its statute pertaining to public education in accordance to the new laws enacted by the government.

*   *   *

9. The discussion and drafting of proposals relating to the settlement of all open questions shall be within the jurisdiction of the joint committee established under the Section 1.

Budapest, October 7, 1948.

On behalf of the Government
of the Hungarian Republic:
Gyula Ortutay
Minister of Religion and Education

On behalf of the Synod of the
Hungarian Reformed Church:

Dr. Jenö Balogh
President of the Synod

Dr. Imre Révész
Reformed bishop,
Ecclesiastic President of the Synod

2. Unitarian Church

An agreement similar to that concluded with the Reformed Church was concluded between the Government of the Hungarian Republic and representatives of the Hungarian Unitarian Church on the same day and published in the same issue of the Official Gazette.

3. Evangelical Church

Agreement between the Government
of the Hungarian Republic and the Synod
of the Evangelical Church in Hungary

(*Magyar Közlony,* No. 276, December 16, 1948)

The agreement was concluded on December 14, 1948 and signed by
Gyula Ortutay, Minister of Religion and Public Education and by Zoltán
Turótzy, the Evangelical Bishop, and Zoltán Mády, Supervisor-General.
In general, the agreement conforms with those previously concluded
between the State and the Reformed and Unitarian Churches. Concerning
certain Evangelical schools, Paragraph (d) of Section 6 provides that
legal relations existing up to that time between the theological faculty
of Sopron and the Ministry of Religion and Public Education shall continue. Paragraph (e) of Section 6 provides that the Government agrees
that two secondary schools, one for boys and one for girls, in Budapest,
remain denominational provided that they do not exceed their present
size. According to Paragraph (f) of Section 6, "the Government of the
Hungarian Republic recognizes and secures to the Evangelical Church as
a matter of right that compulsory religious instruction in government
schools shall be held in full freedom."

4. Roman Catholic Church

Agreement between the Government of the
Hungarian People's Republic and the Roman Catholic
Bench of Bishops

The Budapest Daily *Magyar Nemzet,* No. 202,
August 31, 1950, Page 1.

The Government of the Hungarian People's Republic and the Hungarian Catholic Bench of Bishops, moved by the desire to ensure peaceful
cooperation between the State and the Catholic Church and thus to
promote unity, the constructive work of the Hungarian people, and the
peaceful development of our country, concluded after negotiation the
following agreement:

I.

(1) The Bench of Bishops recognizes and, in accordance with its
civic duties, supports the political order and the Constitution of the
Hungarian People's Republic. The Bench of Bishops declares that it will
proceed under ecclesiastical laws against ecclesiastical persons who may
act against the legal order of the Hungarian People's Republic or against
the constructive work of its government.

(2) The Bench of Bishops emphatically condemns all subversive activities, regardless of their source, directed against the political and social order of the Hungarian People's Republic. It declares that it shall not permit the religious feelings of the Catholic believers to be misused for political purposes against the State.

(3) The Bench of Bishops calls upon the Catholic believers as citizens and patriots to assume their share with all their strength in the great work which is being done by the whole of the Hungarian people under the leadership of the Government of the People's Republic by carrying through the Five-Year-Plan, for the purpose of increasing the standard of living and making social justice effective. The Bench of Bishops particularly calls upon the clergy not to resist the movement of agricultural productive co-operatives, because, these being voluntary associations, it [the movement] is founded on the moral principle of human solidarity.

(4) The Bench of Bishops supports the movement for peace. It approves the efforts of the Hungarian people and the government of the Hungarian People's Republic to protect peace, condemns every kind of warmongering, and the use of the atomic weapon, and consequently it holds guilty of a crime against humanity any government which will be the first to use the atomic bomb.

II.

(1) The Government of the Hungarian People's Republic guarantees complete religious freedom to Catholic believers according to the Constitution of the People's Republic and similarly guarantees freedom of activity to the Catholic Church.

(2) The Government of the Hungarian People's Republic agrees to restore [to the Church] eight secondary Catholic denominational schools (six schools for boys and two for girls) and agrees that the religious teaching orders for men and women may work in the Catholic denominational schools in numbers required for teaching.

(3) The Government of the Hungarian People's Republic, in the spirit of agreements already concluded with other denominations, is willing to take care of the financial needs of the Catholic Church by assigning an appropriate sum for Catholic ecclesiastic purposes, during a period of eighteen years, that is until the Catholic Church is able to meet its financial needs from its own resources, and according to a scale proportionally decreasing every three or five years respectively.

The Government of the Hungarian People's Republic particularly emphasises that within the [above] limits of material support an adequate minimum subsistence should be secured for the clergy performing pastoral work.

A committee shall be established for the actual carrying out of the present agreement consisting of an equal number of representatives of the government of the Hungarian People's Republic and of the Bench of Bishops.

Budapest, August 30, 1950.

In Behalf of the Cabinet
Council of the Hungarian
People's Republic:

/s/ József Darvas

Minister of Religion and Education
In Behalf of the Hungarian
Catholic Bench of Bishops:

/s/ József Grösz

Archbishop of Kalocsa

C.   Excerpts From the Speech of József Revai
Minister of People's Education
(*Szabad Nép*—No. 129, June 6, 1950)

On June 6, 1950, József Révai, Minister of People's Education, in a speech before the Central Committee of the Hungarian Workers Party (Communist Party) stated:

The various male and female religious orders are the most influential organizations of the reactionary mass agitation carried out by the clergy. In Hungary, there are 23 male religious orders with 2,582 members and 40 female orders with 8,956 members, that is, a total of 63 orders with a total of 11,538 members. These 63 religious orders owned 636 convents of larger or smaller size. Do we need them any longer? Some of the male and female religious orders voluntarily withdrew from fulfilling the tasks which allegedly had been their profession [this refers to the teaching orders]. Or their former jobs have become useless [this refers to those orders whose purpose was taking care of the poor and nursing]. Or they deceitfully misuse their activity as members of religious orders for political purposes [this refers to the overwhelming majority of the members of the missionary orders]. This situation cannot be tolerated. It cannot be permitted that the members of the teaching orders, upon their refusal to teach, should begin to exercise pastoral functions, thereby swelling the number of priests. For in the term 1949/50, the People's Democracy has introduced free religious instruction in the nationalized schools, that is to say, has introduced a system that leaves it up to the parents to decide, according to their own free choice, whether or not their children should receive religious instruction.—We must put up a firm and determined defense against the reactionary incitement going on during the lessons of religious instruction. The working parent who sends his child to religious instruction in schools entrusts his child's soul, in most cases, to the care of the people's foe, the agents of the imperialist war-mongers. To send children to church or to religious education in schools given by reactionary priests means at the same time, be it intentionally or not, to take a stand against the People's Democracy. Optional religious instruction in schools is not the final solution in the application of democratic principles to this question. We shall change this. At the universities, too, there may be no room any more for theology schools, because scholastic teaching on the basis of Marxism-Leninism cannot be carried on within the framework of an organization where theology is taught. We shall in the future, as we did in the past, respect religious conviction, and proclaim and realize full freedom of religion within the life of the State, based on the principle that religion with respect to the State is a private matter. At the same time we shall naturally, in an increasing scale, put into effect the doctrine of Marxism-Leninism, according to which religion, within the Party, is not a private matter. We shall patiently explain to our Party members and must, by the means of education and propaganda, finally succeed in making clear to them, that: by going to church, by sending their children to religious instruction in schools, they, even if unintentionally, promote the efforts of the reactionary clergy. It was shown by the Polish example that, in principle, an agreement between the Church and the People's Democracy is possible. The Polish Bench of Bishops declared—I am quoting from the text of the agreement—that it "shall urge that the clergy in the course of its pastoral duties call upon the faithful to intensify their work for the reconstruction of the country and the advancement of the nation's welfare." Our own Bench of Bishops is urging the clergy to do the opposite. The Polish Bench of Bishops declared that "the principle that the Pope is the competent and supreme authority of the Church refers to matters of faith, morals, and Church jurisdiction; in other matters, however, the Episcopate is guided by the interest of the Polish State." The Hungarian Episcopate is not guided by the interests of the Hungarian State, but conforms to the policy of the Vatican, which serves the imperialists. The Polish Bench of Bishops declared that it would explain to the clergy that it should not oppose the development of the cooperatives in rural areas. The Hungarian Bench of Bishops does the contrary: it encourages the priests to protect the *Kulaks* and to attack the cooperatives. The Polish Episcopate declared that "in condemnation of all acts against the Polish State, the Church shall particularly oppose the misuse of religious feelings for anti-State purposes." The Hungarian Episcopate does the contrary: it misuses religious feelings for anti-State purposes. The Polish Bench of Bishops declared that "the Church shall denounce and punish under Canon Law those clergymen who are guilty of participation in any underground activities against the Polish State." The Hungaraian Bench of Bishops does the contrary: it has not yet dissociated itself from the American spy Mihalovics and even now it gives the conspirator against the State, Mindszenty, the honor of calling him 'Cardinal Prince Primate.' It is impossible to pursue a policy of peace and appeasement with such a Bench of Bishops. The government, however, is ready to make an agreement with, and give material support to, priests who collaborate with the People's Democracy.

Mr. Révai finally pointed out four tasks which should be performed by the Party. They are:

(1) To expose the reactionary clericalism of the Catholic Bench of Bishops, the enemy of peace;

(2) To support and help those priests who by opposing the bishops are true to the people and to support peace and the People's Democracy;

(3) To see to it that adequate measures of self-defense be taken by the State, combined with an enlightening campaign, against reactionary clericalism;

(4) To achieve the goal that our Party functionaries and the bulk of our Party members stop sending their children to religious instruction in schools, to increase the propaganda against reactionary clericalism among the people, to increase the enlightening work against Church ideology within the Party. In order to safeguard our socialist work of construction and in defense of our country and the peace and of the unity of our people, we are determined to liquidate this Fifth Column of the imperialists: reactionary clericalism.

D.   Excerpt From the Article of Bishop Bertalan Badarik.
     ("Kereszt," June 23, 1951)

"Why did the Bench of Bishops take the oath? It did so primarily out of love for our country and our people. If we examine the different kinds of relations between the State and the Catholic Church in the course of the 2000 years of its history, then we may establish that the Church has always been loyal to the State as long as it could do so without giving up its principles. And it could not act otherwise because Christ, its founder, claimed this loyalty from the Church. St. Paul, the apostle of the nations who preached the gospel in the world empire which was utterly opposed to Christianity, admonished the believers of the Church community of

Rome with the following words: 'Let everybody be subject to the higher authorities, for there is no authority except from God, and those who exist have been appointed by God.' (Rom. 13, 1).

"This, however, would be only a negative attitude. The Bench of Bishops is ready also to contribute in a positive way to the maintenance of the social order and the establishment of domestic peace necessary for building up the country. And it actually does so. It is acting so not only for the sake of fulfilling a given promise, but by continuing its activity as before. Through the pastoral clergy it teaches the Hungarian people to practice those virtues of the Gospel without which neither the order of the state nor security nor peace nor constructive work can be safeguarded. These virtues are: respect for authority, stressing loyalty to the state, obedience to laws, love of fellow men, solidarity, mutual reliance upon each other, respect for man as the highest value, respect for man's inherent rights, cherishing freedom above all, stressing on the part of the Church the mandatory divine command to work, and an ever increasing positive contribution of the Church [in furthering these virtues].

"The Bench of Bishops has taken the oath of allegiance to the new Constitution also because therein freedom of religion is guaranteed without restriction. Freedom of religion is an indispensable precondition of the activity of the Church. The Church actually does not claim anything else from the State than that this freedom be safeguarded. It leaves to Divine Providence everything else it needs for its activities. However, the Church must expect and receive from the State the warrant to enable it to struggle for this freedom. Now, since the new Hungarian Constitution actually warrants this, the Bench of Bishops did not act contrary to its conscience in pledging allegiance to this Constitution.

"We hope that the fact that we took the oath shall strengthen the confidence of the responsible leaders of the country in the Catholic Church in Hungary. Both of us need this confidence, for the letter and the spirit of the new Constitution must be transplanted into actual life, and also that part [of the Constitution] warranting freedom of religion must actually be secured for [everyday] life. This, however, is a practical task which the contracting parties cannot realize without mutual confidence.

"Summing up, the Bench of Bishops has taken the oath of loyalty to Hungary and our people in order that freedom of religion which has been warranted without any restriction in the Constitution shall be realized in practice and in order to maintain peace within and without.

"It took the oath with the knowledge that the oath is not contrary to Catholic doctrine or to our pastoral duty. In taking the oath, the Bench of Bishops has proclaimed in unmistakeable words: The Catholic Church, confessing its doctrine, maintaining its discipline, unshaken in its loyalty, prevails. We took the oath not for the sake of material profit, not because we are clinging to power, but in order to be able to continue to render our services to our beloved Hungarian people."

NOTES

1. Law No. II of 1723.
2. Sec. 4 of Law No. XXXI of 1504 and Law No. XV of 1536.
3. Law No. I of 1920 on the Restitution of Constitutionality and the Provisional Regulation of the Exercise of the Supreme State Power.
4. See Kubinszky, Lajos, Outline of the Law of Administration of matters of Religion and Public Education, (In Hungarian), Budapest, University Press, 1947.
5. *Ibidem.*
6. Law No. I of 1608, enacted before the coronation; and Law No. V of 1647, ratifying the Peace Treaties of Vienna and Linz. Religious freedom for these churches was further regulated by Law No. XXVI of 1791.
7. Law No. XX of 1848.
8. Law No. XXVII of 1791, confirmed by Sections 6-8 of Laws No. XX of 1848.
9. Law No. X of 1792.
10. Law No. VII of 1885.
11. Law No. IX of 1868.
12. Law No. XX of 1848.
13. Section 6 of Law No. XLIII of 1895.
14. Law No. LIII of 1868.
15. Decree No. 77,092 of 1905 V.K.M. of the Minister of Religion and Public Education.
16. Law No. XVII of 1916.
17. Section 54 of Law No. XX of 1949.
18. Decree of the Provisional National Government No. 600 M.E. of 1945, ultimately enacted by the Provisional National Assembly on September 16, 1945, by Law No. VI of 1945. The Provisional National Government was constituted with the assistance of the Political Section of the Headquarters of the Soviet Russian Occupation Forces of Hungary in Debrecen, Eastern Hungary, on December 22, 1944. The Provisional National Assembly was constituted of members appointed by the approval of the Russian Occupation Forces by the following five political parties: Communist, Social Democrat, Labor Union (considered as forming a political party of their own), National Peasant Party and the Smallholders; these parties distributed the mandates in the Provisional National Assembly in equal shares among themselves. Later they were joined by the Civic Democratic Party.
19. One cadastral hold equals 1.42 acres.
20. Sec. 54.
21. Law No. XX of 1949 (adopted on August 20), Sec. 54, Para. 1 and 2.
22. Law No. II of 1939.
23. Decree No. 752 of 1945 M.E. (May 10, 1945).
24. Numerous lists of the dissolved religious associations appeared in the *Magyar Közlöny* since 1946, e.g. No. 206, September 11, 1946; No. 4, January 3, 1947; No. 230, October 10, 1947; No. 49, February 28, 1948.
25. Dr. György Vadas, *Handbooks of the Democratic Administration.* Vol. IV. Certain Administrative Branches and the Development of the Public Administration. (Outline and Tetxbook for the Introductory Administrative Course by the Council of Trade Unions. [established] according to Decree of the Prime Minister No. 10,070 of 1945). (In Hungarian) Budapest, 1947, p. 41.
26. Decree No. 3180 of 1948. Korm.
27. Decree No. 55,746 of 1949 Bk. M.

28. Resolution of the Cabinet No. 1,012 of 1952.
29. Edict No. 1 of 1950 (January 25, 1950).
30. Law No. I of 1222 on the "Annual Celebration of the Day of King Stephen."
31. by Law No. XXXIII of 1948, in force since June 16, 1948.
32. See *Supra* II, A, 1 Land Reform.
33. The denominational schools had to obtain the approval of the Minister for Religion and Public Education for their textbooks.
34. Early in the same year one of the most important Catholic organizations, the St. Stephen Society, was dissolved and its printing shop, the Stepheneum, nationalized, as were all printing shops belonging to the Catholic Church.
35. Law No. XXXIII of 1948 was enforced by Decree of the Minister of Religion and Public Education No. 8,000 of 1948 V.K.M. (June 27, 1948).
36. Decree No. 750 of 1949 Korm. (in force since January 22, 1949).
37. Decree No. 4,105 of 1949 Korm. (June 26, 1949).
38. See Article 7(h) of the Agreement between the Government and the Reformed Church of October 7, 1948, and Art. 6(h) of the Agreement with the Evangelical Church of December 14, 1948, in the Appendix.
39. Edict No. 23 of 1950, transferring the Divinity Schools of the Universities to the Churches.
40. Introduced in the Parliament on June 15, 1948.
41. Art. 3.
42. Edict No. 5 of 1949.
43. Decree No. 1101/1 of 1949 V.K.M.
44. See the speech of Mr. József Révay, Minister of People's Education, on June 5, 1950, delivered before the Central Committee of the Hungarian Workers Party, in which he said: "To send children to Church, to religious instruction in schools * * * means at the same time, be it intentionally or not, to take a stand against the People's Democracy. Optional religious education in schools is not the final solution of applying democratic principles to this question. We shall change this." (In the Appendix)
45. Decree No. 1101-11-1 of 1950 V.K.M.
46. Decree No. 4288 of 1949 M.T. (October 22, 1949).
47. Tomcsányi Móric, The Public Law of Hungary. (In Hungarian) p. 195; Móra Mihály, The Greek Orthodox Church Laws, The Catholic Church and the State (In Hungarian) p. 15, Kubinszky, op. cit., p. 250.
48. Law No. IX of 1868.
49. Kubinszky, op. cit., p. 250.
50. Notice No. 1161-1-K4 of 1950 Eln. No. 6.
51. Law No. XXI of 1092.
52. Law No. CII of 1715, Sec. 3.
53. Decree No. 110 of 1951 M.T. Sec. 1, Subsec. 1, Par. (f) and (i) enforcing Law No. I, of 1951.
54. *Magyar Közlöny*, No. 77, May, 1951, p. 435.
55. Decree No. 1016 of 1952 M.T. (June 1, 1952).
56. Edict No. 20 of 1951.
57. Decree No. 170 of 1951 M.T.
58. See II. A, General Survey, 1.
59. Magyar Nemzet, April 28, 1951, p. 5. (In Hungarian)
60. The Accord between the Hungarian Church and State, published by the Legation of the Hungarian People's Republic, Washington D.C., p. 3.
61. No. 214 of 1951 M.T. (December 21, 1951).
62 Decree No. 212 of 1951 (XII. 15) M.T.
63. In 1940 out of the total population of 9,317,000, there were 6,120,000 Roman Catholics, 233,672 Greek Catholics, 1,935,000 Reformed, 557,000 Evangelical, 38,300 Orthodox, 17,917 Baptists, 400,980 Jews, 8,465 Unitarians and 5,515 others or, expressed in percentages, 65.6 per cent Roman Catholic, 2.5 per cent Greek Catholic,

20.8 per cent Reformed, 6 per cent Evangelical, 0.1 per cent Unitarian, 0.4 per cent Orthodox, 0.2 per cent Baptist and 4.3 per cent Jewish. Hungarian Statistical Manual XIIIth year of issue, 1910-1941, Magyar Statisztikai Zsebkönyv, Hungarian Central Statistical Office, Magyar Központi Statisztikai Hivatal, Budapest, 1948, Pátria, p. 50.

64. *Szabad Nép*, No. 112, May 15, 1948.
65. R. H. Markham, *Communists Crush Churches in Eastern Europe*, Boston Year, p. 89.
66. See Appendix, B, 1.
67. Markham, *op. cit.*, p. 89.
68. *Ibidem*, p. 90.
69. *Ibidem*, p. 87.
70. Since Mr. Lázár was arrested without charge this fact was not published, as similar cases never have been.
71. *Szabad Nép*, No. 108, May 12, 1948.
72. See note 63; in comparison, a considerably large part of Hungarians living in Transylvania (Romania) are Unitarians.
73. October 7, 1948.
74. See Appendix, B. 3. Agreement with Evangelical Church.
75. Markham, *op. cit.*, p. 88.
76. *Népszava*, No. 227, October 2, 1948.
77. *The Four Years Struggle of the Church is Hungary*, published by the order of Joseph Cardinal Mindszenty, Longmans, Green & Co., London, 1948, p. 152.
78. *Szabad Nép*, No. 112, May 16, 1948.
79. *Op. cit. supra*, note 77, p. 153.
80. Supra note 24.
81. Sigismund Mihalovich, *Mindszenty, Ungarn, Europa*, Badenia Verlag, Karlsruhe, 1949, p. 207.
82. *Op. cit. supra*, note 77, p. 155.
83. *Ibidem*, p. 156.
84. *Szabad Nép*, No. 136, June 16, 1948.
85. June 16, 1948.
86. *Szabad Nép*, No. 137, June 17, 1948.
87. Keesing's *Contemporary Archives*, Keesing's Publications Ltd., London, 1948-1950, p. 9721.
88. *Op. cit. supra*, note 77, p. 181.
89. Keesing, 1948-1950, p. 9721.
90. *Op. cit. supra*, note 77, p. 183.
91. Keesing, 1948-1950, p. 9721.
92. *Ibidem*, p. 9721.
93. *Népszava*, No. 286, December 11, 1948: Rákosí's speech, No. 275, Nov. 28, 1948.
94. *Ibidem*, No. 289, December 15, 1948.
95. Keesing, 1948-1950, p. 9721.
96. *Ibidem*, 9721.
97. *Népszava*, No. 299, December 28, 1948.
98. *Op. cit. supra*, note 77, p. 189 and Keesing, 1948-1950, p. 9880.
99. *Népszava*, No. 302, December 31, 1948.
100. Keesing, 1948-1950, p. 9721.
101. *Ibidem*.
102. Markham, *op. cit.*, p. 83.
103. *Katolikus Szemle* (Catholic Review, published by the Catholic Action of Hungarians Abroad), Rome, 1950, No. 3, p. 130.
104. *Ibidem*, p. 129.
105. See Appendix, C; *Szabad Nép*, No. 129, June 6, 1950.
106. *Katolikus Szemle*, 1950, No. 3, p. 130.
107. *Ibidem*, p. 131; the Archbishop's letter, p. 115.

108. See Appendix B, 4.
109. Edict No. 34 of 1950.
110. See Appendix, A. 4, Edict No. 34 of 1950.
111. *Katolikus Szemle*, 1950, No. 3, p. 131.
112. V. Korpinski, *The Social and State Structure of the U.S.S.R.*, Moscow, 1950.
113. Law No. X of 1092.
114. March 31, 1783.
115. Law XXXVIII of 1791.
116. Law No. XXIX of 1840.
117. Law No. XVII of 1867.
118. Law No. XLII of 1895.
119. Law No. VIII of 1942.
120. Law No. XXVII of 1940 (Section 2).
121. Decree No. 200 of 1945 M.E.
122. Dated July 30, 1868.
123. The "Congressional Jewish" congregations are almost the same as the "Conservative Jewish" congregations in the U.S.A.; "Orthodox Jewish" congregations correspond in both countries; "Status-quo-ante Jewish" congregations take an intermediary position between them.
124. June 14, 1869.
125. Decree No. 26, 915 of 1871 V.K.M.
126. Decrees No. 22, 331 and 35, 874-II of 1928 V.K.M.
127. Decree No. 2, 727 of 1945 V.K.M.
128. Decrees No. 62,000 and 110,000 of 1947 V.K.M.
129. Decree No. 34,000 of 1948 V.K.M.
130. Magyar Közlöny, Hivatalos Lap, No. 271, Dec. 10, 1948.
131. The discussion of Cardinal Mindszenty's and Archbishop Grosz's trial is limited to the examination of material published by the Hungarian Government. It included:

1. The so-called "Yellow Book" (*Documents on the Mindszenty case*. Budapest, January, 1949) published before the trial, which included all the evidence the prosecution had collected "to prove tangibly and irrefutably . . .that Mindszenty and his company were guilty," as the preface to the book announced hereafter cited as "Yellow Book";

2. The so-called "Black Book" (*The Trial of József Mindszenty*. Hungarian State Publishing House, Budapest, 1951) containing excerpts of the minutes of the Mindszenty-trial hereafter cited as "Black Book";

3. The so-called "Gray Book" (*Trial of József Grösz and his Accomplices*. State Publishing House, Budapest, 1951) containing the proceedings of Archbishop Grösz's trial, hereafter cited as "Gray Book."

All these documents were published and distributed by the Hungarian Government in English and in several other languages.

It is doubtful, however, whether these publications are impartial and factual accounts of what actually took place. In the first place, the fact must be considered that even prior to the public hearings effort was made to influence public opinion against the Cardinal. Secondly, it seems certain that the account contained in the "Black Book" differs materially from the account given daily by the Hungarian radio and that the minutes of the trial seem to be edited. No control is possible on the book concerning the Grösz proceeding.

The review of the laws concerned is based on texts published in the Hungarian Collection of Laws of 1930, 1939, 1945 and 1946 as well as in the Official Collection of Laws and Decrees of 1949 and 1950. The messages accompanying the bills are attached thereto.

These messages are of importance for they are considered by Hungarian courts as evidence for the interpretation. The *Commentary on Law No. VII of 1946 on the Criminal Protection of the Democratic State Order and the Republic* (Atheneum,

Budapest, 1946) may also be considered as an official interpretation since Istvan Riesz, the Minister of Justice, wrote the preface and Police-Colonel István Timár, the deputy-chief of the Political Police, and Mózes Ábráhám, Honorary Attorney of the District Pest, compiled, this booklet.

132. Preamble of Decree No. 81 of 1945 M.E. enacted by Law No. VII of 1945, and amended by Law No. XXXIV of 1947.

133. Section 11 of Law No. VII of 1946.

134. Riesz-Timár-Ábráhám, [*Commentary of*] *Law No. VII of 1946 on the Criminal Protection of the Democratic State-Order and the Republic*. In Hungarian [Budapest], 1946, p. 5.

135. Law No. XI of 1949 on the "Participation of the People, in Criminal Jurisdiction and Simplification of the Procedure of Appeals."

136. Decree No. 4172 of 1949 Korm.

137. Law No. XX of 1949.

138. This is the English translation of the charges as printed in *The Trial of József Mindszenty*, published by the Hungarian State Publishing House, Budapest, 1949, p. 162-163:

"1. József Mindszenty, the first accused, is guilty of:

A) the crime of leading an organization aimed at the overthrow of the Republic and the democratic State order, committed once, falling under Law VII:1946, Article 1, Paragraph 1;

B) of the crime of treason, committed once continuously, falling under Law III:1930, Article 58; and guilty of

C) the crime of treason defined in Law III:1930, Article 60, Paragraph 3, and qualified according to Law XVIII:1934, Article 2, Paragraph 1, committed once; and guilty of

D) the crime of failing to deposit into a blocked account foreign currency, and failing to declare foreign assets, committed once and continuously, defined in the Decree 8400/1946, Article 1, Paragraph 1, Item (a) further owing to the infringement of the obligation comprised in Paragraph 2, Item (b) and considering Article 17, Paragraph 1, qualified according to Paragraph 2, of the said Article; and guilty of

E) the crime of speculation with foreign currency, committed once continuously, defined and punishable in consideration of Law XXVI:1922, Article 1, Paragraph 1, Item 1, and of Law XIV:1939, Article 1, as set out in P.M. Decree No. 8800/1946, Article 20, Paragraph (2); and guilty of

F) the crime of having sent out of the country foreign currency without a permit, committed once, defined under the infringement of the prohibition comprised in P.M. Decree No. 8400/1946, Article 4, Paragraph 1, Item (d), and Article 17, Paragraph 1, of the same Decree; and guilty of

G) the crime of disposing without a proper permit of valuables falling under declaration, committed once, and defined under the prohibition laid down in P.M. Decree No. 8400/1946, Article 3, Paragraph 3 and Article 17 of the same Decree Paragraph 1, Item I."

The charges against Archbishop József Grösz as formulated in the sentence were translated into English in *The Trial of József Grösz and his Accomplices*, published by the State Publishing House, Budapest, 1951, p. 367, as follows:

"The first accused József Grösz was found guilty of

1. the crime of leading a conspiracy aimed at the overthrow of the democratic order of the State, as defined in Article 1, paragraph 1, of Act VII:1946;

2. the crime of speculating with foreign currency, as defined in Article 57, points a) and b), of Law Decree 1950:30, as qualified in Article 58, paragraph 3, of the same;

3. the crime of abetting escape from the country as defined in Article 48, paragraph 4, of Act XLVIII:1948; and

4. the crime against the People, committed by being accessory after the fact, as defined in Article 12, point 6, of Order 1440/1945. M.E., passed in Parliament under Article 1 of Act VII:1945."

139. Law No. VII of 1946. Section 1, Subsection 1.

140. Law No. V of 1878, Section 127, Subsection 2 and Law No. III of 1921 were the laws dealing with sedition before the new regime.

141. Law No. VII of 1946. Sec. 1.

142. Riesz-Timár-Ábráhám, op. cit.

143. Message accompanying the bill.

144. Law No. III of 1930. "Black Book," p. 178.

145. Law No. XVIII of 1934 and Law No. II of 1939.

146. Decree No. 4338 of 1949 M.T.

147. Law No. XXVI of 1922.

148. Edict No. 30 of 1950.

149. "Black Book" p. 169.

150. Ibidem, p. 170.

151. Ibidem.

152. Ibidem, p. 171.

153. Ibidem, p. 172.

154. Ibidem, p. 173.

155. Ibidem, p. 173.

156. "Gray Book," p. 371.

157. Ibidem, pp. 371, 373.

158. Ibidem, pp. 374, 375.

159. Joseph Henry Beale, Jr. *A Treatise on Criminal Pleading and Practice,* Boston, Little, Brown and Co., 1899: p. 57.

160. See P. Beat Ambord, S. J., *Der Vatican und die Kirche Hinter dem Eisernen Vorhang,* Eichstatt i. Bay., Roma Verlag; p. 48.

161. Vladimir Gsovski, "The Legal Status of the Church in Soviet Russia," *Fordham Law Review,* January, 1939.

162. Stephen K. Swift, *The Cardinal's Story.* New York, 1949. p. 288.

TABLE OF STATUTES

BIBLIOGRAPHY

Beale, Joseph. *A Treatise on Criminal Pleading*. Boston: Little, Brown & Co., 1899.

Beat, Ambrose. *Der Vatikan und die Kirche hinter den eisernen Vorhang*. Eichstätt i. Bayern: Roma Verlag, 1949.

Documents in the Mindszenty Case. Budapest: Atheneum, 1949.

Gsovski, Vladimir. "The Legal Status of the Church in Soviet Russia," *Fordham Law Review*, VIII (1939), 1-28.

Katolikus Szemle. Rome, 1946—present.

Kereszt. Budapest, 1949—present.

Keesing's Contemporary Archives. London: Keesing Publication, Ltd., 1945.

Korpinski, V. *The Social and State Structure in the U.S.S.R.* Moscow, 1950.

Kubinszky, Lajos. Outline of the Law of Administration of matters of Religion and Public Education. *Vallás- és kőzoktatasűgyi igazgatas vázlata*. Budapest: Egyetimi nyomda, 1947.

Markham, R. H. *Communists Crush Churches in Eastern Europe*. Boston: Meador, 1950.

Mihalovich, Sigismund. *Mindszenty, Ungarn, Europa*. Karlsruhe: Badenia Verlag, n.d.

Móra, Mihály. The Greek Orthodox Church Laws, the Catholic Church and the State. *A gőrőgkeleti egyházjog, a kat. egyház és az állam*. Budapest: Stephaneum, 1943.

Népszava. Budapest.

Statistical Yearbook—1940. *Statisztikai Évkönyv*, Budapest, 1940.

Swift, Stephen. *The Cardinal's Story*. New York, 1949.

Szabad Nép. Budapest, 1945—present.

Ries, Istvan, Timár, István; and Abrahám, Mozes. [Commentary of] Law No. VII of 1946 on the Criminal Protection of the Democratic State Order and the Republic. *A demokratikus államrend és kőztársaság védelméről szóló 1946. évi VII.t.c.* Budapest, [1946 or 1947?].

The Four Years Struggle of the Church in Hungary. London: Longman, Green & Co., 1948.

The Trial of József Grősz and His Accomplices. Budapest: Hungarian State Publishing House, 1951.

The Trial of József Mindszenty. Budapest: Hungarian State Publishing House, 1949.

Tomcsányi, Móric. The Public Law of Hungary. *Magyaroszág közjoga.* Budapest: Egyetemi nyomda, 1940.

Vadas, György. Handbooks of the Democratic Administration, *A demokratikus közigazgatás kézikönyve.* Vol. 4. *Egyes közigazgatási ágak és a közigazgatás fejlesztése. (A Szakszervezeti Tanács által a 10070/1945 M.E. sz. rendelet értelmében rendezett közigazgatási bevezető tanfolyam vezérfonala és tananyaga.)* Budapest, Budapest székesfővárosi irodalmi és müintézet, 3rd edition, 1947.

Stefan Rosada and *Józef Gwóźdź*

CHURCH AND STATE IN POLAND

Vladimir Gsovski, *editor*

CHURCH AND STATE IN POLAND
by Stefan Rosada and Józef Gwóźdž

ABBREVIATIONS

Dz. U.—*Dziennik Ustaw Polskiej Rzeczypospolitej Ludowej* (Journal of Laws of the Polish People's Republic).

Dz. Urz. Min. Ośw.—*Dziennik Urzędowy Ministerstwa Oświaty* (Official Gazette of the Ministry of Education).

Monitor Polski—*Monitor Polski, Dziennik Urzędowy Polskiej Rzeczypospolitej Ludowej* (Official Gazette of the Polish People's Republic).

INTRODUCTION

This study aims to trace the position of the Church in Poland as it has developed from 1944 to July 1, 1954. During this period the Government proceeded to bring public and private life in the country into alignment with the Soviet system and systematically eradicated all democratic institutions, thereby isolating Poland from the free world. At the same time, Church policy was being shaped to accord with Communist ideology, the final aim of which is the creation of a non-religious society. However, with regard to the Church in general and the Roman Catholic Church in particular, the Government showed a cautious attitude at the beginning. It was difficult for the Communist regime to put its ideology into practice at once. Existing conditions made it impossible for the Communists to make an immediate and direct attack upon the Church.

Without dwelling upon the historical ties of Poland with the Roman Catholic Church and the exceptionally strong religious feeling of the Polish people, it is to be noted that Poland within its present boundaries emerged from World War II more Roman Catholic than ever. At present over 95 per cent of the population is Catholic. This denominational uniformity is partly the result of Poland's loss of Eastern provinces in which the population embraced a large number of members of the Russian Eastern Orthodox Church (*prawosławni*). These form now only a small fraction of the total population within the present boundaries of Poland, variously estimated from 50,000 to 400,00O (*see infra* Chapter IV, A). Hitler's brutality reduced also the number of Jews of whom only approximately 40,000 are left in present Poland.

As for other religious groups, which were always only small minorities, Protestants of all kinds may number a third of a million, of whom most are Lutherans. National Catholics who do not acknowledge the authority of the Vatican, other denominational groups and non-believers do not exceed 100,000. Practically all the rest of the inhabitants are Roman Catholics. Almost all the Catholics now in Poland are those following the Latin Rite because the Uniates who follow the Greek Catholic Rite are mostly Ukrainians who inhabited the Eastern Provinces now included in the Soviet Union. It is estimated that not more than 100,000 Greek Catholics remain in Poland.

Thus, an analysis of the present relationship of the Government with the Church and of its attitude toward religion in general may be reduced in fact to its relations with the Roman Catholic Church. The majority of the population acknowledges a supreme spiritual authority of a non-national character, the Holy See. This alone makes the relationship of the Communist government to the Church more complex than it is in the case of independent national churches, as in some other countries behind the Iron Curtain. Today the Roman Catholic Church is the only organization not yet absorbed by the Communist regime and still permitted to function within Poland. The tactics used against the Church have varied and the intensity of the attacks has fluctuated.

The rising tension within the country is best illustrated by the fact that although the Government found it prudent in 1945 to exempt church land from nationalization, it passed a statute in 1950 nationalizing Church land, and in 1953 it did not hesitate to issue a decree aimed at complete control of the Church.

Certain distinct stages in the Church and State relationship in Communist Poland may actually be observed in the period between 1944 and 1953 from an analysis of the factual situation as well as statutes and executive orders. These stages are characterized by a subtle policy observed also in other aspects of life in Poland: alternation of benevolence and pressure, of tolerance and hostility.

The first stage dates from the time of the establishment of the Council for National Liberation[1] in 1944 to the conclusion of the Agreement of April 14, 1950, between the Government and the Roman Catholic Episcopate in Poland. During the second stage, the new Constitution of July 22, 1952, was enacted. However, the new Constitution did not clarify the status of the Church in Poland. The third stage dates from February 9, 1953, when the Decree on the Appointment of Clergymen to Ecclesiastical Offices was enacted.

Legal provisions alone do not show the true status of the Church. A wide discrepancy between the rules of law and their application is in evidence. Therefore, to obtain a true picture, important developments and official statements made by the Government and by the Polish Episcopate are reviewed in connection with the laws and decrees enacted.

Finally, it should be borne in mind that postwar Poland has boundaries different from those which it had prior to World War II. The present study covers the situation as it exists within the postwar boundaries. It does not treat the situation in the area which formed the eastern part of Poland and which is now within the Soviet Union.

I. CONSTITITUTIONAL PROVISIONS AND THE CONCORDAT OF 1925

A. *Situation Prior to the Enactment of the New Constitution of July 22, 1952*

1. *Provisions of the 1921 Constitution*

A confusing situation resulted from the fact that the constitutional provisions of present-day Poland were not, until July 22, 1952, embodied in any single act called "Constitution." The provisions may be found in several acts which were put into effect both before and after the present regime came into being. Thus on February 19, 1947, the Polish Legislative Assembly passed a "constitutional statute" commonly called the "Small 1947 Constitution." [2] It is, however, confined to the regulation of the structure and jurisdiction of the supreme authorities of the Polish Republic. These provisions were declared to have been formulated in accordance with the fundamental principles of the 1921 Constitution and were designed to apply until the enactment of a new Constitution.

Among the sources of law by which the Legislative Assembly was supposed to be guided pending the adoption of the new Constitution only one was mentioned which contains provisions relating to the Church (Art 1). This is the Constitution adopted in 1921. It is true that on the eve of World War II another constitution was in force, *viz.*, that of 1935. However this constitution was repudiated *in toto* for postwar Poland by the "Manifesto" of the Polish Committee of National Liberation of July 21, 1944, which called it "fascist and illegal." With regard to the status of the Church, this was of no consequence, since the 1935 Constitution upheld in this respect the provisions of the 1921 Constitution.

Before analyzing these provisions it may be mentioned that

by a separate resolution of February 22, 1947, dealing with the basic civil rights and liberties, "the Polish Legislative Assembly as the Supreme authority of the Polish Nation solemnly declared that it will continue to safeguard . . . 3) freedom of conscience and religion."[3]

In referring to the 1921 Constitution, "the Small 1947 Constitution" mentioned only that "the fundamental principles of the 1921 Constitution" continue to be valid without any further specifications. It was left to interpretation what provisions of the 1921 Constitution relating to the Church were fundamental. We will quote therefore from the 1921 Constitution Articles directly relating to the Church:

> 111. Freedom of conscience and religion shall be guaranteed to all citizens. No citizen shall, by reason of his faith or religious convictions, be limited in his access to rights enjoyed by other citizens.
>
> All inhabitants of the Polish State shall have the right to profess their creed freely in public and in private and to practice the precepts of their religion or ritual, provided that this is not contrary to public order or public morals.
>
> 112. Freedom of religion shall not be utilized in a manner contrary to law. No one shall evade performance of his public duties by reason of his religious faith. No one shall be compelled to participate in religious activities or rituals, unless subject to parental or guardian's care.
>
> 113. Every religious association recognized by the Government shall have the right to hold collective and public religious services, to conduct its internal affairs independently, to possess and acquire, to administer and dispose of personal and real property, to hold and to utilize its foundations and funds, and also to establish institutions for religious, scientific, or philanthropic purposes. A religious association may not, however, remain in opposition to the laws of the State.

Thus the 1921 Constitution not only established as a matter of general principle the freedom of citizens "to practice the precepts of their religion," but also guaranteed to churches independence in internal affairs and the right "to hold and utilize foundations and funds and also to establish institutions for religious, scientific, or philanthropic purposes." The Churches enjoyed full corporate status, were legal entities. In addition, there

were special provisions relating to the Roman Catholic Church
in particular and to other non-Catholic denominations.

> 114. The Roman Catholic faith, being the religion of the great
> majority of the nation, occupies a leading position in the State
> among other religions, which, however, also enjoy equal rights.
> The Roman Catholic Church is governed by its own laws. The
> relation of the State to the Church shall be determined on the basis
> of an agreement with the Holy See, which shall be subject to
> ratification by the *Sejm*.

By virtue of this article the Roman Catholic Church retained a privileged position and was not required to be recognized
by the Government, whereas all other denominations, if they
were to constitute a Church or religious association, had to
obtain recognition. The Roman Catholic Church was governed
by its own laws, acknowledged *ipso facto* by the State. Other
Churches were also governed by their own statutes, but these
statutes had to be recognized specifically by a legislative act.
Moreover, the Roman Catholic Church also held a leading position among other denominations, although all were equal before the law.

Articles 115 and 116 dealt with Churches other than the
Roman Catholic Church. Three groups are distinguished: first,
Churches of religious minorities; second, legally recognized
religious associations; and third, all others. The first group embraces the non-Catholic Churches which were already established
on the territory of Poland prior to the Constitution. Neither
these Churches nor the religious associations which had already
obtained recognition by the State required any special act of
recognition (Article 115).

> 115. The Churches of religious minorities and other legally rec-
> ognized religious associations shall be governed by their own laws,
> which the State shall not refuse to recognize, provided that they do
> not contain provisions contrary to law.
> The relation of the State to these Churches and religious denom-
> inations shall be determined by legislation after an understanding
> has been attained with their authorized agencies.

In compliance with the principle of freedom of conscience,

Article 116 enabled new or hitherto unrecognized denominations to obtain a status equal to those already recognized.

> 116. Recognition of a new religious denomination or one not hitherto legally recognized shall not be refused to religious associations whose organization, teaching, and structure are not contrary to public order or public morals.

Article 121 of the Constitution provided for mandatory religious instruction in schools, to be supervised by the Churches concerned.

2. Concordat of 1925

The legal status of the Catholic Church in pre-war Poland was determined, in addition to the Constitution, by the Concordat concluded between the Holy See and the Polish Government on February 10, 1925.[4] This is the outline of its principle provisions:

The Roman Catholic Church was guaranteed freedom to exercise its ecclesiastical authority and jurisdiction as well as freedom to administer and manage matters relating to its property according to the principles of canon law. Free contact with the Holy See was assured to bishops, the lower clergy, and members of the Church. The Church was also assured the right to issue directive orders to subordinate agencies and to the faithful without special permission from the Government authority.

The Concordat further provided for diplomatic relations with the Holy See through an Embassy at the Vatican and a Papal Nuncio to be accredited to the Polish Government.

Moreover, the assistance of the civil authorities was promised to the Church in the execution of its regulations and decrees; the clergy was assured protection by the Government in its official duties; and the inviolability of Churches was guaranteed.

The Concordat also guaranteed legal protection to the clergy's property, objects of artistic and historic value, and the like.

The Government recognized the right of ecclesiastical legal

entities to all property, whether real or personal, investments, capital, income, and interest, as well as other rights which these corporate bodies of the Church then possessed within the territory of the State. Special clauses of the Concordat dealt with matters of compensation for property which the Church had lost or was required to give up for the purposes of the land reform then planned.

In all schools except the higher educational institutions, religious instruction was declared mandatory, the Church authorities having the right to supervise religious instruction.

The Concordat of 1925 was in force as the basis of the relationship between Church and State at the end of World War II. The Polish Government-in-Exile has maintained its representative at the Vatican, who is still accredited to the Holy See.

3. Attitude of the Postwar Government to Provisions dealing with the Church in the 1921 Constitution and the Concordat

The Soviet-sponsored Polish Government took a definite negative attitude toward the Concordat almost as soon as it came into being. It did not take, or a least did not announce, any customary diplomatic steps for direct repudiation or denunciation of the Concordat. Nevertheless a statement appeared in a publication of the Ministry of Foreign Affairs, in the daily press and by radio to the effect that the Polish Provisional Government decided on September 12, 1945 that "the Concordat between the Polish Republic and the Vatican was no longer binding following the one-sided breach on the part of the Holy See."[5] It was also printed in the semi-official law review that such a stand was taken on the basis of the legal opinion prepared by a special committee appointed for this purpose by the Minister of Justice. The opinion itself was also made public.[6]

In this opinion it was alleged that, contrary to the provisions of the Concordat, the Vatican appointed a German priest as the apostolic administrator of the Archbishopric of Gniezno-Poznań and entrusted the administration of the Diocese of

Chełmno to the German bishop of Gdańsk. The opinion stressed also that because of the postwar changes in the political conditions of Poland, the Concordat lost its binding force in accordance with the maxim of *rebus sic stantibus.*

The Council of Ministers also declared that the Holy See, contrary to the attitude of most other countries, had not yet recognized the Provisional Government, and that consequently no regular relations existed between the Holy See and the Polish Government.

No official statement was made by the postwar government indicating which of the provisions of the 1921 Constitution retained their force. Only one discussion of the problem in the legal press was disclosed.[7] Stefan Rozmaryn, a law professor and open supporter of the regime, voiced the opinion that: "The contents of Article 112 (last words), Articles 114, 115, 117-121, are binding only insofar as they are put into effect by ordinary legislation, and then only by force of such ordinary laws. . . . If ordinary legislation does not contain provisions putting into effect the above mentioned articles 114, 115, 117 through 121, then the respective provisions of the Constitution do not apply at all. What is not contained in ordinary statutes does not apply and that which does apply may be changed or abolished by an ordinary legislative act." It is noteworthy that the author does not mention any legal provision upholding Article 120 of the 1921 Constitution, which provides for mandatory religious instruction in all public schools. But a circular letter of the Ministry of Education of September 13, 1945 treated Article 120 as still in force.

This discussion merely shows the uncertainty of constitutional guarantees in Poland prior to the enactment of the new Constitution. It may be stated that the status of the Church in particular was then no longer governed by definite, generally recognized constitutional provisions.

Likewise an article by S. Piotrowski appeared in the official law review insisting that all regulations based upon the Concordat had lost their binding force simultaneously with its renunciation. Therefore, contended the article, the conditions existing prior to the Concordat have been restored, and thus the Canon Code applies and retains its binding force as the internal law of the Church insofar as it is consistent with the laws effective in the State.

That the view denying the validity of the Concordat is questionable to say the least is evident from the discussion of the general nature of concordats in a learned treatise on canon law which appeared in Warsaw in 1948 and reads as follows:

> Concordats are also binding upon successors of the parties who concluded them; they do not lose their validity because of a change in the form of government or dynasty in a state. They do, however, cease to be binding when in a given territory new States are formed different from the former State; Poland is not bound by concordats concluded by powers which partitioned Poland in the 18th century.

The present Polish Government does not claim to be the government of a new country. Consequently, in the light of the above interpretation it may not unilaterally withdraw from the Concordat.

A rather exhaustive answer to the charges brought against the Vatican by the Polish Government as the reason for which it denied the validity of the Concordat of 1925 was offered by Professor Oscar Halecki, a noted Polish historian in exile, in his book published in New York in 1951.[8] Professor Halecki says:

> The Vatican answered the charges made by the Communist regime in its declaration of September 12. It was easy to prove that in neither of the two specific instances cited by Warsaw had the Concordat of 1925 been violated by the Holy See. If, toward the end of December 1939, the administration of the Polish diocese of Chelmno had been entrusted provisionally to the Bishop of Danzig, that measure was "imposed by inescapable necessity and dictated solely for the welfare of souls. After nearly three months of occupation the diocese was in a disastrous condition: the Bishop being absent, the Auxiliary gravely ill, the Curia sealed up and almost all the clergy dispersed"; and the nearby Bishop of Danzig[9] was selected as administrator precisely because his own diocese, not belonging to any German ecclesiastical province, was immediately subjected to the Holy See and in accordance with the concordat was within the sphere of competence of the Nuncio to Poland. As to the second charge, the statement that a German priest, Father Breitinger, had been nominated Archbishop of

Gniezno and Poznan, was simply untrue. This priest who before the war had been a chaplain for the German Catholics of the archdiocese, had been made Apostolic Administrator for the Germans of the "Wartheland" (the Polish territories annexed by the Nazis), without receiving any episcopal dignity; on the other hand the only Polish bishop in that archdiocese, Msgr. Dymek, was appointed Apostolic Administrator for the Polish population, since the occupying authorities had imposed the most absolute segregation of the two nationalities in that region, even in the religious sphere. These nominations, too, had an entirely provisional character, "justified by exceptional circumstances and so improvised as to avoid any concordatory category." And the crux of the matter is that the exiled Archbishop of Gniezno and Poznan, Cardinal Primate Hlond, retained his dignity, receiving frequent messages of encouragement from Pius XII.

In any event, if the above declaration of September 12, 1945 is taken as a unilateral discontinuation of the effect of the Concordat and if Articles 114 *et seq.* of the 1921 Constitution were no longer in force, then the Roman Catholic Church in Poland functioned in a legal vacuum. No constitutional provisions, no law or decree defined its status.

A situation of a de facto separation of the Church from the State has arisen. In consequence the State has lost the right to control some of the Church affairs, provided for by the Concordat. Necessary changes in the Church administration were actually made without the government's participation. This is true of the appointment of new bishops, the creation of four separate apostolic administrations with the rights of bishoprics in the recovered territories Wrocław, Opole, Gorzów and Olsztyn to be administered by apostolic administrators and also of placing one archbishop at the head of both the bishopric of Gniezno and that of Warsaw. (It may be noted that an apostolic administration existed also in the diocese of Gdańsk).

In July 1945 Cardinal Hlond, the Primate of Poland who was interned during the last phase of World War II by the Germans, returned to Poland as the head of the administration of the Catholic Church. He consecrated new bishops, re-established seminaries, founded several Catholic papers, revived the activities of convents, and organized the Church administration in the recovered territories. It is to his credit that the Church in Poland was able to reorganize itself after the war within new state boundaries and under a Communist political setup.

Cardinal Hlond died on October 22, 1948, and on January 8, 1949, his successor became Archbishop Stefan Wyszyński, who was elevated to Cardinal in January 1953.

Pope Pius XII appointed Cardinal Hlond, the Primate, as archbishop of Warsaw with the right to retain his Primate's residence in Gniezno. His successor Cardinal Wyszyński retained the same position. This *de facto* situation was neither protected nor denied by law. But in many other respects rights and opportunities afforded to the Roman Catholic Church by the Concordat were gradually withdrawn by the Government, as will be shown below.

With the Concordat pushed aside, the government acquired a free hand in the treatment of the Church, while the Church could not invoke the provisions of the Concordat.

B. *Status of Church and Religion as Provided in the New Constitution*

The status of the Churches has been determined in the new Constitution (Articles 69 and 70), which was enacted by the Legislative Assembly on July 22, 1952.[10] These articles read as follows:

> 69. (1) Citizens of the Polish People's Republic, irrespective of nationality, race, or religion, enjoy equal rights in all fields of public, political, economic, social, and cultural life. Infringement of this principle by any direct or indirect privileges or restrictions of rights on account of nationality, race, or religion, is subject to punishment.
>
> (2) The spreading of hatred or contempt, the provocation of enmity, or the humiliation of a person because of national, racial, or religious differences is prohibited.
>
> 70. (1) The Polish People's Republic guarantees freedom of conscience and religion to its citizens. The Church and other religious bodies may freely exercise their religious functions. It is forbidden to prevent citizens by coercion from taking part in religious activities or rites. It is also forbidden to coerce anybody to participate in religious activities or rites.
>
> (2) The Church is separated from the State. The principles of

the relationship between Church and State, as well as the legal position and the property status of religious bodies, shall be determined by laws.

(3) The abuse of freedom of conscience and religion for purposes endangering the interests of the Polish People's Republic shall be punished.

These constitutional provisions depart in certain essential points from those of the 1921 Constitution discussed above. The Roman Catholic Church is no longer guaranteed the "leading position" among other denominations. There is no longer any statement guaranteeing that the Roman Catholic Church is governed by its own laws. The relations between this Church and the State, which under the 1921 Constitution had to be determined by an agreement between the Holy See and the Polish State, are now relegated to current legislation enacted by the State alone. There is nothing in the new Constitution to prevent the passage of laws which would infringe upon the autonomy of the Church and its property rights. There is no provision in the Constitution relating to mandatory religious instruction in the schools.

Separation of Church and State is declared for the first time in Polish legislation. If this declaration is conceived in the light of the doctrine applied by the Western democracies, it would mean that both the State and the Church function independently. Where such Church policy is exercised without prejudice, the Churches are treated like any other association without particular privileges and are subject to the general provisions of the legislation on associations. The Government is not supposed to interfere with the affairs of the Church, restricting its authority only to the protection of public order among believers of various denominations. This kind of separation of Church and State is followed in the United States of America, where it represents an actual tolerance of religious life in any shape or form, without preference to any given denomination. But the postwar Polish legislation was inspired by a different attitude to Church and religion.

It is not accidental that the legislator refrained from writing into the Constitution any guarantee of the autonomy of the

Church or of a status equal to private associations or corporations. The phrase of the Constitution on the freedom of the
Church to "exercise . . . religious functions" sounds more like a
limitation than the protection of the normal activities of the
Church. It leaves open the question whether Churches may
freely carry on their missionary work and have their organization
established in accordance with canon law. Although separation of Church and State is stated in the Constitution, there is
no provision for a limit to the control of the Church by the State.
Since the renunciation of the Concordat in 1945, the status
of the Catholic Church in Poland has been subject to legislation, upon which the 1952 Constitution sets no restriction for
protecting the independence of the Church. The experience of
the Soviet Union at the time when direct persecution of the
Church took place and was inaugurated by legislation under the
cover of "separation of Church and State" makes one expect
the possibility of interpreting the vague clauses of the Polish
Constitution in the same manner.

Opinions voiced simultaneously with the presentation of the
draft of the new Constitution indicate the trend, as is shown for
instance in the April 1952 issue of *Państwo i Prawo,* where we
read:

> The abolition of class exploitation, depriving the Churches of
> any property of a capitalist (or feudal) nature, together with the
> liquidation of any private property in the means of production,
> relieves religion of the part it used to play, namely that of a
> political ideology in the service of the exploiter classes, and renders
> any compulsion in denominational matters impossible. Only a So-
> cialist State can guarantee full religious freedom in its Constitution.

From this quotation one point stands out, that depriving
the Church of all property is visualized as a normal status of
the Church in a "socialist State," which present-day Poland
claims to be.

In any event the complex status of the Church as it stands
now in Poland cannot be established from the provisions of the
Constitution. It is revealed by an analysis of individual decrees,
especially those of August 5, 1949, and February 9, 1953,
which analysis is given in the next Chapter.

II. POSTWAR LAWS AND DECREES AFFECTING
THE CHURCH

A. *General Survey*

The position of the Church in Poland, and the Roman Catholic Church in particular, is not expressed in any isolated legislative act, but presents itself as a sum total of several measures taken at different times and expressed in several laws and decrees. As is shown in the preceding chapter, the Church in Poland, especially the Catholic Church, enjoyed a well-established legal status. The Church performed several public functions and was free in its internal life. The Church played an important role in education, public welfare, and public health. As soon as the postwar government became established, it proceeded to issue laws and decrees essentially affecting this position.

The jurisdiction over marriage, divorce, and vital statistics was taken from the Church in 1945. The Church was gradually stripped of land and many other possessions. It was also curtailed in several other respects, in particular in taking care of the sick and in public education. The Church was deprived of the material basis for exercising charity. The name of God was stricken from the formula of official oaths, and blasphemy might have ceased to be a punishable offense. A Decree of August 5, 1949 on the Protection of Freedom of Conscience and Religion introduced several other restrictions by implication, especially for the Roman Catholic Church.

The Catholic Church was affected by the new measures more than any other, primarily because of its important activities in various fields of public life, such as social welfare, public health, and education. Secondly, the Catholic Church is a universal church with a well-established universal authority, the Holy

179

See. This is evident from Canon 21 of the Code of Canon Law of 1917, which reads:

> *Canon 218.* As the successor to the primacy of St. Peter, the Roman Pontiff has not only the primacy of honor, but also supreme and full power of jurisdiction over the universal Church, in matters of faith and morals as well as in those pertaining to the discipline and government of the Church throughout the whole world.

Thus the full power of jurisdiction, discipline, and government of the Church is reserved to the Holy See. Woywod in his standard Commentary on the Code of Canon Law[11] emphasizes that

> In matters of faith and morals all Catholics, without distinction of race, nationality, or rite, are bound by the authoritative pronouncements of the Holy See. There can be but one rule in these matters for all who belong to the Catholic Church.

He also states that "in matters of discipline the Supreme Authority of the Church may sanction various rules for various countries, nations, or rites. The Church takes into consideration the particular circumstances under which her children live in the different parts of the world—the manners, customs, and habits of races and nations."

Thus, although concessions to local circumstances can be made, they must be approved by supreme Church authorities.

Almost from the beginning of the postwar Polish regime the activities of the Catholic Church began to be curtailed in one or another respect. The government sought to obtain from the local Episcopate consent for the change in status of the Church as secured by the Concordat. The reluctance of the Episcopate to make concessions on its own accord was followed by additional curtailment of the rights of the Church with regard to real property and hospitals and a decree on freedom of conscience and religion in fact extended protection to atheism. Then the so-called Agreement of April 14, 1950 was signed, under which the Church acquired a new status.

However, all these acts were overshadowed by the Decree of February 9, 1953, regulating the Appointment of Clergymen to Ecclesiastic Offices. The decree sought to bring under government control the organization of the Church and priests and bishops. Moreover, many other steps were taken by the government against the Church and the priests, without knowledge of which the picture of the status of the Church in Poland would be incomplete. All this material is scattered, overlapping, and lacking in consistency. In the next chapter all the successive stages of development are traced as they occurred.

It seems opportune at this point to outline the changes in supreme government bodies specifically charged with the administration of church affairs. Before the war denominational affairs were entrusted to a separate Ministry for Religious Denominations and Public Education, which was established by the Decree of January 3, 1918.[12] Such a ministry also existed in the Polish Government-in-Exile. The self-appointed Council for National Liberation, sponsored by the Soviet Union and claiming to be the sole legislative power of the nation, set up a Provisional Government on December 31, 1944, without providing for a ministry for religious denominations. Denominational affairs were brought under the jurisdiction of the Ministry of Public Administration, Denominational Division. This division was subdivided into three sections: a) for affairs pertaining to the Roman Catholic Church; b) for affairs pertaining to other churches and Christian sects; and c) for affairs pertaining to non-Christian religious associations.

The statutes of March 20 and April 19, 1950, abolished the Ministry of Public Administration and set up an Office for Denominational Affairs under the supervision of the Prime Minister.[13] This office deals with matters pertaining to the relationship between the Government and the particular religious denominations. A Director appointed and subject to recall by the Prime Minister is in charge of the Office for Denominational Affairs.

B. *Laws and Decrees Preceding the Decree on Freedom of Conscience and Religion of August 5, 1949*

During this period new laws and decrees affected the status

of the Catholic Church only to a limited extent. Major changes took place later.

1. Recognition granted to Denominations other than Catholic.

The status of the Catholic Church was indirectly affected by the official recognition of various other denominations. Thereby the privilege of the Catholic Church—that it does not require special recognition by the State (1921 Constitution, Art. 114) —became obsolete.

Recognition was given on October 16, 1945, to the Methodist Church[14] and on September 5, 1947, to the Reformed Protestant Church of Poland, the Marjavite Church, and the Old Catholic Church.[15] The recognition which these denominations had previously enjoyed only in some parts of Poland was extended to the whole nation.

Discussions of these decrees in the Polish law reviews tried to attach added significance to them.[16] The Government evidently sought to counterbalance the influence of the Roman Catholic Church by placing minor denominations on the same footing. In view of the strength of the Roman Catholic Church, its predominant role in Polish history, and its defiance of Communist ideology, the present Government has directed its attacks mainly against this Church, sometimes by asking the cooperation of some of the other denominations against Catholics. Such cooperation was, however, never carried out on a large scale, because it soon became clear to those concerned that the Government utilized it for propaganda purposes only.

The position of non-Catholic denominations is reviewed *infra,* p. 239).

2. Marriage and Divorce

(a) Prior to 1945

No uniform law on domestic relations (marriage and divorce, parent and child, guardian and ward) was enacted in Poland before 1945. After the formation of Poland in 1918, the pre-

vious laws governing these matters in the individual parts of
the country remained in force. Consequently, in some parts
religious marriage was mandatory and in others civil marriage
was required.

In Western Poland governed by German law only a civil
marriage entered into before an official who kept records of
vital statistics was valid; a religious marriage could be celebrated
only after the conclusion of a civil marriage. Matrimonial cases
concerning annulment of marriage, divorce *a vinculo,* and separation *a mensa et thoro* were in all respects subject to the provisions of the German Civil Code and were within the exclusive
jurisdiction of civil courts. In Central Poland (Kingdom of
Poland) French law and some Russian statutes were in force.
Eastern Poland was under the laws of the Russian Empire.
Here a marriage could be entered into only before a clergyman
of the proper denomination and matrimonial cases were, in
general, decided by the ecclesiastical courts concerned.[17] In
Southern Poland where Austrian law had authority only a religious marriage was valid. Matrimonial cases were subject to
the jurisdiction of civil courts, which in general applied the
rules of the religion concerned. Consequently, divorce was not
permitted for Catholics in the former Russian and Austrian parts
of Poland.

The work of unifying the various legal systems began immediately after the restoration of Poland, and a special committee for the codification of law was set up. This committee
submitted drafts of many statutes, which later were enacted.
However, the draft for the law relating to marriage was not
enacted. The draft provided for a uniform civil marriage ceremony, irrespective of the religious denomination of the parties,
and for the jurisdiction of civil courts in matrimonial cases
(nullity, divorce, separation). This draft was opposed by the
Roman Catholic Church, which objected to the introduction
of compulsory civil marriage and the transfer of jurisdiction in
matrimonial cases to the civil courts. Negotiations were conducted in this matter with the Vatican, but the outbreak of
the war in 1939 prevented a settlement.

(b) First Postwar Law on Marriage and Divorce

The Government of postwar Poland made great use of the work already done by the prewar committee on the codification of law and enacted several uniform laws for the entire country in 1945 and 1946. Among them was the Marriage Law of September 25, 1945, which went into effect on January 1, 1946.[18] This law established for the whole of Poland the rule that "only a civil marriage entered into before an official of the Civil Status Registry shall have legal effect as far as the State is concerned" (Art. 12, para. 2). The law also contains the following provision:

> Art. 37. The provisions of the law do not deprive the parties of the possibility of adding also [to the civil marriage] the performance of ceremonies resulting from their membership in a religious association.

Consequently, the religious celebration of a marriage was expressly allowed. However, it had no legal effect, and could not precede the civil marriage. The new Marriage Law, Art. 24-35, also provided for a uniform divorce law for the whole of Poland, regardless of the religion of the spouses. Divorce could be granted only by the civil court, but only for reasons specified in Art. 24.

The decree enacting the marriage law[19] repealed all previous laws on marriage and divorce, in particular the provisions pertaining to entering into marriage and to jurisdiction in matrimonial cases.[20]

Prior to the enactment of this uniform marriage law, records of vital statistics were maintained in parts of Poland where religious marriage was mandatory by the ministers of religion according to law. The Decree of September 25, 1945[21] established the keeping of records on vital statistics by the civil authorities in the whole of Poland. Consequently, the ministers of religion were relieved of their official function of keeping records of vital statistics. Furthermore, the decree enacting the new Law on Records of Vital Statistics[22] superseded all heretofore existing statutory provisions relating to the subject. Ecclesiastical authorities and offices which kept records of vital statistics prior to the enforcement of the new law were ordered to turn over all records and registers to the offices entrusted with the keeping of records of vital statistics, in accordance with Art. 20 of the law.[23]

(c) The New Code of 1950 on Domestic Relations

A new Code of Domestic Relations was enacted by the Law of June 27, 1950[24] and went into effect on October 1, 1950. The provisions enacting this Code are laid down in the Law of June 27, 1950,[25] which repeals all previous statutes on domestic relations. According to Art. 1 of the new Code:

> A marriage is considered valid only when both parties declare their intent to enter into marriage jointly before an official of the Civil Status Registry. If the declaration is not given before an official of the Civil Status Registry, no marriage comes into being.

The new Code on Domestic Relations omits the provision of the former Code which stated that a religious ceremony may follow (Art. 37, Marriage Law of September 25, 1945). Art. 29 of the new Code contains provisions regulating divorce. This article reads:

> If for important reasons a complete and lasting discord has occurred in the marital relations, either spouse may ask the court to dissolve the marriage by divorce.

This is the only provision of the Code relating to divorce. All the usual legal grounds for divorce are replaced by an extremely broad formula, "a complete and lasting discord in the marital relations." Thus, the new Code in fact leaves the granting of a divorce to the discretion of the court. This change in divorce law is similar to that enacted in the Soviet Union in 1944.

3. Church Property

The noncommittal attitude and the avoidance of vital issues which characterized the Government's policy towards the Church during the early period of the new regime was perhaps most apparent in the nationalization of land under the Decree of September 6, 1944, on Execution of the Land Reform.[26]

The law contained a provision which empowered the Legislative Assembly *(Sejm)* to make the final disposition of landed property owned by the Catholic Church and other denominations. This provision in fact postponed the nationalization of Church land until March 20, 1950, when the Sejm passed a statute in which it resolved the problem of land owned by the Church.[27]

But it must be mentioned that even before the nationalization of land owned by the Church, religious associations and societies active in hospital work lost their property rights to hospitals and medical institutions. The Statute of October 28, 1948 on Social Institutions of Public Health and Their Administration declared that the Minister of Health may also consider medical institutions owned by religious associations and societies as social institutions of public health (Art. 1). Social institutions of public health were defined as medical institutions maintained by the central and local government agencies, and agencies of social insurance.

In certain instances the Council of Ministers may resolve that medical institutions owned by religious associations and societies either be nationalized outright or placed under government administration (Art. 13). The Council of Ministers may likewise decide that such institutions either be administered or taken over as property of the then still existing local government authorities. This authority was widely used. For example two resolutions of the Council of Ministers to this effect, of September 21, 1949, list 52 hospitals and medical institutions taken over without compensation by public authorities.[28] Numerous similar resolutions were passed later.[29]

4. The Duty of Clergymen to Keep Special Books for Income Tax Purposes

This duty was established in the Executive Order of the Minister of Finance of July 5, 1949.[30] Secs. 2 and 6 of the executive order require clergymen of all religious denominations to keep special account books, and to enter therein all revenues obtained and expenditures made in connection with any activities designed to meet spiritual needs, such as performance of religious ceremonies and other religious functions. The entries must be made not later than the day following the receipt of the revenue or the expenditure. Failure to comply with this strict rule may easily lead to prosecution for tax evasion.[31]

5. *Religious Instruction in Schools*

Religious instruction in all public schools was mandatory under Art. 120 of the 1921 Constitution and under the Concordat of 1925, Art. XIII, which states that religious instruction shall be mandatory in all schools except in institutions of higher learning. It gave the church authorities the right to supervise religious instruction. In accordance with this provision, the Minister of Religious Denominations and Public Education issued the Executive Order on Teaching the Roman Catholic Religion in Schools on December 9, 1926.[32] Sec. 1 of this executive order provided for the "mandatory religious instruction of Catholic pupils in all schools (except in institutions of higher learning), in State schools, public and communal schools, as well as in private schools which are subsidized by the national Government, by local government funds, or those which enjoy the rights of a State or public school."

A circular by the Minister of Education of September 13, 1945[33] expressly upheld Art. 120 of the 1921 Constitution, making religious instruction in all public schools mandatory for pupils belonging to a church recognized by the State. However, the circular emphasized that if the parents of a child so desire, he may be exempt from religious instruction. This circular was based on a legal opinion of August 29, 1945, prepared by a special Committee appointed by the Ministry of Justice.[34] On careful reading of the legal opinion and the subsequent circular of the Minister of Education, it becomes obvious that parents and guardians are rather encouraged not to have their children attend religious instruction at school.

The new Constitution of July 22, 1952, is silent on the subject of religious instruction in schools. Religious instruction is officially still included as a subject in the curricula of public and secular schools. To circumvent the legal provisions on religious instruction in these schools, a Government-sponsored Society of Children's Friends (*Towarzystwo Przyjaciół Dzieci*) began in 1947 to open secular schools without religious instruction. Great pressure has been brought on parents to register their children in these schools, while the clergy on their part have sought to counteract this influence.

The *Trybuna Ludu* of November 26, 1950 explains that "a secular school represents the basic change of ideology, the new method of teaching and education, and is organized free from the elements hostile to the People's Poland." *Życie Warszawy* of October 9, 1951 reports on the activity of the *Towarzystwo Przyjaciół Dzieci* as follows:

> In 1947 we had in the whole country only 5 schools maintained by the Society; in 1951-52 there will be 463 such schools. In the current year 93 elementary schools, 36 secondary schools, 45 teachers' colleges, 42 schools, and 9 secondary schools for children's nurses in kindergartens, will be opened.
>
> By means of a mass action of cultural and recreational activity, as well as children's summer camps, the Society will take care of 300,000 children.

C. *Decree of August 5, 1949 on Freedom of Conscience and Religion*[35]

The Decree on Freedom of Conscience and Religion actually deals with this subject matter only in the first Article (Art. I), where it merely repeats the rule, stated in Art. 111 of the 1921 Constitution, that the Republic of Poland guarantees all citizens freedom of conscience. Otherwise the decree is essentially a penal statute; out of thirteen articles containing substantive provisions, twelve are penal clauses dealing with offenses and penalties. The decree does not deal with the status of the church and religious bodies at all. Therefore, it should be compared with the criminal legislation in force prior to the decree. This is to be found in the Criminal Code of 1932 and the so-called "Small Criminal Code" of 1946 which supplemented the Code.[36] It is a particular feature of the Decree of 1949 that it does not replace these sources outright, but only "insofar" as the new decree "regulates the subject

matter." Thus the decree leaves open the question which provisions of previous sources are no longer in effect. Blasphemy,
for example, punishable with a sentence up to five years under
the Code of 1932 (Art. 172), the decree of 1949 does not mention. Does this mean that blasphemy is no longer an offense, or
that Art. 172 of the Criminal Code of 1932 is still in force?
Moreover, the maximum penalties for various offenses against
the free practice of religion run, under the Code of 1932, from
two to three years. The more or less standard penalty under the
Decrees of 1946 and 1949 is higher, up to five years. But the
Decree of 1949 places under the same penalty not only infringement upon the rights of a citizen because of his religion, but also
such acts committed "because of his lack of religion" (Art. 2).
The Decree of 1949 also punishes "whoever publicly insults, ridicules, or humiliates a group of individuals . . . because of lack of
religion" (Art. 7). Any fight against atheism may easily be regarded as such an offense, atheism being the official creed of
Communists.

Another provision of the Decree of 1949 directly interferes
with the autonomy and spiritual jurisdiction of the Church. If
the Church is separated from the State, the Church must have
the right to exercise the right of discipline over its members.
Admission to rites and religious ceremonies is unquestionably a
part of the internal spiritual jurisdiction of the Church. Article
4 interferes with this right of discipline and spiritual jurisdiction.
This article imposes a penalty of imprisonment of up to five years
for denying a person "access to a rite or religious service because
of his activities or his political, social, and scientific views."

This interference is given a peculiar interpretation in the official English issue of the *Review of Polish Law*:[37] "Article 4 of
the Decree in protecting the privileges of citizens has in view the
prevention of religious fanaticism, which might impede the
development of social conditions and scientific research as it
used to do in the Middle Ages."

Article 8 of the Decree is the most remarkable in providing
for punishment by imprisonment not less than 3 years for abusing freedom of conscience and religion to pursue aims hostile to

the form of government of the Polish Republic.[38] But the Constitution of July 22, 1952, in its provision concerning the abuse of freedom of conscience and religion for purposes prejudicial to the interests of the People's Republic, offers wider opportunities for criminal prosecution. The decree limits prosecution to "acts directed against the form of government of the Polish Republic," whereas the new Constitution provides for punishment of "any act endangering the interests of the Polish People's Republic." Any announcement or discussion in which a clergyman criticizes the conduct of the Government or an act of public authority might be brought under this provision.

D.   Developments Immediately Preceding the Agreement of April 14, 1950

1.   The Case of Caritas

In consequence of the renouncing of the Concordat, the legal basis for the functioning of the Church in Poland was destroyed and a joint committee, consisting of representatives of the Government and the Episcopate, was created in August 1949. As intermittent meetings of the joint committee were held, the Government acted, and its attacks upon the Church became more intensive. Within the first few weeks of 1950, the Government made a drive towards forcing the issue to the point of an open conflict with the Church.

The opening attack was directed against the Church welfare organization, known as "Caritas" which under the care of bishops had already for years before the war conducted on a wide scale charitable work all over the country.

On January 22, 1950, the press published some documents which were to prove that Caritas had used its funds for the support of members of its own administration instead of for the support of really destitute people.[39] The following day this charge was indirectly brought against the ordinaries.[40] It was alleged that the ordinaries violated their duty to exercise due supervision over this organization and therefore did not prevent these abuses. The Government placed Caritas under forced administration on

January 23, 1950.[41] Primate Wyszyński and Cardinal Sapieha replied by a letter to the President on January 24, 1950, protesting against this measure. A conference of Catholic bishops held in Kraków on January 30, 1950 submitted a written statement to the President of Poland on the Caritas case. This statement contains a detailed protest to the President of the Republic against the hostile campaign instigated through both the press and radio against the institution of Caritas.[42] The Polish Episcopate has emphatically refuted the false charges of misuse, embezzlement, and detrimental administration of funds. The pertinent parts of the statement read:

> ". . . In adherence to the teachings of the Gospel, Caritas has always endeavored to reach anyone in need, irrespective of his political or ideological affiliation. Funds were derived from contributions of the Relief Committee of the American Episcopate, the Catholic League, and the National Committee of Americans of Polish Descent. In distributing these funds Caritas had not only to take into consideration the needs of the wards entrusted to it, but also to follow the explicit will of the donors. Thus, according to the will of the benefactors, help was also given to monasteries, theological seminaries, and other Catholic institutions. The Episcopate headed by Cardinal Sapieha saw to it that the relief action was conducted honestly and fairly.
>
> In view of the foregoing facts we cannot but declare the following:
>
> 1) When Caritas was placed under Government-enforced administration, the organization ceased to perform the social welfare activities of the Church.
>
> 2) Under these circumstances the bishops are faced with the regrettable necessity of proceeding with the liquidation of the charitable institution patronized by the Church and known as the Caritas Society.
>
> 3) The clergy and the members of congregations, who have added to the progress of Caritas by their generous contributions and devoted work, are sincerely encouraged by the Episcopate to continue their support of the work of Christian charity in the spirit of Christ's commandment to love one's neighbor . . ."

The bishops ordered the clergy to read the foregoing statement to their congregations. This was carried out wherever the security police did not prevent it.

On the same day, January 20, 1950, party officials convoked

a conference of the so-called "patriotic clergy" in Warsaw. The participants branded the abuses within Caritas and acknowledged their confidence in the actions of the Government.

Caritas has been reorganized under Government control and now acts independently of any Church authority. In 1951 the nationalization of Caritas was completed and today it maintains about 1100 branches. The present personnel is required to undergo special Marxist training.[43]

The Caritas affair was only a pretext to bring the conflict with the Church to a head. It is now clear that the true issue was to place the Church in a situation which would make it necessary to come to an understanding with the Government in order to forestall further curtailment of Church activities. The situation as it then existed is summed up in a statement of Primate Wyszyński and Cardinal Sapieha, which was submitted to the President of Poland on February 16, 1950.[44] The pertinent passages read:

> . . . Your repeated assurances, Mr. President, and those of the Prime Minister and Minister Wolski, claimed that there neither is nor will be any conflict with the Church in Poland. We have accepted these assurances at their face value. Today, however, painful experiences of recent events have caused us to doubt the meaning of assurances made by the highest authorities.
>
> We must declare that the conflict with religion in Poland has already been under way for some time, with the results exceeding the results of any means heretofore known of waging war against God.
>
> The fact that churches remain open and are frequented by a greater number of people than ever does not disprove that there is a conflict. People go to church because they seek refuge there from the continuous suppression endured at work, in offices, and at political meetings, at which they are incessantly harassed in their very personal feelings towards God.
>
> All that we stated above is evident in the curricula of preparatory and regular schools, in textbooks for schools, in the methods used in the educational work of young people, in party rules, in resolutions passed at meetings of various organizations, in outlines of talks prepared for so-called "activists," and in complaints and grievances by people who are forced to listen to words full of hatred of everything relating to religion. Further proof as to the

persistent supervision of religion can be seen in the fate of the Catholic schools, hospitals maintained by the Church, religious associations and brotherhoods, in the rebuilding of churches, and so forth.

Moreover, we find other proof of suppression in observing the fate of the Catholic press and publications. Many have been closed down since they are unable to cope any longer with the imposed censorship. Manuscripts of Catholic writings are accumulating and piling up in censorship offices. This alone is an indictment of the regime for suppressing religious thought in Poland and attempting to erase from the national literature and culture thousands of works which are not permitted publication. Mr. President, the suppression of the Church, of religion, and of God is quite clearly evident in Poland.

. . . At present we again find some odd news items in the press; having dropped the phrase "reactionary episcopate" the press today refers to a "reactionary faction of the episcopate." This is but a new attempt, endeavoring this time to stake hopes on "patriotic bishops." All these attempts serve but one purpose—they reveal the true character of the campaign against the Church.

. . . Exceptions are also to be taken to the peculiar method of terrorizing the bishops. The Minister admitted that by means of regulations directed against the Church he intends to exert a decisive pressure upon the bishops. The continuous terror has achieved just the opposite result. In consequence, the episcopate has become more confirmed in its belief that the Government has no intention whatsoever of abiding by its word, but that it is aiming rather to bring about accomplished facts directed against the freedom of the Church.

The repeated protests of the Episcopate against the obviously hostile policy of the Government towards Church and religion have not brought relief in the mounting conflict. On the contrary, on February 28, 1950 the government brought further charges against the Primate and the Episcopate, reproaching them with hostility towards the new Poland and lack of patriotic loyalty in siding with the policy of the Vatican.[45]

In particular the statement of the Government alleged that:

The episcopate refuses to reconcile itself to the fact that power in Poland is now in the hands of the masses, that the form of government in which a handful of capitalists and landowners exploited and dominated the nation has been eliminated once and for all, and that the medieval privileges of the Church hierarchy—which have long since been removed in many European countries—cannot be maintained . . .

. . . It is generally known that the Vatican has taken political measures to back the revisionist tendencies of the imperialists in the Western Zones of Germany and that these measures coincide with the activities of warmongers. They are, therefore, aimed at Poland's most vital interests. Clearly, under such conditions, the execution by the Polish clergy of foreign orders issued by the Vatican on non-religious matters cannot be reconciled with the interests and sovereignty of the Polish State.

2. Nationalization of Church Land

On March 6, 1950, the Prime Minister presented a bill to the Legislative Assembly providing for the nationalization of Church property and the creation of a Church Fund by the Government, which in effect made the clergy entirely dependent upon the government. The Prime Minister, in presenting the bill, made it clear that it was submitted in consequence of the resistance and non-subordination of the Episcopate to the demands of the Government, and used the occasion to attack the higher Church hierarchy, the clergy, and the monastic orders. He contended that the landed property of the Church and religious orders was not used for religious or similar purposes, that Church lands had retained a feudal character and served the political aims of hostile international agencies.

The Government press gave great prominence to the confiscation of 375,000 acres of Church lands, stressing, of course, the beneficial character of the bill, both for the clergy and the congregations. Furthermore, the press emphasized that at last the benefits derived from Church lands, until now consumed only by the bishops, would be used by the lesser clergy and the congregations themselves. The press tried to explain that the direct reason for introducing the bill was the selfishness and reactionary character of the hierarchy of the Catholic Church in Poland and its dependence upon foreign agencies. The debate on the bill took place on March 20, 1950, whereupon the Legislative Assembly passed it unanimously.[46]

In consequence of the statute of March 20, 1950, all land

held thus far by religious associations was nationalized. The so-called real purpose of this statute as stated by the legislator was "to remove the last vestiges of feudal privileges held by religious associations and at the same time to secure the material needs of the clergy."

The statute considers as landed property of a religious association any real property of every kind owned by a Church or other denominational associations, its institutions, convents, societies, or any kind of organized units and organs; the statute holds as immaterial the legal status of the religious association and the aims for which its income from the property was designated. Such land holdings are transferred to Government ownership *without any compensation,* together with any buildings, existing enterprises, and establishments thereon, as well as all appurtenances and chattels free from any liabilities. The Minister of Public Administration shall exclude from the expropriation places designated for purposes of worship, as well as dwelling quarters of convents, bishoprics, archbishoprics, consistories and headquarters of other religious associations.

Land which constitutes farm holdings of parish priests is exempt from nationalization. The Government guarantees parish priests possession of farm holdings insofar as it considers such holdings the basis for the parish priests' maintenance, provided they do not exceed 50 hectares, or, in the provinces of Poznań, Pomerania, and Silesia, 100 hectares. Where a priest's farm holdings exceed the above size, then only the acreage in excess of the established limits is subject to nationalization.

The law, in declaring that the farm holdings are left to the parish priests as the basis of their maintenance, shows that the Government continues for the time being to be more favorable to the lower clergy. This policy is connected with the attempts made by the Government to separate the lower clergy from the higher church hierarchy.

Furthermore, the Council of Ministers may decide that some categories of landed property or certain parts thereof may remain under the management of a Church institution, establishment, association, or other organized unit or organ of the Church. The

Council may also transfer such landed property to the management of another Church organization, the proceeds being used for the benefit of the particular unit. Such transfer of land may be granted against payment of compensation to the Church Fund or may be granted free. All income derived from the nationalized land is to be designated entirely for Church and charitable purposes. The Minister of Agriculture and Land Reform is to evaluate the revenue derived from the land according to the standards of the Government Land Fund. Such Fund will be under the supervision of the Minister for Public Administration.

The Council of Ministers defines the rules providing for the formation of the Church Fund, establishes methods of instituting its agencies, and sets forth the principles of its activity. The established Statute of the Church Fund is to provide the allocation of revenues for purposes of a given religious association and to secure the participation of the clergy and congregations in the administrative organs of the Fund. The allocated amount shall correspond to the income which the land of the particular association will yield under nationalization.

The Church Fund is to be designated for purposes which the statute enumerates as:

1) to maintain and rebuild churches;
2) to render material and medical assistance to the clergy and to provide rest homes for them;
3) in justifiable instances, to include the clergy in the health insurance scheme at the expense of the Church Fund;
4) to grant special pensions to clergymen who rendered services of great merit in the field of social work;
5) to carry out charitable and social welfare services.

The Council of Ministers may extend the scope of the Church Fund and also include other needs of either a religious or a charitable nature.

The Statute on the Nationalization of Church Lands provides criminal punishments for frustrating or opposing the enforcement of the statute. Acts aimed against the carrying out of the statute or public sanction of acts of this nature are also liable to punishments. Persons found guilty under this statute are to be punished in the same manner as offenders obstructing the carrying out of the land reform.[47]

The above-outlined provisions of the statute clearly show the intentions of the present Government to dispose altogether of the Church as an obstacle to the sovietization of the country. Later developments prove that the Government planned by confiscating Church lands to create a medium of exerting material pressure on the clergy for political ends. By assuming the right to dispose freely of the confiscated land, it is also possible for the government to transfer the land at its discretion to another religious organization, which may serve and become subordinated to the Government's doctrine.

Altogether the basic policy of the Government in nationalizing Church lands aims at the creation of conditions favorable to conversion of the Catholic Church into a separate national organization with a Government-controlled episcopate and clergy.

A later Decree of April 24, 1952 abolishes all foundations established for charitable purposes and provides that all assets become State property.[48] However, the use of the nationalized property, which constituted farm holdings of parish priests or was established for the advancement of the religious cult, is guaranteed by the State for such purposes, within the limits and according to the principles defined in the Statute of March 20, 1950.

E. *Agreement of April 14, 1950, concluded between the Representatives of the Polish Government and the Roman Catholic Episcopate of Poland*

1. *Attempts at a "Concordat on a Lower Level"*

The steps taken by the government and described in the preceding chapter were also followed by negotiations which Wolski, Minister of Public Administration, carried on directly with the lower clergy. The episcopate objected to this in a letter of February 16, 1950 to the President: "When the Minister induces the subordinate clergy to disregard the bishops and to enter into what is termed a concordat concluded on a lower level, we cannot remain silent. We submit, therefore, our exceptions to the adopted methods of conducting the talks."

The offer by the Minister proposed that: the lower clergy should recognize the administration of Caritas as set up by the Government and cooperate with it, disregarding their ecclesiastical superiors. The Holy See should break diplomatic relations with the Polish Government-in-exile and recall its ambassador. The Holy See should recognize the western boundaries of Poland and establish regular dioceses on the recovered territories in place of the present apostolic administrators. The clergy should issue an official statement withdrawing all charges on the persecution of the Church. Bishops should renounce their "feudal privileges" and refrain from interference in parochial administration. The Church should be independent from the Holy See except in purely religious matters; the bishops and the clergy should above all be guided by the interests of the People's Poland and should refrain from all contacts with international religious bodies. They should devote themselves to the work of establishing a People's Poland in the spirit of progressive socialism.[49]

Undoubtedly the conclusion of such a "concordat" would result in the establishment of a schismatic national Church and would bring the Church under the complete domination of the Communists.

Oscar Halecki, gives the following picture of the situation:[50]

> From the outset it had been well known to the Vatican that the relentless struggle against religion and in particular against the Catholic Church in the satellite countries was being directed from Moscow. It was also evident that the Moscow-controlled international organization of the Communist party, revived soon after the war under the guise of an information center, the Cominform, was responsible for the whole campaign. The Vatican pointed out that the intensification of the struggle against Catholicism in Poland had been decided on at a Cominform meeting held in Silesia in July 1949, the ultimate aim of which was to create in that country a schismatic national church. A similar decision with regard to all countries in the Russian orbit was taken at a Cominform meeting held in Budapest in January 1950. At the same time a new, specialized organization was created under the name of "Orginform," with the objective of provoking religious confusion in the Catholic

countries and of training, in four special schools, the military leaders of the Communist action against the Church. That center was established in Warsaw under a Russian chief—one more evidence that it was Moscow which was responsible for all these developments in the unhappy countries under her control.

2. Agreement of April 14, 1950

In spite of the intensified action of the Government against the Church the open conflict was apparently averted when on April 15, 1950 it was announced in Warsaw by the joint committee of representatives of the Polish Government and of the Roman Catholic episcopate of Poland that an agreement had been concluded on April 14 covering the relationship between the Government and the Church.[51]

This agreement does not replace the concordat renounced by the government. It was reached between the episcopate of the Church in Poland—not the Holy See—and the Polish Government. However, this does not mean that bishops exceeded their authority. The Holy See had no direct relations with the Polish Government since the renunciation of the concordat. The episcopate acted as a body of bishops of Poland.

The agreement is laid down in a declaration and an attached protocol. The first nine sections of the agreement set out the duties of the Church toward the State; sections 10-19 contain concessions and guarantees of the Government to the Church.

On April 29, 1950 the bishops expressed their opinions on the agreement in a joint statement announcing that the agreement signed on April 14 was merely a declaration to clarify relations between Church and Government and not a pact or treaty, and that therefore it required no approval by the Vatican.

The value of the agreement lies, of course, in the interpretation of its clauses. The loose wording of the provisions in the agreement has already given rise to further disputes as to their interpretation and accusations that the Church does not fulfill its promises.

It can only be presumed that under the conditions which have arisen in Poland, the episcopate attempted to save as much of its position as possible. Although the Polish episcopate certainly must have known that the Government did not actually want a lasting settlement of the problem of Church and State, there was strong motivation for concluding the agreement. The negotiators of the Polish episcopate still wanted to come to terms with the Government as long as it gave at least a promise that conditions essential for the normal activities of the Church would not be changed. Also, it may have been considered that the conclusion of the agreement would show the peaceful intentions of the episcopate and at the same time make it possible to receive financial support for the Church.

The best and most authoritative explanation of the motives which guided the episcopate in signing the agreement was given later in the Protest of the Polish Episcopate of May 8, 1953.[52] We read:

> . . . There were important reasons against the agreement. We heard about the fate of the Church in other People's Democracies. One could therefore have doubts whether the other party to the agreement would have the goodwill to keep its pledges. The Marxist doctrine itself is alarming, as far as religion is concerned, not to mention the fact that people from many parts of the country cautioned the Episcopate on the pertinency of reaching an agreement.
>
> But the Polish bishops neither wanted to consider foreign experiences, nor pass judgment in advance upon the goodwill, nor omit the occasion for an understanding, by basing themselves on theoretical consideration about the principles or consequences of Marxism, nor submit to the suggestions of external voices. They wanted first of all to give an answer by their deed to the accusations that the episcopate does not want an agreement, that it is a partner to political reaction and capitalism, that it is beforehand hostile to the present regime. At the same time we wanted to give an irrefutable proof of our goodwill and our sincere wish for peaceful co-existence . . .
>
> . . . The Episcopate took a great risk, but it did not fear that the fact alone of reaching an agreement will open for the opposite side an enormous gain as far as world opinion is concerned, as an unheard-of precedent, which could give it a strong basis for rehabilitation in the eyes of Catholicism both at home and abroad. The Episcopate did not fear that rehabilitation. On the contrary it sincerely hoped for it, but it hoped for a rehabilitation honestly deserved, and that was the spirit from which the agreement was born. . . .

To return to the contents of the agreement, it may be stated that in general the obligations undertaken by the Church were couched in a language perfectly compatible with the normal exercise of the Church mission. This is true of the obligation "to teach the faithful respect for law and state authorities," especially because it was to be performed "in accordance with the teaching of the Church" (Art. I). Likewise hardly any objection could be made by the Church against the making "a call upon the faithful to intensify their work for reconstruction of the country and the advancement of the nation's welfare." (Art. II). It may be noted that no reference is made to "people's democracy," "socialist reconstruction," "class warfare" and the like, but merely "respect for law," "reconstruction of the country," "nation's welfare" and similar terms are mentioned instead. With reference to the recovered territories the bishops did not undertake to make changes in the church administration themselves but merely "to approach the Holy See" in this matter. (Art. III). Likewise it was rather a tradition of the Catholic Church in Poland "to be guided by the interests of the Polish state," especially when the government recognized "the principle that the Pope is the competent and supreme authority of the Church" not only "in matters of faith and morals" but also in the "Church jurisdiction." (Art. V)

Further legal bonds of the agreement correspond in general to the basic duties of a citizen and do not conflict with the principles of the Church. The provisions of the agreement have obliged the Episcopate to oppose activities hostile to Poland and the misuse of religious feelings for anti-state purposes (Art. IV and VII), to support all efforts towards strengthening peace, and to oppose any attempts to provoke war (Art. IX), and not to oppose the development of the cooperatives in rural areas. (Art. VI).

Provisions regulating the so-called farming cooperatives provide for a variety of forms, from the collective farms of the soviet *kolkhoz* type to loose associations for joint tilling which are compatible with a considerable economic independence for their members. Therefore, no objection could be raised against "the development of cooperatives in rural districts" in general. On the other hand, no particular sympathy for the soviet type of farms could be required from the clergy on the basis of the agreement.

But the provision that "the Church shall combat criminal activities of underground bands and denounce and punish under Canon Law clergymen guilty of participation in any underground activities against the Polish State" is far-reaching in its implications. This provision was, for example, invoked when Archbishop Stefan Wyszyński was later accused of failure to condemn Bishop Kaczmarek and was banned from his office.

Moreover, the Protocol imposes upon the Episcopate the duty to facilitate the activity of the clergy willing to work in the reorganized "Caritas" and to assist the poor and needy, and to cooperate in the enforcement of the statute on the nationalization of Church land.

On the other hand, the government made a number of important concessions and guarantees. Mandatory religious instruction was to remain in schools and it was provided that lay and clerical instructors of religion in schools be treated on an equal footing with teachers of other subjects and supervisors of religious instruction be appointed by school authorities upon consultation with the episcopate. The Government guaranteed not to prevent students from participating in religious practices outside the schools. Schools run by the Catholic Church were guaranteed enjoyment of the privileges of State schools. Where a school is established with no religious instruction or where a school is transformed into one of that type, Catholic parents who so desire shall have the right and the opportunity to send their children to schools where religion is taught (Art. X). Also, the Catholic University of Lublin was permitted to continue its present activities (Art. XI). Catholic associations were to enjoy the same rights as before, after satisfying requirements set in the decree concerning associations (Art. XII). The Catholic press was to be treated on an equal basis with other publications (Art. XIV). The Government gave the Church the right to conduct its activities in the field of charity, welfare, and religious education (Art. XIII). Further, the Government guaranteed that no obstacles be placed in the way of public worship, traditional pilgrimages and processions, that the status of military chaplains be defined by a special regulation, that religious ministrations in hospitals and penal institutions be in the hands of specially appointed chaplains, and that religious orders have full freedom of activity (Art. XV-XIX).

In addition, the protocol imposed upon the Government the duty to appropriate to the Ordinaries the necessary money from the Church Fund. This in itself is important, for it was to prevent the lower clergy from becoming directly dependent upon the Government. Finally, priests and monks were not to be called to active military service, but attached to the reserves and assigned to auxiliary services.

The practice of the past three years shows that the existence of the agreement does not prevent the Government from taking steps inspired by the enmity of the communists toward religion in general and towards Catholicism in particular, even where these steps are contrary to the agreement. This was taken up point by point in the Protest of the Polish Episcopate of May 8, 1953 which was handed to Bierut as the head of the Government. To mention but a few of these points: though stabilization of Church conditions in the Recovered Territories was agreed upon (Art. III), the Government removed apostolic administrators from the particular dioceses and did not admit new bishops in their place. It is explained in the Protest of May 8, 1953 that "instead of approving such nominations, the [Government] authorities introduce vicars capitular into the Western Provinces, thus promoting a temporary organization instead of one fully permanent and stabilized."

The collection of signatures for the Stockholm peace appeal, sponsored widely by the Soviet bloc, gave grounds for condemning the Polish bishops for their refusal to sign this appeal. The Government considered this a breach of the Agreement (Art. IX), in which it is provided that the Episcopate shall support all efforts to preserve peace.[53] With regard to this charge, the Polish Episcopate in the above mentioned protest states that the Government authorities "do not want and yet proclaim slogans of

peace. Why do they then try to spread the senseless idea that
the Pope is an enemy of peace? It is a falsehood which reveals
the character of the leaders of the World Council of Peace. It
is a dangerous falsehood, which discredits the campaign for
peace, by preventing millions of the faithful from sincerely
joining it."

A number of new trials against the so-called reactionary clergy
also took place. Again, the higher hierarchy was accused of not
condemning the alleged underground activities of which these
priests were accused. The Government construed this as a violation of Art. VIII of the Agreement, in which the hierarchy
pledged to punish under canon law clergymen who are guilty of
participation in any underground activities against the Government. With reference to this alleged violation of the agreement
of 1950 by the Episcopate, the protest of May 8, 1953 refuted
the Government's accusation, pointing out:

> The Polish Episcopate not only made it possible, but is keeping
> the agreement completely and with consistency. Only in one point
> has it been hindered from keeping it. The Government authorities
> expressed the desire that priests and bishops issue sentences of
> condemnation upon ecclesiastics arrested or condemned by secular
> courts. But the bishops were not allowed either to look into the
> records of the case, or to hear the accused without constraint.
> Everybody understands that it is neither possible nor morally per-
> missible to pass a verdict in such conditions.

Contrary to the explicit guarantees of Art. X of the agreement
regarding the status of Catholic schools, "a large number of
them have since been liquidated in the country, while others
are doomed to a slow disappearance by the liquidation of separate grades. The situation of the Catholic University whose scope
of activities was to continue [Art. XI] has in fact become uncertain. More than 10 professors have been removed from the
faculty for unknown reasons and the school of law and economics
liquidated altogether."

Despite the basic stipulation on the status of religious instruction in public schools [Art. X], "religion is systematically removed from public schools under the pretext of transforming
them into schools of the Society of Children's Friends, without

any religious instruction at all. In the remaining schools the number of hours for religious instruction is being reduced. Teachers of religion are being dismissed without reason and no replacements are made in their place."

Moreover, despite the stipulation of Art. X-b of the agreement, that the authorities will not place obstacles in the way of religious practices outside of school, the protest states that in fact "these are hindered or rendered altogether impossible by the school authorities, who deliberately arrange all sorts of school and athletic events during the time when religious services are held. Catholic youths are in fact prohibited from belonging to religious organizations which consequently were altogether disbanded, while on the other hand pressure has been exerted for them to join the Government-directed Marxist Polish Youth League. Thus, through application of diversified methods the present school policy in Poland has rendered the guarantees of the agreement meaningless. Crosses were removed from school rooms and hospital wards although the students and patients resisted their removal."

The protest further emphasizes that "In even more glaring contradiction to the guarantees of the agreement is the plight of the Catholic press and publications." Despite the stipulation of Art. XIV that it is to enjoy the same treatment on an equal basis with other publications, "it has become subject to crippling censorship and has been all but suspended altogether, so that today it is in fact disappearing." The situation is illustrated by official statistics[54] which show the steady decrease of Catholic publications over the years as follows:

1947	Jan.-June 253	June-Dec. 263	Total 516
1948	235	248	483
1949	221	241	462
1950	102	42	144
1951	37	34	71
1952	28	30	58
1953	45	—	45

The press in Poland is controlled by the Government and is openly utilized in attacking the Roman Catholic Church. The attacks are centered mainly on the Vatican. The Catholic publications are today limited largely to diocesan weeklies which are concerned only with strictly religious matters and local affairs of the diocese. There are still a few periodicals being published, like *The Priests' Ateneum (Ateneum Kapłańskie), Homo Dei, Polonia Sacra,* and *The Biblical and Liturgical Review (Ruch Biblijny i Liturgiczny),* which deal with subjects of such a special nature that in effect they appeal only to a very limited circle of readers. The circulation of popular religious periodicals, which before reached the masses, is now curtailed. The nationalization of printing establishments and all restrictions resulting therefrom make religious publications dependent on the Government even in purely technical matters of printing.

The protest also relates that "while the Catholic press and publications are disappearing, the dissidents' press, ostentatiously appearing as Catholic, is given all possible official support. This is true of the weekly *Dziś i Jutro* (Today and Tomorrow) and the daily *Słowo Powszechne* (Universal Word), mouthpiece of the so-called "Committee of Catholic Intellectuals and Leaders" and the Government-sponsored "Committee for Catholic Priests," which was established in February 1951 to control the newly formed "Union of Patriotic Clergy." This organization was to mobilize the pro-Government clergy against the prelates of the Church, and simultaneously to publish a periodical under the title "The Citizen Priest" *(Ksiądz Obywatel),* with the aim of winning the lower clergy to the side of the Government. Among the Catholic publications of a wider scope was the *Tygodnik Powszechny* (General Weekly), published by the Metropolitan Chapter in Cracow, which was recently suspended and resumed publication after its editorial board had been removed. "This systematic destructive action against the Catholic printed word is further aided by the State agency *Ruch,* which holds the complete monopoly for the distribution of books and newspapers, and also by withholding allotments of paper and through press censorship. Paper is short for Catholic publications but plentiful for others. The Office of Censorship causes severe economic loss by condemning whole issues of already printed magazines and books." (Protest cited *supra*).

Art. XIX of the agreement upholds full freedom of activities for religious orders—in fact "the fate of monastic clergy has become more uncertain and threatened than heretofore. Religious orders are restricted in their activities or even forbidden to continue these activities which they used to carry on in keeping with their vocation. They are being systematically dispossessed of their means of existence and the possibility of apostolic work. In 1952 minor seminaries were liquidated and their property, including personal effects of their members and sometimes even the monastery buildings, were frequently confiscated. It was from these seminaries that the monastic orders were largely receiving their monastic appointments."

With reference to the hospitals and charitable institutions, the Protest states that "Religious orders of sisters are being removed from hospitals and charity institutions, even those which they owned and in which they had worked for the good of the sick, the orphans and the destitute. Without any consideration whatsoever for their present or future fate, they are being deprived of their financial means and support, although they often cannot be properly replaced."

This shows that in spite of the agreement, the process of restricting the activities of the Church continues.

It may also be mentioned that reference to God was dropped in the formula of oath. The military oath underwent a rephrasing in statutes in 1950 and 1952.[55,56] The Decree of 1944 and the Statute of 1947 still included in the military oath the closing phrase: "So help me, God![57,58] The formulae of the 1950 and 1952 statutes omit the mention of God altogether. Instead, the military oath reads: "I swear . . . to stand unyielding in defense of peace, in brotherly alliance with the Soviet Army . . ."

In an equal manner, the mention of God has been removed from the oath of a witness in the Codes of Civil and Criminal Procedure. The term "oath" has been replaced by the term "solemn promise," which reads:

> Conscious of the importance of my words and my responsibility before the law, I solemnly promise that I will honestly speak the truth, concealing nothing.[59,60]

Similar promises without the mention of God had already been substituted for oaths for the officials of the executive and judicial branch.[61, 62]

F.   *Church Administration in the Recovered Territories*

Events in Poland after the agreement show that the attacks of the Government upon the Church have not ceased. The problem of Church administration in the so-called "Recovered Territories" became the chief target because the Vatican had maintained only a provisional administration in these territories involving five dioceses. These territories, approximately 39,000 square miles in area, are former German provinces, assigned to Poland in compensation for the loss of her eastern provinces to the USSR. The principle that Poland should be compensated by substantial accessions from the eastern provinces of Germany was adopted at the Yalta (Crimea) conference. The area of the Recovered Territories was outlined at the Potsdam Conference. The Recovered Territories were placed under Polish administration "pending the final delimitation of Poland's western frontiers," which was relegated to a future peace treaty with Germany. Poles consider these territories as historically Polish, and have thus coined the name of "Recovered Territories" to designate them. Polish public opinion is unanimous in considering the assignment of the territory to Poland as final and the reservations concerning its ratification in a future peace treaty as a formality. While the Soviet Union and the Polish Government have adopted an attitude that the frontier of the Recovered Territories is finally settled, the Western Powers seem to maintain the position that the entire problem must await settlement in the peace treaty with Germany. These circumstances have been used by the Communist Government in its effort to interfere with the administration of the Catholic Church in that part of Poland and thus the administration of the Church in these territories became a vital issue.

Upon the incorporation of the Recovered Territories into Poland, their remaining German population was moved to Germany and replaced by Poles, to a large extent those from the eastern part of Poland which had been annexed by Russia. After the creation of the German Democratic Republic for Eastern Germany, Poland signed an agreement with this republic on July 6, 1950[63] regulating the marking of the established and existing Polish-German frontier.

Normally the bishopric is administered by a bishop appointed by the Pope. If a bishop is "inhabilitated to do so, the administration is performed by the Vicar General whom the bishop appoints to substitute him, or by another priest delegated by the bishop, unless the Holy See made other provisions." [64]

In addition, canon law provides for other emergencies. Thus the bishop may delegate the administration to several persons who are to succeed each other in turn. If all such persons are impeded, the cathedral chapter of canons elects a vicar, called a capitular vicar, in contrast to a vicar general. For grave and special reasons the Holy See may appoint apostolic administrators to administer a canonically erected diocese, e.g., in case the ordinary is incapacitated from governing the diocese, or in case of his expulsion, imprisonment, etc. by the civil power, or for any other reason that the Holy See deems proper (Canon 312 of the Code of Canon Law). A cathedral chapter may be in brief defined primarily as a body of clerics specially appointed to assist the bishop as his council and to administer the diocese during a vacancy. Moreover, in dioceses where it is impossible to establish or revive the cathedral chapter of canons, the bishops may appoint diocesan consultors. The body of such consultors then takes the place of the chapter.

In the instance of the Recovered Territories the German bishops and their vicars left their dioceses at the end of World War II. Primate Hlond, following special instructions from the Holy See, organized the administration in the dioceses of Wrocław, Opole, Gorzów, and Olsztyn. He also established apostolic administrators in these dioceses, thus a temporary form of administration of the dioceses was set up. This arrangement was a form of "other provisions" which the Holy See may make in the absence of a Vicar General. The protest of the Polish episcopate of May 8, 1953 remarks in this connection that "the [post-war Polish] government itself at one time had words of praise for the great significance this had for State life, for social and psychological stabilization, for the work of settlement, and for reconstruction."

Nevertheless the Polish government later intensified its demands on the Polish episcopate for a permanent administration. It may be observed that no hasty action could be expected from the Holy See in view of the international situation. It has been the policy of the Vatican always to await a final peace settlement before definitely adjusting the affairs of the Church to new political frontiers. Therefore, the Holy See may have refrained at the very beginning of the post-war period from establishing regular bishops prior to the conclusion of a final peace treaty with Germany. But, on the other hand the above-mentioned protest also relates definite steps taken later by the Holy See toward the appointment of bishops which was frustrated by the Polish government. To quote the protest:

> And when, in the further stage of the stabilization of ecclesiastical relations in the Western territories, the Polish Primate [the late Cardinal Hlond] had obtained from the Holy See appointments of bishops for Wrocław, Opole, Gorzów and Olsztyn, who would have had the duty to reside in the Western territories, the government took a hostile attitude toward this achievement, and did not permit them to take office. This did not stop the party press from heaping abuse on the Holy See and the hierarchy, claiming that they were doing nothing for the Western territories.

As an example of such accusation the following passages from the *Trybuna Ludu* of January 25, 1951 may be quoted:

> German bishops whose jurisdiction formerly extended to the territories which at present form a part of the Polish State demonstrate that they still continue to regard these territories as formally under their jurisdiction.
>
> The responsibility for the existing temporary character of the Church administration in the western territories, which is contrary to the interests of the Polish Nation, lies entirely with the Polish episcopate. In April, 1950 the Polish episcopate, in agreement with the Polish Government, undertook the obligation to take appropriate steps to put an end to the temporary character of the Church administration in the western territories. The episcopate, moreover,

agreed to oppose anti-Polish activities, and especially the anti-Polish and "revisionist"[65] pronouncements of a part of the German clergy. The signature of the episcopate under the agreement concluded with the Government has remained a dead letter.

The Polish episcopate has done literally nothing to fulfill its obligations, and representatives of the episcopate are doing everything in their power to minimize the issue and to spread confusion among the faithful.

Thus, genuine patriotic feelings of the population are played up against the loyalty of the people to the hierarchy of the Church. Moreover, on January 27, 1951, the Polish Government issued a direct order for immediate removal of the apostolic administrators and ordered priests who held these offices to leave the Recovered Territories. Consequently, it became necessary to replace the apostolic administrators with capitular vicars in each of the dioceses involved. This act of the removal of the apostolic administration was a direct government interference with the ecclesiastical administration, as is evident from the statement of the Government made on January 27, 1951:[66]

The Polish Government has ordered the liquidation of the provisional status of the ecclesiastical administration in the Recovered Territories as represented by the apostolic administrators, and the removal from those dioceses of clergymen who fulfilled the functions of apostolic administrators.

Furthermore, on January 30, 1951, the press published an announcement of the official Polish news agency. It states as an already accomplished fact that the apostolic administrators "have left the Recovered Territories." The announcement reports also that: "capitular vicars have been elected in accordance with provisions of canon law to assume government in the particular dioceses . . . The capitular vicars have commenced to appoint permanent parish priests for parishes in the Western Territories to remove the temporary character of the Church administration on all levels and to manifest that the western territories are inseparably united with the rest of Poland as regards Church administration also."

As stated in the official announcement, Archbishop Stefan Wyszyński conferred with the President of the Republic on Feb-

ruary 3, 1951, on the Church administration in the Recovered
Territories.

On February 18, 1951, the Catholic weekly *Tygodnik Powszechny,* published by the Metropolitan Chapter in Cracow,
made public the following announcement:

"The Episcopate announces for the benefit and information
of the clergy and the faithful, that as a result of the changes
which have been made in the Church administration in the western territories, capitular vicars were elected by the diocesan
consultors,[67] who from now on hold the Church office in accordance with the rules of canon law. The clergy and faithful should
give their confidence to those now in charge of the diocese and
render them necessary assistance."

The Polish Episcopate in its later protest of May 8, 1953,
with reference to the removal of the Apostolic administration
and the election of capitular vicars states, that "the administrative authorities have—removed—Apostolic administrators . . .",
and "interfered with the election of capitular vicars, thus depriving the elections held in such circumstances of all legality."

Thus, under pressure from the Government the diocesan consultors were compelled to name permanent appointees as capitular vicars immediately. The Episcopate evidently assented to
the Communist regime in this matter to remove one of the
grounds causing friction between State and Church.

In connection with the appointment of capitular vicars as
well as other bishops in Poland, the new formula of oath to be
taken by them has been formulated as follows:

> I swear solemnly to be faithful to the Republic of Poland and
> her People's Democratic Government. I promise that I shall not
> undertake anything which might be contrary to her interests or
> endanger the security and integrity of her frontiers. I shall see to
> it that the clergy under my jurisdiction shall not act to the detri-
> ment of the Polish State or against the existing public order. I shall
> take care of the welfare and interest of the State, and endeavour
> to protect it from all possible threatening perils of which I might
> be aware.[68]

The oath was taken before the Officer in Charge of the Office
for Denominational Affairs.

Towards the end of 1951 the Polish Government renewed the campaign against the Church on the issue of the Recovered Territories. This time the reported anti-Polish revisionist attempts of the government of the Federal German Republic and the proposed remilitarization of Western Germany were used as the basis of the attack. With this in view, on December 12, 1951, the Government sponsored a convention of the clergy and Catholic leaders in Wrocław (Breslau). The convention wound up with a resolution now demanding the installation of regular bishops in the Recovered Territories instead of capitular vicars. But the situation remains unchanged at the time when the present report is concluded.

It seems appropriate to conclude this chapter with the voice of the Catholic Church answering the accusations of lack of a patriotic stand on the issue of the Recovered Territories. It is fully presented in the statement made by Archbishop Wyszyński, Primate of Poland on November 29, 1951,[69] a few days prior to the convention in Wrocław. The following excerpts are worthy of quoting:

> . . . Cardinal Hlond has gone, but the trend of his thought and the conduct of the Polish bishops has in no way changed. The evidence of this policy is the agreement reached between the Government of the Polish Republic and the Episcopate of Poland, in particular with its significant Point 3, which I think noteworthy to recall: The Episcopate of Poland declares that economic, historical, cultural, and religious rights, as well as historical justice, demand that the Recovered Territories remain with Poland forever. This is an expression of the stand taken by the whole Polish Episcopate, for all of the Episcopate made efforts to reach the "agreement," and considered it indispensable for peaceful coexistence of the Church and the State in Poland.

> . . . The opinion of the Polish people, the Polish Episcopate, and the Polish Government with regard to the western territories is unanimous. The Holy See is aware of it, takes it into account, and has full understanding for our attitude.

> The Holy See is not inclined to issue statements. There is, however, no lack of facts, which sometimes are more expressive than words. So, for instance, it is an indisputable fact that the Holy See has taken due notice of the revival of Church life in the western territories promoted by Cardinal Hlond. Moreover, the Holy See

consented to the establishment of ecclesiastical organs, as provided
for ecclesiastical corporations in canon law. With the consent of
the Holy See diocesan curias, ecclesiastical courts, and theological
seminaries have been organized. Thus the Holy See acknowledges
and assumes that Polish Church life will continue to develop in
the Recovered Territories, that it will consolidate and take a better
organized form.

The Holy See has also taken due notice of our proposals regarding Church organization in the western territories. It has even
made decisions which are of great significance for a favorable
settlement of Church affairs. And though some time may still be
required for these decisions to be put into effect, they nonetheless
constitute historical facts and an additional proof that the Holy
See has due regard for the rights and needs of Polish Church life
in the western territories . . .

The Polish people are rightly perturbed by the echoes of anti-
Polish propaganda, which raises its voice stronger every day against
the Polish frontier on the Odra and Nysa Rivers. We share this
anxiety for these anti-Polish voices constitute a threat to peace.
Our country needs first of all the opportunity to work in peace
in order to rebuild its economic life and to heal the wounds dealt
to our biological and cultural life. We have even a right to expect a
different attitude from the German people, in particular from the
German Catholics. After all, Catholic ethics demand an admission
of responsibility for instigating the war, of which Poland, among
others, became a victim. German Catholics must be conscious of
the grave wrongs which were done to the Polish State and the
Polish national culture in the course of that war. What reasons
can possibly justify the murder of so many millions of Polish citizens? What can explain the unparalleled destruction of such a
great city as the capital of Poland, Warsaw? Even today these
crimes cry out for justice. If God's Providence destined that we
are to be again in the Recovered Territories, then I see in this
striking fact not only the fulfillment of our historical rights, but
also a sign of justice which brings restitution.

G.   Decree on the Appointment of Clergymen
to Ecclesiastical Offices

1.   Events which Precipitated the Promulgation
of the Decree of February 9, 1953

The campaign of the Government against the Church abated
somewhat from towards the end of 1951 until the elections to

the new National Assembly were over in October 1952. After the new Constitution was adopted and the elections were over, the campaign against the Church was resumed but in a different manner. Heretofore, the campaign had been aimed primarily at the Vatican, as one of the presumed agencies of the "imperialist camp." The Polish clergy was not attacked directly. Now an outright purge of the rank and file of the clergy began.

The new attacks opened in November 1952 with the removal from office of Stanisław Adamski, Diocesan Bishop of Katowice, and his two Auxiliary Bishops, Herbert Bednorz and Juliusz Bieniek.[70] At the time of the general elections the bishops circulated a petition asking the Government to enforce properly the law on mandatory religious instruction in schools. This action was labeled by the Government as "political sabotage." An intensive press campaign was launched against them; also, a number of mass meetings of protest were staged.

The Warsaw publication *Trybuna Ludu* on November 12, 1952, reported that active members of the "National Front" and leading agitators of the Province of Silesia had called a mass meeting and in a resolution condemned the activities of the three bishops referred to above.

During November of 1952, also, arrests were made among the priests of the Cracow Metropolitan Curia. These arrests were followed by a spy trial in January 1953. Prior to the trial another event evoked new attacks, i.e., the elevation of Archbishop Stefan Wyszyński to a Cardinal of the Roman Catholic Church in January 1953. Because of possible repercussions the Primate did not go to Rome to receive his Cardinal's hat, although he was not formally prevented from doing so. An outstanding example of the attacks aroused by Wyszyński's elevation, is found in the *Trybuna Ludu* of December 8, 1952. The editorial in the official Communist Party organ was entitled "The Political Significance of the Vatican Nomination" and accused the Vatican of an anti-Polish attitude. In particular it reiterated the usual charges that its policy "is conducted not in the interest of faith but in that of American imperialism," that "it challenges the Polish right to the Recovered Territories and renders support for a rebuilding of the Wehrmacht, lending support to the sinister forces of reaction and fascism." The editorial then goes on to attribute a deliberate link between the Vatican's policy and the elevation of Primate Wyszyński. In fact the paper broadly intimates that the Polish Episcopate's ties and loyalty to the Holy See are tantamount with treason of Polish national interests.

These accusations were followed by the Cracow trial which took place on January 21-26, 1953, before the Court Martial of the Military District of Cracow. Certain offenses committed by civilians are tried before courts martial in the same manner as high treason committed by members of the armed forces.[71] The indictment charged the accused with carrying on espionage on orders from the Vatican, of being in the service of the United States, of illicitly hiding arms, and of illegally dealing in foreign currencies. On January 27, 1953, the military court in Cracow passed sentences asked for by the prosecution. A priest, Rev. Lelito and two Catholic laymen were sentenced to death; Rev. Szymonek to life imprisonment; Rev. Brzycki to 15 years' imprisonment; Rev. Pochopień to 10 years' imprisonment. The court proceedings themselves went on in true Soviet fashion, the accused not only pleaded guilty but indulged in self-accusations, setting themselves up as a warning to others. The trial was highly publicized in the press and at numerous public meetings which were especially convened to discuss it. The whole case was handled in a short time. The trial took place within 7 weeks after the arrest of the suspects. The reports on the trial published in the Polish press carried in detail passages from the indictment, testimonies of witnesses and the prosecutor's pleadings which were obviously designed to discredit the whole Polish clergy as agents of foreign intelligence and as enemies of the People's Poland, and to justify beforehand the promulgation of the Decree of February 9, 1953, which brought all the clergy under direct control of the Government. Many press editorials commented on the charges involved in the trial, even prior to the formal indictment of the accused and the actual opening of the case in court. For example, the *Trybuna Ludu* came out on January 18, 1953 (three days before the start of the trial) with an editorial entitled:

"Centers of a Hostile Conspiracy Against the Nation Cannot be Tolerated—Comments on the Espionage Affair in the Curia of the Archbishop of Cracow." The article contained practically everything subsequently presented in the trial as judicial confessions of the accused. In addition, the editorial intimated the real designs of the Government towards outright control of the clergy. We read:

> The problem is not confined just to the Cracow affair . . . the Church hierarchy has not broken away from an orientation towards the forces of reaction and did not take a stand together with the People's Poland . . . Thus, those who take their political inspiration from such a poisoned source as the Vatican can only act to the detriment of our country . . . Let us examine what kind of men were maintained in and appointed to responsible posts in the Church hierarchy . . .

In addition to the individual priests already under arrest, the article also enumerates the following leading members of the episcopate: Archbishop Jabłrzykowski, former Metropolitan of Wilno; Archbishop Baziak, formerly Metropolitan of Lwów and currently Capitular Vicar of the Diocese of Cracow; Bishop Świrski of Siedlce; the Auxiliary Bishop of Warsaw, Majewski, the Auxiliary Bishop of Cracow, Respondek. The charges against them include, among others, discrimination against the so-called "patriotic" priests among the lower clergy, and may be indicative of a planned elimination of all the key dignitaries of the Church. In fact, later reports from Poland tend to confirm the fact that some have already been removed from office.[72]

After the trial, meetings of the so-called "Priests' Committee of the Union of Fighters for Freedom and Democracy"[73] were held, both in Warsaw and other regional cities. On January 30, 1953, a meeting of the enlarged Presidium of this committee adopted a resolution relative to the ". . . espionage and antinational and anti-State activities of priests disclosed at the Cracow trial."[74] The steps suggested in their resolution were later embraced in the decree of February 9, 1953. This resolution, signed by some "patriotic priests," was meant to create the impression of a "popular demand" among the rank and file of the clergy for control of the hierarchy.

All this was a mere prelude to the promulgation of the Decree of February 9, 1953 on the Appointment of Clergymen to Ecclesiastical Offices.

2. Decree of February 9, 1953[75] and Enforcing Provisions of May 5, 1953[76]

a) Basic Rules of Appointment of Clergymen to Ecclesiastical Offices under Canon Law and the Concordat of 1925

In order to assess the significance of the decree of February 9, 1953, this study is introduced by a brief outline of the provisions of canon law and the Concordat which deal with appointment to ecclesiastic offices.

According to canon law, bishops are freely appointed by the Pope. The ordinary has the right to fill ecclesiastical offices within its own diocesan territory. The so-called consistorial benefices, i.e., sacred offices which have the right to receive revenue from the endowment of such office, can be erected by the Holy See only. The ordinaries may create non-consistorial benefices in their respective territories. The local ordinaries may, generally speaking, convert and suppress benefices and change their jurisdiction; only in some exceptional cases is the decision reserved to the Holy See. The ordinary may deprive a clergyman of his office for any just reason, according to his prudent judgment. Thus, prior to the conclusion of the concordat the Roman Catholic Church was, in accordance with constitutional provisions, empowered to handle all these appointment matters without asking for the consent of the Government. In particular, appointments of clergymen to ecclesiastical offices did not require the consent of government authorities; the duty to take an oath of allegiance was not imposed upon the clergymen; the Church could establish, convert, and suppress ecclesiastical benefices without the consent of State authorities. A clergyman could be deprived of his office by the ordinary upon his own initiative.

By the Concordat the Roman Catholic Church received the guarantee of the free exercise of its ecclesiastical authority and jurisdiction according to the principles of canon law. However, the Concordat provided that in dealing with some of the matters referred to above the Government must be consulted. According to the Concordat only the appointment of archbishops and bishops required the consent of Government authorities and only these ordinaries had to take an oath of allegiance. Appointments of clergymen to ecclesiastical offices within a diocese did not require the consent of government authorities. In these cases the ecclesiastical authority, prior to the appointment, merely requested the administration to furnish information that the candidate is a citizen, had studied theology in Poland or in papal institutes, and had engaged in no activities endangering the safety of the State. Aliens or persons who had not studied theology in Poland or in papal institutes could obtain pastoral benefices only with the permission of the Government. The Roman Catholic Church could freely erect and convert ecclesiastical benefices. The consent of the Government was required only in cases where financial support was needed. In cases where charges were brought by the Government against a clergyman and the decision to be rendered would in all probability comply with the request presented by the Government, the ordinary decided the case. In the event of a difference of opinion between the ordinary and the government, a special procedure was devised in which an equal number of clergymen and representatives of the Government functioned as a deciding body.

When the Concordat was unilaterally renounced by the postwar Government, the episcopal administration, and appointments of diocesan ordinaries were conducted according to canon law.

b) Principles of the Decree and its Enforcing Provisions

The decree of February 9, 1953 and the enforcing provisions of May 5, 1953 brought about a radical change in the situation and laid down several new rules. The important regulation on the enforcement explained *ex post facto* the reasons for issuing the Decree. It states that the purpose of the decree is "to see to it that persons who hold ecclesiastical offices perform their functions in accordance with the principles and requirements of the constitution of the Polish People's Republic." It is now required "that clergymen in the performance of duties resulting from their ecclesiastical offices show a social and patriotic attitude consistent with the principles of the Constitution of the Polish People's Republic." Thus, not only is loyalty required from the clergy as heretofore, but the Government demands from them a direct contribution to its policy. This is also implied in the text of the oath quoted below.

Moreover, "government agencies should not permit ecclesiastical offices held by clergymen to be used or abused as a cover either for an attitude or action averse to the Polish People's Republic or for overt or covert political activity inconsistent with the basic law of the Constitution and with regulations issued by Government agencies on the basis of the provisions of the Constitution."

Effective February 10, 1953, any appointment of clergymen to ecclesiastical offices was made subject to Government approval. Before an ecclesiastical office is filled by a clergyman, consent to the candidate must be obtained in advance from the competent Government authority. Similar consent is also required for the release of a clergyman from an ecclesiastical office or his transfer to another such office. The Presidium of the Government (Office for Denominational Affairs) has the authority to issue the consent to the appointment of diocesan ordinaries, but in all other cases this authority is vested in the Presidium of the Provincial People's Council concerned. (Art. 3, 4). The term "ecclesiastical offices filled by clergymen" comprises all ecclesiastical offices, according to the regulation. They may be of permanent or provisional character, and auxiliary or substitutive.

Every appointee, without exception, must take a special oath. Bishops and titular bishops shall be sworn in by the Office for Denominational Affairs at the Presidium of the Government, and all other clergymen by the appropriate Presidium of the Provincial People's Council. Two formulas of oath are prescribed, one for bishops and titular bishops and the other for all other clergymen. Both consist of four paragraphs. The first, third and fourth paragraphs are identical and read:

> 1) I affirm solemnly to be faithful to the Polish People's Republic and her Government. I promise to do everything for the development of the Polish People's Republic and for the strengthening of her power and security.
>
> 3) I promise not to undertake anything which might be contrary to the interests of the Polish People's Republic or endanger the security and integrity of her frontiers.
>
> 4) Having in mind the welfare and interest of the State I shall endeavor to avert from it any threatening perils of which I might be aware.

Paragraph two of the formula for the bishops reads:

> 2) I shall make every effort that the clergy under my jurisdiction in accordance with their civic duties appeal in their sacerdotal activities to the faithful to obey the law and government authority, to intensify their work on the development of the national economy and on the improvement of the nation's welfare.

For other clergymen this paragraph reads:

> 2) In conformity with the duty of a citizen I shall appeal in my activity as a clergyman to the faithful to respect the law and governmental authority, to increase the work in developing the national economy and in increasing the prosperity of the nation.

The Regulation is explicit and states that all clergymen without exception who hold ecclesiastical offices have to take the oath of allegiance. The oath is, therefore, required also from holders of ecclesiastical offices who were appointed prior to the Decree.

Only a Polish national may be appointed to the ecclesiastical office of clergyman. The law does not provide any exception to this rule (Art. 1).

Any erection, conversion and suppression of an ecclesiastical office, as well as any change in its jurisdiction, is subject to the approval of the Government (Art. 2) and cannot be made before consent is given by the competent Government authority, the Presidium of the Provincial People's Council and, in cases relating to episcopal matters, by the Office for Denominational Affairs. The regulation provides that the petitioner should receive an answer within a month, but otherwise leaves the decision to the discretion of Government authorities.

A clergyman who "acts contrary to law and public order, or supports, or conceals, such activities, will be removed from his office either upon the initiative of his superior ecclesiastical authority or upon the request of Government authorities." (Art. 6). The wording of this provision now makes the removal of a clergyman mandatory in cases where the Government authority so demands. The ordinary no longer has the right to examine whether the reason stated in the request presented by the Government for removal is just, nor does he have the right to decide according to his own best judgment. The regulation contains a plain-spoken provision, which reads: "The Presidium of the Provincial People's Council or the Office for Denominational Affairs shall direct the demand for the removal of a clergyman from office within a prescribed time to the appropriate Curia."

The power to demand the removal of clergymen from office may easily be used gradually to eliminate all clergymen not fully submissive to the regime, thereby reducing the spiritual power of the Holy See.

An appeal against the decision of the Provincial People's Council demanding removal may be taken by the ordinary or the person concerned to the Office for Denominational Affairs. Appeals from decisions relating to the erection, conversion and suppression of ecclesiastical offices and from decisions which disapprove the filling of an ecclesiastical office by a proposed candidate also lie with the Office for Denominational Affairs. The decrees rendered by this Office in these matters are final. Thus, the final decision is always with a Government agency which makes the decision at its discretion.

The decree and the regulation create conditions under which only priests directly approved by the Government may officiate.

It seems obvious that the provisions of the Decree of February 9, 1953, conflict with the separation of Church and State as this principle is traditionally understood in America. Since this principle is written in the new 1952 Constitution, the Polish Government press tries to explain away the features of the decree contradicting the principle. Thus, *Głos Pracy* (The Voice of Labor) of February 13, 1953, in an article on the Decree of February 9, 1953 states:

> The decree in no way infringes upon freedom of conscience and religion; it in no way restricts the rights of the Church and clergy. But at the same time it puts an end to the abuse of religion and to the abuse of ecclesiastical appointments for ends hostile to the whole nation.

The Polish Episcopate in its protest of May 8, 1953, gives strong reasons to prove that the Decree of February 9, 1953, on the Appointment of the Clergy contradicts the principle of separation of Church and State announced in the Constitution. The pertinent passage reads:

> . . . the decree of February 9, 1953, is most obviously in contradiction to the previous and more general decree about freedom of conscience and religion and moreover and above all it is contrary to the newly adopted Constitution of the People's Republic. For the Constitution introduced the separation of Church and State. And the separation of Church and State, as President Bierut, the main author of the Constitution, has authoritatively stated, means that "the Church has its own autonomous organization and organizational structure." How then is it possible that today when the Church has been constitutionally separated from the State and isolated as an autonomous organism, the State can allow itself continuous legal interference with the Church's internal structure? No authority has ever done such a thing in Poland, even without attempting to establish separation of Church and State. Even the authority of the People's Poland did not issue such a decree at the time when, from its standpoint, the possibility of such interference was held not to be ruled out by the Constitution. A decree which is in contradiction to the Constitution cannot be legally binding. The ratification of the decree by the Sejm cannot provide the decree with legal force as long as the Sejm has not amended the Constitution itself.

The Episcopate likewise attacks the legality of the demand imposed by the decree that the clergy take an oath of loyalty to the People's Poland before National Councils:

> This demand is also not justified as there is no Concordat in the People's Poland, and the Agreement did not foresee any "oath."

> Under the present conditions the demanding of an oath can mean
> either that the priests are considered State employees, which is not
> right, since the present pastor is not even a civil employee, or that
> in the eyes of the Government authorities, the Catholic clergy is
> considered an uncertain, suspicious element, which again could be
> a visible expression and unfounded discrimination against the
> Catholic priests, when taking into consideration that such an "oath"
> is not required from other citizens of the State.

After reading these passages one is forced to conclude that
separation of Church and State declared by the Constitution is
practiced by the present government to bring about the submission of the Church to the State.

H. *Recent Developments*

The tension between the Government and the Church steadily
mounted and after the enactment of the Decree of February 9,
1953 developments have been extremely grave. The persistent
campaign against the episcopate and its ties with the Vatican
was given considerable attention by all propaganda media and
at a series of "conferences of the clergy and lay Catholic leaders.[77]
The third anniversary of the 1950 agreement between the Government and the Catholic episcopate was utilized to bring to
the fore further charges against those who, as the paper *Życie
Warszawy* puts it, "cynically abuse religion and the Church for
dirty political ends." [78] While attacks against religion or the practice of worship are insidiously avoided, the press states that the
episcopate, being "guided by the Vatican's orders, does not want
to reconcile itself, for political and not religious reasons, to the
fact that the power in Poland is forever in the hands of the
people." Thus, it became clear that the prime objective of the
Government's tactics was to remove from the episcopate persons
unwilling to become tools of the Communist domination of the
country. The official organ of the Communist Party insists that
"all citizens of the country are bound to absolute loyalty to the
People's State, a patriotic attitude, and a total recognition of the
raison d'état of the People's Poland."[79]

This was echoed also at the numerous meetings of "Catholic

lay activists and clergy" organized in various parts of the country. From various statements voiced at these meetings by members of the clergy and stressed in the propaganda campaign, it is clear that the Government now attempts to make the clergy an instrument of its own anti-religious aims. This is best illustrated by the following pronouncements.[80]

> As a social worker, the priest should support the cooperative farm movement and point out that it is in accordance with the basic principles of the Catholic religion on the law of property, which may belong either to the individual or the community.
>
> Marxism and Catholicism can coexist . . . the basis of an understanding between the followers of the two creeds could be the respect they hold for one philosophical outlook: the love of the people and the profoundest esteem for the socialist progress of mankind.
>
> Our next task is to achieve the final severance of Catholicism in Poland from the policy of abusing religion for purposes contrary to the principles of Catholicism and opposed to the present *raison d'état* of the Polish nation.

These and numerous other statements in the same vein are quoted by the official Polish Press Agency and attributed to members of the "patriotic clergy" who are named as participants in these meetings.[81] To accentuate the wedge which the Government strives to drive between the lower clergy and the episcopate, the Council of State on the eve of the National Day, July 22, 1953, conferred upon a number of Catholic priests and lay leaders high State decorations[82] for their "social work." The priests named in this announcement are those most active in the so-called "Union of Catholic Intellectuals."

In September 1953 the direct attacks against the episcopate crystallized in the trial of Bishop Kaczmarek of Kielce and the "suspension" of Stefan Cardinal Wyszyński as Primate of Poland. It seems that the two events were timed by the Government for a definite purpose. Bishop Czesław Kaczmarek of Kielce was under arrest for two years before his trial by the Court Martial in Warsaw on September 14, 1953. Together with three other priests and a nun, the Bishop was charged with "anti-State activities and espionage" and the whole proceedings of the trial were given the widest possible coverage in the press and radio. All the defendants were reported to have pleaded guilty. Their elaborate confessions followed the usual Soviet pattern of self-accusation, and among the confessed "criminal activities," alleged contacts with the U. S. Embassy (under former Ambassador Arthur Bliss Lane) became one of the major charges. The indictment and arguments of the prosecution tried to make a case out of the defendants' activities when they were still students in theological seminaries and their priestly activities between the two world wars. The whole trial aimed to discredit the Polish episcopate and to attribute all evils that befell Poland to the Vatican.

Bishop Kaczmarek and the other accused were sentenced on September 22, 1953 for espionage for the U. S. A. and the Vatican. The Bishop received 12 years' imprisonment, the other defendants 10, 9, 6, and 5 years. The propaganda value of the trial is dubious since the people are by now fully cognizant of the inevitable outcome of such political trials. However, it may be said that the trial served as a pretext for the removal of Stefan Cardinal Wyszyński as Primate of Poland.

On September 28, 1953, a week following the sentencing of Bishop Kaczmarek, the Presidium of the Government published the following communiqué:[83]

> In consequence of persistent abuse by Father Archbishop Stefan Wyszyński of his ecclesiastical functions, despite frequent warnings; for his violation of the principles of the agreement; for carrying out a campaign of incitement and creating a poisoned atmosphere which, as Bishop Kaczmarek's trial showed, favors hostile activities and is especially harmful in view of the designs on the inviolability of the frontiers of the Polish People's Republic; the Presidium of the Government, basing itself on its legal powers and in its anxiety for a complete normalization of relations between the Government and the Church hierarchy, has banned Archbishop Stefan Wyszyński from performing functions connected with his previous ecclesiastical posts.

Simultaneously with this statement the Official Polish Press Agency announced:

> In connection with the Government decree depriving Archbishop Stefan Wyszyński of his functions, the Episcopate, having made

decisions safeguarding the continuity of leadership of the Episcopate, applied to the Government for permission for Archbishop Wyszyński to live in one of the monasteries. The Government has agreed to this.

It may also be observed that the Government announcement of September 28, 1953 does not speak of the "removal" of the Primate, but states "that he has been forbidden to carry out his functions." This careful phrasing sounds somewhat milder than the wording of Art. 6 of the February decree, which reads: "Clergymen . . . shall be removed from office . . . upon the request of Government authorities." It is also noteworthy that the Government gave heed to the arguments of the episcopate expressed in the protest of May 8, 1953, that the decree is in conflict with the provision of the Constitution promising that the Government will not interfere in affairs of ecclesiastical administration. In fact, the Government invokes only the agreement of 1950 in removing the Primate.

Confronted with the fact that the leader of the Roman Catholic Church in Poland was removed, the episcopate was left to its own devices and could but regroup its ranks so as not to be cut off altogether from ecclesiastical jurisdiction over the clergy and faithful. The official Polish Press Agency claimed that the episcopate yielded. The agency published a statement attributed to the Polish episcopate, which declares:[84]

> In its care for the good of the Church and Nation and at the same time in the interests of the unity of our Nation, the episcopate is determined to prevent in the future the distortion of the intentions of the agreement of April 1950 and to create conditions favorable for the normalization of relations between the State and Church. The episcopate, which condemned the establishment and operation of diversional centers directed against the State, repudiates the atmosphere favoring such activities and is of the opinion that it must be radically changed.
>
> The regrettable facts disclosed at the trial of the Bishop of Kielce, Czesław Kaczmarek, demand determined condemnation. The episcopate will not tolerate activities harmful to the State on the part of any member of the clergy, and will impose proper punishments in accordance with canon law, on those guilty.
>
> The episcopate also opposes the linking of religion and church with the egotistic political aims of foreign circles hostile to Poland

which would like to abuse religious feelings for political ends. The Polish episcopate states that now, at a time of increased efforts on the part of German revisionists directed against the inviolability of our frontier on the Odra and Nysa rivers and at the time of increased activities by diversionary centers hostile to Poland, a complete consolidation of the nation is necessary.

That is why the episcopate is firmly opposing the political attitude and actions of certain factions of the hierarchy and the large majority of the German clergy who are the motive power behind the anti-Polish, revisionist activities and who at the same time quote as their authority the Holy See and the Vatican.

The activities of international circles aiming at unleashing a new war call for the mobilization of all forces, intellectual and moral, to safeguard peace and strengthen Poland and her capabilities of resistance. The episcopate, together with the Government, thinks it right to create such conditions as, in the interests of the State and the Church, would remove the obstacles on the road to the full implementation of the agreement and to the strengthening of unity and the nation's consolidation.

The declaration is, in contrast to the protest, cautious and conciliatory, and may be explained by the desire of the clergy to remain at its post. On the other hand, no less conciliatory was the statement published by the Government[85] on September 29, 1953, which reads:

The Deputy Prime Minister, Jozef Cyrankiewicz, made the following statement in connection with the Episcopate's declaration:

"The Government acknowledges the episcopate's declaration dated September 28, 1953, and expresses the conviction that this declaration will effectively prevent practices aimed against the interests of the State and Nation and create a basis for permanent normalization of relations between the State and Church.

"It is the Government's concern that the rights and duties of the citizens, guaranteed by the Constitution, as regards religious freedom and freedom of conscience, be fully observed by all institutions and all citizens. The State authorities stand on the basis of the agreement of April 14, 1950, and, taking into consideration the episcopate's declaration dated September 28, 1953, will adopt a friendly attitude toward the Church hierachy's postulates, being of the opinion that these will make a real contribution to the cause of strengthening the unity and consolidation of the Nation."

The prominence given to this latest act of conciliation is accentuated by the fact that Boleslaw Bierut, as head of the government personally received a delegation of the episcopate on September 28, 1953. It was reported that during the conversation the implementation of tasks resulting from the episcopate's declaration and the Government's statement were discussed.

On December 17, 1953, the Warsaw radio broadcast a report that the Polish bishops had sworn loyalty to the Government. The announcement stated that the ceremony of taking the oath took place in the office of the Council of Ministers and that the oath was accepted by the Deputy Prime Minister on behalf of the government. In his address to the bishops, the Deputy Premier, speaking on behalf of the government stated that "the agreement dated April 14, 1950 was an expression of the State's attitude aimed at the normalization of relations between State and Church and the Episcopate's declaration dated September 28, 1953 was an expression of appreciation of the correctness of this attitude and the need for a consistent implementation of the agreement on the part of the Polish episcopate."

The Vatican's *L'Osservatore Romano,* commenting on the foregoing report, said that "if it turns out to be true, conditions existing in Poland are by themselves sufficient to make us understand that the gesture performed by the Bishops was not free, but the result of long moral, administrative, and physical violence, that probably included even blackmail." [86]

Such was the status of the Church at the end of April 1954. Whatever developments the future may yet bring, it is certain that the conflict will not abate as long as Communist doctrine remains incompatible with religion of any kind. The Roman Catholic Church in her long and proud history of fulfilling her mission has weathered many a persecution, no matter how hopeless the struggle has appeared.

III. TRANSLATIONS OF STATUTES AND DOCUMENTS

1. Concordat of 1925 (Excerpts)

Art. X. The erection and conversion of ecclesiastical benefices, congregations, and religious orders, as well as their houses and institutes, shall be determined by the competent ecclesiastical authority, which, whenever the above decisions involve expenses to be paid by the Government, shall make such decisions in agreement with the Government. An alien shall not receive the post of a Provincial without a proper permit from the Government.

Art. XI. The Holy See shall appoint archbishops and bishops. His Holiness consents to consult the President of the Republic prior to the appointment of archbishops and diocesan bishops, coadjutors *cum iure successionis,* as well as the Bishop of the Armed Forces, to be certain that the President shall raise no objections of a political nature to such an appointment.

Art. XII. The above mentioned ordinaries [archbishops and diocesan bishops] shall take an oath of allegiance before the President of the Republic prior to taking over their duties . . .

Art. XIX. The Republic of Poland guarantees to the competent [ecclesiastical] authorities the right to confer duties, offices, and ecclesiastical benefices according to the provisions of canon law. The following principles should be observed when pastoral benefices are conferred:

> If the permission of the Polish Government has not been received, pastoral benefices may not be obtained in the territory of the Polish Republic
>
> 1. by aliens, as well as persons who have not studied theology in theological institutes in Poland or in papal institutes, [and]
> 2. by persons whose actions endanger the safety of the State.

Prior to the appointment of such benefices, the ecclesiastical authority shall consult the competent Minister of the Republic of Poland in order to ascertain that there are no objections similar to those which were mentioned above under 1 and 2. In cases where the above mentioned Minister does not present such objections within 30 days against the nominee, the ecclesiastical authority shall make the appointment.

Art. XX. In cases where the authorities of the Republic of Poland charges a clergyman with activities endangering the safety of the State, the competent Minister will present the above mentioned charges to the ordinary, who, upon agreement with this Minister, shall render the appropriate decision within three months. In the event no agreement between the ordinary and the Minister is reached, the Holy See shall refer the matter for settlement to two clergymen appointed by it; these two clergymen will render the final decision in agreement with two representatives of the Republic of Poland.

2. Criminal Code of 1932 (excerpts)

Art. 172. Whoever publicly blasphemes God shall be punished by imprisonment not to exceed five years.

Art. 173. Whoever publicly profanes any ecclesiastical or religious body recognized by law, or its teachings, beliefs, or rituals, or whoever profanes any object of religious rites, shall be punished by imprisonment not to exceed three years.

Art. 174. Whoever maliciously interferes with a general public performance of a religious act of a church or religious body recognized by law shall be punished by imprisonment not to exceed two years.

3. *Decree of June 13, 1946 (excerpts)*

Art. 30. Whoever publicly instigates or advocates national, denominational, or racial quarrels shall be punished by imprisonment not to exceed five years.

Art 31. (1) Whoever publicly abuses, ridicules, or humiliates a group or an individual because of his national, denominational, or racial affiliation shall be punished by imprisonment not to exceed five years.

(2) Whoever maltreats another or inflicts minor bodily injury upon another because of his national, denominational, or racial affiliation, shall be liable to the same punishment.

Art. 32. Whoever commits a crime directed against a group or an individual because of his national, denominational, or racial affiliation shall be punished by imprisonment for not less than three years, by imprisonment for life, or by death if the crime results in death, a serious bodily injury, a breach of the public peace, or a threat of common danger.

Art. 33. Whoever participates in a conspiracy which includes among its objectives the commission of crimes defined in Art. 31, Par. 2, or in Art. 32, or joins a mob which commits such a crime collectively, shall be punished by imprisonment.

Art. 34. Whoever, contrary to his duty, fails to intervene against the commission of crimes defined in Arts. 30-33 shall be punished by imprisonment not to exceed five years or by confinement in custody.

4. *Decree of August 5, 1949, on the*

Protection of Freedom of Conscience and Religion

In accordance with Article 4 of the Constitutional Act of February 19, 1947, concerning the Structure and Jurisdiction of the Supreme Authorities of the Polish Republic and the Act of July 2, 1949, Authorizing the Government to Issue Decrees with Force of Law (*Dz. U.*, 1949, No. 41, Law No. 302) The Council of Ministers has resolved and the People's State Council confirmed, the following:

Art. 1. The Polish Government guarantees freedom of conscience and religion to all citizens.

Art. 2. Whoever infringes upon the rights of a citizen because of his religious denomination, his religious convictions, or because of his lack of religious profession shall be punished by imprisonment not to exceed five years.

Art. 3. Whoever, in any manner, compels another to participate in religious activities or rites or whoever unlawfully prevents another from taking part in them shall be punished by imprisonment not to exceed five years.

Art. 4. Whoever abuses religious freedom by denying another access to a rite or religious ceremony because of his activities or his political, social, or scientific views, shall be punished by imprisonment not to exceed five years.

Art. 5. Whoever offends the religious feelings of others by publicly desecrating an object of religious worship or a place designed for the performance of religious rites shall be punished by imprisonment up to five years.

Art. 6. Whoever publicly foments enmity on religious grounds or sanctions such enmity shall be punished by imprisonment up to five years.

Art. 7. (1) Whoever publicly insults, ridicules, or humiliates a group or an individual because of such group's or individual's religious denomination, religious convictions, or lack of religious profession, shall be punished by imprisonment up to five years or detention.

(2) Whoever commits physical violence against another because of his religious denomination, religious convictions, or lack of religion, shall be punished in a like manner.

(3) Whoever commits any other criminal act directed against a group or an individual because of religious denomination, religious convictions, or lack of religion, shall be punished by imprisonment.

(4) If an act specified in paragraph (3) above results in death, serious bodily injury, disturbance of the normal course of public life, or danger to public safety, then the offender shall be punished by imprisonment for not less than three years, or for life, or by death.

Art. 8. (1) Whoever abuses freedom of conscience and religion to pursue aims hostile to the form of government of the Polish Republic, shall be punished by imprisonment for not less than three years.

(2) Whoever undertakes preparations to commit the criminal act defined under paragraph (1) shall be punished by imprisonment.

Art. 9. Whoever misuses freedom of religion for personal, pecuniary, or other benefit, exploits human credulity by way of spreading false rumors, or misleads other persons by fraudulent or deceitful actions, shall be punished by imprisonment.

Art. 10. Whoever participates in a conspiracy which has for its aim the commission of a crime defined in Articles 3-9, or whoever deliberately joins a crowd which collectively commits such a crime, shall be punished by imprisonment or by confinement in custody.

Art. 11. Whoever, contrary to his duty, fails to intervene in order to prevent the commission of a crime as defined in Article 10, shall be punished by imprisonment not to exceed five years or detention.

Art. 12. Whoever in any manner instigates or encourages the commission of acts defined in Articles 2-11, or recommends or publicly sanctions their commission, shall be punished by imprisonment.

Art. 13. In case of punishment by imprisonment for a crime provided for in this law, the court may decree loss of public and civic rights.

Art. 14. The court of appeals shall have original jurisdiction in criminal matters dealt with in this law.

Art. 15. The provisions of the Criminal Code of 1932 and of the decree of June 13, 1946, concerning Crimes Particularly Dangerous During the Period of National Reconstruction (*Dz. U.* 1946, No. 30, Law No. 192) are abolished insofar as the provisions of this decree regulate the subject matter.

Art. 16. The enforcement of this law is entrusted to the Minister of Justice.

Art. 17. This law shall go into effect on the day of its promulgation.

5. *Agreement Concluded Between the*
Representatives of the Polish Government and of the Roman Catholic Episcopate of Poland

For the purpose of assuring the People's Poland and its citizens the best opportunity for development and peaceful work the Polish Government, which advocates respect for religious freedom, and the Polish episcopate, which is concerned with the welfare of the Church and the interests of the State, agree to regulate their relationship in the following manner:

I.

The episcopate shall urge that the clergy in the course of its pastoral duties and in accordance with the teachings of the Church teach the faithful respect for law and the authorities of the State.

II.

The episcopate shall urge that the clergy in the course of its pastoral duties call upon the faithful to intensify their work for the reconstruction of the country and the advancement of the nation's welfare.

III.

The Polish episcopate states that economic, historic, cultural, and religious reasons and also historic justice demand that the Recovered Territories should belong to Poland forever. Basing itself on the premise that the Recovered Territories form an inseparable part of the Republic, the episcopate shall address a request to the Holy See that those Church administrations now holding the rights of residential bishoprics shall be converted into permanent episcopal dioceses.

IV.

To the extent of its ability, the episcopate shall oppose activities hostile to Poland and particularly the anti-Polish revisionist actions of a part of the German clergy.

V.

The principle that the Pope is the competent and supreme authority of the Church refers to matters of faith, morals, and Church jurisdiction; in other matters, however, the episcopate shall be guided by the interests of the Polish State.

VI.

Basing itself on the premise that the mission of the Church can be fulfilled within various social and economic systems established by the secular authority, the episcopate shall explain to the clergy that it should not oppose the development of cooperatives in rural areas since the cooperative movement is based essentially on that ethical element in human nature directed toward voluntary social solidarity, which has as its goal the welfare of all.

VII.

In accordance with its principles and in condemnation of all acts against the Polish State, the Church shall particularly oppose the misuse of religious feelings for anti-State purposes.

VIII.

The Church, which condemns all crime in accordance with its principles, shall combat the criminal activities of underground bands and shall denounce and punish under canon law those clergymen who are guilty of participation in any underground activities against the Polish State.

IX.

In accordance with the teachings of the Church, the Episcopate shall support every effort toward strengthening peace and oppose to the extent of its ability every attempt to provoke war.

X.

Religious instruction in schools:

A. The Government does not intend to change the present status of religious instruction in schools; the program of religious instruction will be worked out by school authorities, together with representatives of the episcopate; the schools will be supplied with appropriate textbooks; lay and clerical instructors of religion shall be treated on an equal footing with teachers of other subjects; supervisors of religious instruction shall be appointed by the school authorities in consultation with the episcopate.

B. The authorities will not place obstacles in the way of students wishing to participate in religious practices outside the schools.

C. While existing schools which are Catholic in character shall be continued, the Government shall require that these schools carry out instructions loyally and fulfill the program as determined by State authorities.

D. Schools run by the Catholic Church shall enjoy the privileges of State schools in accordance with the general principles defined by the appropriate laws and the regulations of the school authorities.

E. Where a school is established which provides no religious instruction or where a school is transformed into one which does not provide for religious education, those Catholic parents who so desire shall have the right and the opportunity to send their children to schools where religion is taught.

XI.

The Catholic University of Lublin shall be permitted to continue the present scope of its activities.

XII.

Catholic associations shall enjoy the same rights as before after satisfying all requirements provided in the decree concerning associations. The same principle shall apply to the Sodality of St. Mary.

XIII.

The Church shall have the right and the opportunity to conduct its activities in the fields of charity, welfare, and religious education within the framework of existing regulations.

XIV.

The Catholic press and Catholic publications shall enjoy privileges as defined by appropriate laws and the regulations of the authorities on an equal basis with other publications.

XV.

No obstacles shall be placed in the way of public worship, traditional pilgrimages, and processions. In accordance with the requirements for maintaining public order, arrangements for such ceremonies shall be made in consultation between Church and administrative authorities.

XVI.

The status of military chaplains shall be defined by a special regulation to be worked out by military authorities in agreement with representatives of the episcopate.

XVII.

Religious ministrations in penal institutions shall be in the hands of chaplains appointed by appropriate authorities upon recommendation of the diocesan bishop.

XVIII.

In State and community hospitals religious ministration for patients who desire it will be in the hands of hospital chaplains who shall be remunerated through special agreement.

XIX.

Religious orders shall have full freedom of activity within the limits of their calling and within the framework of existing laws.

Signed in Warsaw on April 14, 1950

Wladysław Wolski
Minister of Public Administration

Bishop Zygmunt Choromański
Secretary of the Episcopate

Edward Ochab
Vice-Minister of National Defense

Bishop Tadeusz Zakrzewski
(Płock Diocese)

Franciszek Mazur
Deputy to the Sejm

Bishop Michał Klepacz
(Łódź Diocese)

The Protocol of the joint committee of the representatives of the Roman Catholic episcopate and the Polish Government concerning the concluded agreements reads as follows:

1. In consequence of the settlement reached between the representatives of the Government of the Polish Republic and the Polish episcopate in the matter of Caritas and the desire to normalize the relations between State and Church, the Church organization Caritas will be transformed into an Association of Catholics to bring aid to the poor and needy. The Association shall base its activity on field offices which shall correspond to the administrative and territorial division of the country. The episcopate, in accordance with the charitable aims of the Association, shall facilitate, in conformity with the teachings and practice of the Catholic Church, the activity of the clergy who are willing to work with the Association.

2. The Government of the Republic of Poland, enforcing the statute on nationalization of land owned by the Church according to Art. 2, Par. 3 and Art. 7, Par. 1 of the statute, shall review the needs of Bishops and Church institutions in order to take into account these needs and grant them the necessary assistance.

3. The Church Fund shall place appropriate sums of money at the disposal of bishops in charge of a diocese.

4. In carrying out the statute on military service the military authority will grant deferments to the alumni of theological seminaries to give them the opportunity to complete their studies. Priests after their ordination and monks after taking their vows will not be called to active military service, but shall be attached to the reserves and assigned to auxiliary services.

Signed in Warsaw, April 14, 1950

Władyslaw Wolski
Min. of Public Administration
Edward Ochab
Vice-Min. of National Defense
Franciszek Mazur
Deputy to the Sejm

Bishop Z. Choromański
Secretary of the Episcopate
Bishop T. Zakrzewski
Ordinarius, Diocese of Płock

Rev. Bishop M. Klepacz
Ordinarius, Diocese of Łódź

6. Decree of February 9, 1953, on the Appointment of Clergymen to Ecclesiastical Offices

Art. 1. Only Polish nationals may be appointed to the ecclesiastical office of a clergyman.

Art. 2. The erection, conversion, and suppression of ecclesiastical offices held by clergymen as well as a change in the jurisdiction of these offices shall require the previous consent of competent Government authorities.

Art. 3. (1) Before an ecclesiastical office may be taken over by a clergyman, prior consent of the competent Government authorities must be obtained.

(2) Paragraph 1 shall also apply in cases of release of a clergyman from an ecclesiastical office or transfer to another office.

Art. 4. The following Government bodies shall have the authority to give consent: in matters relating to diocesan ordinaries, the Presidium of the Government shall have the authority; in all other cases the authority shall be vested in the Presidia of the Provincial People's Councils (the People's Councils of the Capital City of Warsaw and the City of Łódź) concerned.

Art. 5. Clergymen holding ecclesiastical offices shall take an oath of allegiance to the Polish People's Republic. This oath shall be administered in the Office for Denominational Affairs, or in the Presidium of the Provincial People's Councils (the People's Councils of the Capital City of Warsaw and the City of Łódź) concerned.

Art. 6. Clergymen holding ecclesiastical offices who act contrary to law and public order, or support and conceal such activities, shall be removed from office, either upon the initiative of the superior church authority, or upon the request of Government authorities.

Art. 7. The Prime Minister shall be entrusted with enforcement of the decree.

Art. 8. The decree shall go into effect on the day of its publication.

Chairman of the People's State Council:
A. Zawadzki
Secretary of the People's State Council:
M. Rybicki

IV. NOTES ON OTHER RELIGIOUS DENOMINATIONS

A. *The Polish Orthodox Church*
(Russian Eastern Orthodox Church in Poland)

The organization of the Orthodox Church in Poland comprises today: a Metropolitan See in Warsaw and 4 bishoprics: Białystok, Łódź, Wrocław, and Gdańsk.

The autocephaly of the Polish Orthodox Church was established at the Synod of Bishops in Warsaw (June 12-14, 1922), when the Orthodox Church in Poland made itself independent from the superior authority of Moscow. This position of the Polish Orthodox Church was recognized by Gregory VII, the Patriarch of Constantinople, by the decree of November 13, 1924. In certain respects this decree also established the dependence of the Church on the Patriarch of Constantinople. The legal status of the Autocephalous Orthodox Church in Poland was afterwards definitely defined by the decree of November 18, 1938.[87] By this decree the Polish Autocephalous Orthodox Church retained—in dogmatical and canonical matters—a full unity with the Universal Eastern Orthodox Church, but was made independent of any spiritual or secular authority outside the country. A statute governing the internal affairs of the Polish Autocephalous Orthodox Church was enacted by the Executive Order of the Council of Ministers on December 10, 1938.[88]

Prior to World War II, the Orthodox Church in Poland was administered by the Metropolitan Dionisius, the head of the Church. He performed his duties until 1948, when the Government no longer recognized him. The duties of the Metropolitan were then taken over by an interim council with Archbishop Timotheus at its head. In June 1948 this council sent a delegation to the Patriarch of Moscow with the following petition:[89]

1. Whereas the Polish Autonomous Orthodox Church declares its autocephalous status of 1924 contrary to canon law and therefore invalid, it asks the blessings of the Russian Mother Church for an ecclesiastical autocephaly.

2. Whereas the Metropolitan Dionisius stubbornly has upheld the previous autocephaly and separated himself from the religious community in Moscow, the Polish Church cannot continue any religious or ecclesiastical relations with him and cannot continue to recognize him as the head of the Church.

3. The Polish Church severs all religious ties with any of the clergy and lay members of the Polish Church, who share the errors of the Metropolitan Dionisius until they expiate for them.

This petition was of course accepted very favorably in Moscow, and the Moscow Patriarch was prompt to announce, on June 22, 1948, that in view of the fact that the Polish Orthodox Church declared the previous autocephaly contrary to canon law, the spiritual union with the Russian Orthodox Church is now revived and the right to full self-government will be granted to the Polish Orthodox Church. Soon afterward the synod of bishops of the Russian Orthodox Church formally bestowed autocephaly upon the Polish sister Church.

The Patriarch of Constantinople, who had been informed of this move, treated it as a mere affirmation by the Russian Orthodox Church of the autocephalous status of the Polish Orthodox Church, and asked that the Metropolitan Dionisius be reinstated in his functions as the head of the Orthodox Church in Poland. In the meantime the Metropolitan Dionisius repented before the Patriarch of Moscow Alexei on August 22, 1948. As a result of this action the Patriarch of Moscow lifted all ecclesiastical interdictions from the Metropolitan Dionisius and restored his ties with the Russian Orthodox Church with the title of Metropolitan *ad personam* but without the right to be addressed as "Most Venerable," which was symbolic of the autonomy of the Polish Autocephalous Orthodox Church. In effect this decision left the Church without a Warsaw Metropolitan.

In 1951 the synod of bishops of the Polish Orthodox Church declared that there is no person in Poland worthy of the high office of Metropolitan and appealed to the Moscow Patriarch to select someone from among the Russian hierarchy to head the Orthodox Church in Poland. On June 15, 1951, the synod of bishops in Moscow granted the request and transferred Makary, the arshbishop of Lwów-Tarnopol, to the Autocephalous Orthodox Church in Poland.

It is noteworthy that the act of the Moscow synod was not only signed by the Russian Patriarch and six other Russian bishops, but also by the Metropolitan of Czechoslovakia and the Bishop of Germany. This indicates that Moscow tends to uphold the authority of the Moscow-dependent Orthodox bishops in Central Europe. It also explains why Moscow decided against outright incorporation of the Polish Orthodox Church into the Russian Church, leaving it only an illusory independence.

B. *Protestant Denominations*

The Protestant denominations in Poland number about 330,000 members, most of whom adhere to the Augsburg-Protestant Church (about 250,000). The Protestants are centered mainly in Warsaw, the region of Mazury, and the Cieszyn part of Silesia. After 1945 the government treated the Protestant denominations quite favorably. However, events which took place during 1951 indicate that the policy of the Government towards the Protestants does not differ from the policy applied to other denominations. It began with the refusal to approve the head of the Augsburg-Protestant Church. After 1945 Jan Szeruda was temporarily in charge of Augsburg Protestant Church affairs, acting in the capacity of a deputy bishop. In 1950 the Church assembly elected Szeruda to the office of bishop. However, the government declined to approve the appointment, asserting that he was not sufficiently 'positive towards the State." As a result of this refusal the Church assembly afterwards elected Pastor Kotula from the Zaolzie region in Cieszyn-Silesia to this office. But the government informed the Augsburg-Protestant Church that it will refrain from approving any candidate to the office of bishop or as head of the Protestant Church in Poland. Thus the Protestant Church remains without its own bishop and administrative head, since under the law regulating the status of the Augsburg-Protestant Church in Poland, an elected candidate must be approved by the President of the Republic.

It should be mentioned that the prewar Statute of 1936 on the relationship between the State and the Augsburg Protestant Church of Poland[90] was amended in 1946[91]. The amendment provided that all Old Lutheran parishes, Protestant-Lutheran parishes belonging to the United Evangelical Church in Upper Silesia, and all Protestant parishes of the Augsburg and Helvetic Confession, were included in the Augsburg Protestant Church of Poland. The Augsburg-Protestant Church of Poland comprised parishes of the Augsburg-Protestant Church and the Lutheran (Old Lutheran) Confessions which were then in existence wherever situated within Poland. This Church also included the Moravian Brothers, the so-called Herrnhutters. A later statute of 1947[92] repealed all provisions which relate to matters regulated by it. According to the 1947 statute, the Augsburg-Protestant Church of Poland consists of the Augsburg-Protestant parishes in existence throughout Poland. This Church also comprises Lutheran and Augsburg parishes (Congregations, Protestant Churches) which belonged to the United Evangelical Churches and also to the Old Lutheran and Protestant Church of the Augsburg and Helvetic Confessions; it also includes the Moravian Brothers (Herrnhutters).

C. *The Old Catholic Church and the Polish National Church*

The Old Catholic Church and the Polish National Church had such small congregations of followers that they played a minor role. Prior to 1945 the Old Catholic Church was recognized only in certain parts of Poland. In 1945 it received general recognition throughout all of Poland, as stated before. The Polish National Church on the other hand received no recognition whatsoever at any time in Poland. In 1947, by executive orders[93] of the Minister of Public Administration, records kept up to January 1, 1946 by clergymen of the Old Catholic Church and the Polish National Church for the purpose of showing births, marriages, and deaths, were officially recognized for the first time as legal proof.

D. *Jewish Denominational Group*

No special legislation was enacted regarding the status of the Jewish religion. Thus it comes under the new legislation dealing with churches and religion. Since this legislation does not cover all problems, it seems that prewar provisions remain in force insofar as they were not repealed by new legislation.

There are about 40,000 Jews in Poland today, who are located chiefly in the cities of Łódź, Warsaw, Wrocław and Wałbrzych. The Jewish denominational communities have been restricted in their activity to purely religious work. All Jewish denominational schools have been closed, and only in larger Jewish centers are pupils allowed to attend extracurricular instruction in Yiddish. Jewish religious holidays are not acknowledged.

NOTES

1. *Dz. U.* 1944, No. 1, Law No. 1.
2. *Dz. U.* 1947, No. 18, Law No. 71.
3. *Review of Polish Law,* Year 2, No. 1, 1948.
4. *Dz. U.* 1925, No. 72, Law No. 501.
5. *Information on Poland,* published by the Ministry of Foreign Affairs Press and Information Department, in English, Warsaw 1949.
6. This opinion was published in the legal periodical *Demokratyczny Przeglad Prawniczy,* (Democratic Law Review), No. 1, Year 1, November 1945, a publication of the Ministry of Justice.
7. *Panstwo i Prawo* (State and Law), No. 1, January 19, 1948. Monthly review published by the Polish Lawyers Association, Warsaw.
8. Halecki, Oscar. *"Eugenio Pacelli, Pope of Peace",* New York, 1951.
9. Bishop of Danzig Splett was indicted under the Decree of the Polish Committee for National Liberation of August 31, 1944 (amended by Decree of February 16, 1945) on the Punishment of Fascist-Hitlerite Criminals for Manslaughter and Ill-treatment of Civilians and Prisoners and of Traitors to the Polish Nation (*Dz. U.* 1944, No. 4, Law No. 16 and *Dz. U.* 1945, No. 7, Law No. 29). The trial took place in Gdansk from January 28 to February 1, 1946, before the Special Criminal Court. The Bishop was sentenced to 8 years' imprisonment. (*vide* "The Case of Splett in the Light of the Canon Law" in *Demokratyczny Przegląd Prawniczy,* No. 3-4, March-April 1946).
10. *Dz. U.* 1925, No. 72, Law No. 501.
11. Woywod, Stanislaus and Smith, Callistus. *A Practical Commentary on the Code of Canon Law,* New York, 1948 vol. I, p. 1.
12. *Dz. U.* 1918, No. 1, Law No. 1.
13. *Dz. U.* 1950, No. 14, Law No. 130, No. 19, Law No. 156.
14. *Dz. U.* 1945, No. 46, Law No. 259.
15. *Dz. U.* 1947, No. 59, Law No. 316.
16. Jaroslaw Demianczuk, Director of the Department for Denominational Affairs. "Unification of Polish Legislation concerning Religion", in *Państwo i Prawo* (State and Law) No. 5/6 May-June, 1948.
17. In the Kingdom of Poland marriages between Orthodox Jews or Mohammedans had to be registered with the official who kept the records of vital statistics, after the religious celebration of marriage. The validity or dissolution of a marriage was subject to the jurisdiction of civil courts, which applied the law of the religion concerned.
18. *Dz. U.* 1945, No. 48, Law No. 270.
19. *Dz. U.* 1945, No. 48, Law No 271.
20. The Decree of September 25, 1945, on the enactment of marriage law also repealed pertinent provisions of: the Executive Order of April 5, 1928 concerning Jewish congregations in Poland except those in the province of Silesia (*Dz. U.* 1928, No. 52, Law No. 500); the Statute of April 21, 1936, concerning the Relationship between the State and the Moslem Religious Association in Poland (*Dz. U.* 1936, No. 30, Law No. 240); the Statute of April 21, 1936, on the Relationship between the State and the Karaism Religious Association in Poland (*Dz. U.* 1936, No. 30, Law No. 241); the Decree of November 25, 1936, on the Relationship between the State and the Augsburg-Protestant Church in Poland (*Dz. U.* 1936, No. 88, Law No. 613); the Decree of November 18, 1938, on the Relationship between the State and the Polish Autocephalous Orthodox Church (*Dz. U.* 1938, No. 88, Law No. 597).
21. *Dz. U.* 1945, No. 48, Law No 272.

22. *Dz. U.* 1945, No. 48, Law No. 273.

23. The Decree of September 25, 1945, on the Enactment of the Law on Records of Vital Statistics also repealed provisions of: the Executive Order of the President of the Republic of March 22, 1928, Concerning the Relationship between the State and the Eastern Church of the Old Rite, which did not possess a clerical hierarchy (*Dz. U.* 1928, No. 38, Law No. 363); the Statute of April 21, 1936, on the Relationship between the State and the Moslem Religious Association in Poland (*Dz. U.* 1936, No. 30, Law No. 240); the Statute of April 21, 1936, on the Relationship between the State and the Karaism Religious Association in Poland (*Dz. U.* 1936, No. 30, Law No. 241); the Decree of November 25, 1936, on the Relationship between the State and the Augsburg-Protestant Church in Poland (*Dz. U.* 1936, No. 88, Law No. 613); the Decree of November 18, 1938, on the Relationship between the State and the Polish Autocephalous Orthodox Church (*Dz. U.* 1938, No. 88, Law No. 597).

24. *Dz. U.* 1950, No. 34, Law No. 308.

25. *Dz. U.* 1950, No. 34, Law No. 309.

26. *Dz. U.* 1945, No. 3, Law No. 13.

27. Statute of March 20, 1950, providing for the transfer to Government ownership of land held by religious associations; for a guarantee to parish priests of the right to possession of lands farmed by them; for the establishment of a Church Fund (*Dz. U.* 1950, No. 9, Law No. 87).

28. *Monitor Polski* "A" 1949, Reg. No. 884, 885.

29. *Monitor Polski* "A" 1952, Reg. No. 421, 1322, 1377.

30. *Dz. U.* 1949, No. 40, Law No. 292.

31. The Executive Order of the Minister of Finance of July 5, 1949, was upheld by the Executive Order of the Minister of Finance of November 26, 1952 (*Dz. U.* 1953, No. 3, Law No. 5) concerning the keeping of special books by those taxpayers not subject to taxation according to the principles applied to the sector of the economic life which has not been socialized.

32. *Dz. U.* 1927, No. 1, Law No. 9.

33. *Dz. Urz. Min. Ośw.*, 1945, No. 4, Reg. No. 189.

34. *Demokratyczny Przegląd Prawniczy*, No. 1, Year 1, November 1945.

35. *Dz. U.* 1949, No. 45, Law No. 334.

36. *Dz. U.* 1946, No. 30, Law No. 192.

37. Review of Polish Law, Year IV, No. 1 and 2, 1950.

38. If the penal clause of a statute indicates the lowest bracket of a penalty, then under the general rule of the Criminal Code (art. 39) the highest permissible term of the particular form of punishment may be imposed by the court in its discretion. Thus, this provision allows the court to impose imprisonment up to 15 years.

39. *Trybuna Ludu* and others.

40. *ibidem*.

41. Order of January 23, 1950, *Monitor Polski*, 1950, Reg. No. 112.

42. Inter-Catholic Press Agency, New York, 1950, No. 15.

43. *Slowo Powszechne*, No. 1, January 1952.

44. Inter-Catholic Press Agency, New York, 1950, No. 12—also *Dziennik Polski*, London, and *L'Osservatore Romano*.

45. *Poland Today*, Publication of the Polish Research and Information Service (Polish Government Agency), New York, April 1950.

46. *Dz. U.* 1950, No. 9, Law No. 87.

47. Art. 20 of the Decree of June 13, 1946 on Criminal Acts Particularly Dangerous During the Period of National Reconstruction (*Dz. U.* 1946, No. 30, Law No. 192) provides: "Whoever frustrates or obstructs the enforcement of land reform or instigates to acts directed against its enforcement, or publicly recommends such acts, shall be punished by imprisonment."

48. Decree of April 24, 1952 on the abolition of foundations (*Dz. U.* 1952, No. 25, Law No. 172).

49. Inter-Catholic Press Agency, New York 1950, No. 15.

50. *Eugenio Pacelli, Pope of Peace*, New York, 1951. Chapter 13.: "Church

Behind the Iron Curtain."

51. *Poland, Documents and Reports,* publication of the Polish Research and Information Service (Polish Government Agency), New York, May 1950, No. 7.

52. Catholic Press Agency Inc. N.Y., October 7, 1953, and was copied from that by Catholic newspapers throughout the world. Among others it appeared in the *L'Osservatore Romano* and in the news-organ of the National Welfare Conference of American Bishops in Washington.

53. *Religious News Service,* February 19, 1951.

54. *Przewodnik Bibliograficzny,* Warsaw, 1947-1953, *passim.*

55. *Dz. U.* 1950, No. 36, Law No. 328.

56. *Dz. U.* 1952, No. 46, Law No. 310.

57. *Dz. U.* 1944, No. 3, Law No. 13.

58. *Dz. U.* 1947, No. 52, Law No. 267.

59. *Dz. U.* 1950, No. 43, Law No. 394.

60. *Dz. U.* 1950, No. 40, Law No. 364.

61. *Dz. U.* 1944, No. 18, Law No. 94.

62. Decree of October 6, 1948, on the Formula of the Oath for Ministers, Government Officials, Judges, Public Prosecutors, and Officials of Public Security. *Dz. U.* 1948, No. 49, Law No. 370.

63. Agreement signed at Zgorzelec, July 6, 1950, and ratified by the Statute of October 28, 1950 (*Dz. U.* 1950, No. 51, Law No. 465—*Dz. U.* 1951, No. 14, Law No. 106, 107.)

64. Canon 366 of the Code of Canon Law provides that whenever the proper government of the diocese demands it, the bishop should appoint a vicar-general, who shall enjoy ordinary jurisdiction in the entire diocese. The vicar-general's appointment is left to the free choice of the bishop, who can also remove him at will.

65. Revisionist is the name for a German movement aiming at the restoration of the boundaries of Germany, which existed before World War I.

66. *Poland Today,* March 951, No. 3.

67. The office of a chapter of canons, of diocesan consulters, and capitular vicars is explained in Woywod, Stanislaus, *A Practical Commentary on the Code of Canon Law* (rev. and enl. ed., New York: Joseph F. Wagner, Inc., 1948) as follows:

p. 158: A Chapter of Canons of a Cathedral is a body of clerics instituted for the purpose of rendering the service of God more solemn and has the additional purpose of assisting the Bishop as his senate and council according to rules of Canon Law, and to administer the diocese during a vacancy.

The creation, reestablishment and suppression of Cathedral Chapters is reserved to the Apostolic See (Canon 392).

p. 173: In those dioceses in which it has not yet been possible to institute or to revive former Cathedral Chapters of Canons, the Bishop shall appoint diocesan consulters. The group of diocesan consulters is established by the Bishop to supply the place and role of the Chapter of Canons, for ordinarily according to Canon 423 the administration of a diocese calls for the establishment in the Cathedral Church of a Chapter of Canons, who assist the Bishop in governing and administering the diocese. It is only by way of exception that a board of diocesan consultors may supply the place of the Cathedral Chapter.

p. 174: The body of diocesan consultors takes the place of the Cathedral Chapter as the Council of the Bishop. Therefore, whatever part in the government of the diocese the Canons give the Cathedral Chapter during the reign of the Bishop, during the time that the exercise of his jurisdiction is impeded, or during the vacancy of the bishopric, is also assigned to the body of consultors (Canon 427).

p. 176: If the Bishop is in captivity, or banished, exiled or otherwise inhabilitated, so that he cannot even by letter communicate with the people of his diocese, the government of the diocese shall rest with the Vicar General or another priest delegated by the bishop, unless the Holy See has made other provisions. The bishop may in such circumstances for grave reasons delegate several persons who are to succeed each other in turn. If all of them fail or are impeded in any of the ways described above, the Cathedral Chapter—or the diocesan consultors where there is no Chapter—shall elect a Vicar who shall assume the government with the powers of a Capitular Vicar. Those called upon to take the government of the diocese in such circumstances shall as soon as possible inform the Holy See of the state of affairs and of their having assumed the government (Canon 429).

68. *Slowo Powszechne,* April 1, 1952.

69. *Tygodnik Powszechny,* December 16, 1951.

70. On November 26, 1952, a Warsaw radio communique announced that on November 25, 1952, the Cathedral Chapter of Canons in Katowice elected as Capitular Vicar the Rev. Filip Bednorz. He is Chairman of the District Board of Priests in Katowice and Vice-Chairman of the Central Committee of Priests attached to the so-called Union of Fighters for Freedom and Democracy.

71. *See* Decree of June 13, 1946 on Criminal Acts Particularly Dangerous During the Period of National Reconstruction and Art. 85-88 of the Military Criminal Code of September 23, 1944 (*Dz. U.* 1946, No. 6, Law No. 27).

72. The Official Polish Press Agency [PAP] reported on December 13, 1952 that Bishop Franciszek Jop had been elected Capitular Vicar of Cracow. The number of Capitular Vicars has increased steadily and now totals eight: five in the Western Territories, and one in Katowice, Kielce, and Cracow.

73. Also referred to as a "Committee of Intellectuals and Catholic Activists." This Committee is a branch of the Union and consists of a regime sponsored faction of "patriotic priests".

74. The Official Polish Press Agency [PAP], Warsaw, February 3, 1953.

75. Published on February 10, 1953 (*Dz. U.* 1953, No. 10, Law No. 32).

76. *Monitor Polski* "A" 1953, No. A-43, Reg. No. 522.

77. April 15, 1953—*PAP* Agency.

78. *Życie Warszawy,* May 5, 1953.—editorial: "Abuse of Religion and Church Authority."

79. *Trybuna Ludu,* May 6, 1953, June 17, 1953, a series of articles attacking the Vatican and the Episcopate.

80. Warsaw, July 1, 1953.—*PAP* report; the so-called "National Conferences of Catholic lay activists and clergy" were also reported held during the earlier part of the year and appear to have become a frequent propaganda outlet for his anti-church policies.

81. *PAP*—editorial reports with quotations on meetings held in Warsaw, Opole, Olsztyn, Bydgoszcz, Wrocław, Gdańsk, Lublin.

82. *PAP*—July 23, 1953.

83. *PAP,* September 28, 1953.

84. *ibidem.*

85. *ibidem.*

86. *L'Osservatore Romano,* December 19, 1953, as quoted in *New York Times,* December 20, 1953, p. 2, col. 2, in article: "Poles' Oath Held Invalid By Vatican"— "L'Osservatore Asks Bishops' Pledge to Regime Be Judged as a Coerced Action."

87. *Dz. U.* 1938, No. 88, Law No. 597.

88. Executive Order of the Council of Ministers of December 10, 1938, containing the Statute for the Internal Government of the Polish Autocephalous Orthodox Church—*Dz. U.* 1938, No. 103, Law No. 679.

89. *Report on Poland (Wiadomości z Polski i o Polsce),* published by the Research and Publication Service, Polish R.I.C., National Committee for a Free Europe, Inc., New York, 1952.

90. *Dz. U.* 1936, No. 88, Law No. 613.

91. *Dz. U.* 1946, No. 54, Law No. 304.

92. *Dz. U.* 1947, No. 52, Law No. 272.

93. Executive Order of the Minister of Public Administration of May 13, 1947, on Making Acceptable as Legal Proof Records Kept by Clergymen of the Polish National Church and the Old Catholic Church for the Purpose of Showing Births, Marriages, and Deaths. *Dz. U.* 1947, No. 41, Law No. 203, 204.

TABLE OF STATUTES

BIBLIOGRAPHY

I. Journal of Laws and Official Gazettes

1. *Dziennik Ustaw Polskiej Rzeczypospolitej Ludowej* (Journal of Laws of the Polish People's Republic), formerly entitled *Dziennik Ustaw Rzeczypospolitej Polskiej* (Journal of Laws of the Republic of Poland).

2. *Monitor Polski-Dziennik Urzędowy Polskiej Rzeczypospolitej Ludowej* (Official Gazette of the Polish People's Republic), formerly entitled *Monitor Polski—Dziennik Urzędowy Rzeczypospolitej Polskiej* (Official Gazette of the Republic of Poland).

3. *Dziennik Urzędowy Ministerstwa Oświaty* (Official Gazette of the Ministry of Education).

II. Articles in Polish legal periodicals

1. Demianczuk-Jurkiewicz. "Unifikacja polskiego prawa wyznaniowego," in *Państwo i Prawo* (State and Law), [miesięcznik, Organ Zrzeszenia Prawników Demokratów w Polsce. Warsaw-Lodź], (May/June, 1948), Year II, No. 5/6.

2. "Dwie Opinie Prawne z Dziedziny Stosunków Kościola i Państwa," in *Demokratyczny Przegląd Prawniczy* (The Democratic Law Review), Centralne Czasopismo Prawnicze Poswięcone Praktyce i Wykladni Prawa oraz Slużbie Wymiaru Sprawiedliwości. Warszawa: November 1945. Year I, No. 1.

3. "Freedom of Conscience and Confession," in the *Review of Polish Law,* published by the Ministry of Justice, Foreign Relations Department. Warsaw. Year IV, Nos. 1 and 2.

4. Grzybowski, Konstanty. "Uwagi o stosunku państwa do Kościola," in *Państwo i Prawo* (April, 1952). Year VII, No. 4.

5. Piotrowski, Stanislaw. "Konkordat zawarty ze Stolica Apostolską z 1925 roku przestal obowiazywać jako wewnętrzna ustawa Krajowa," in *Państwo i Prawo* (December 1947), Year II, No. 12.

6. Rozmaryn, Stefan. "W jakim zakresie obowiazuje dziś Konstytucja z 17 marca 1921 r." *Państwo i Prawo,* (January 1948), Year II, No. 1.

7. Wilanowski, Boleslaw. "Sprawa Spletta" in *Państwo i Prawo,* (March/April 1946), Year II, No. 3-4.

III. Books and Documents

1. Cianfarra, Camille M. *The Vatican and the Kremlin,* New York, 1950.

2. Grabowski, Ignacy. *Prawo Kanoniczne* (Canon Law), Warsaw, 1948.

3. "Information on Poland," published by the Ministry of Foreign Affairs, Press and Information Department. Warsaw, 1949.

4. "In Quest of Peace and Security"—(VII & VIII, Poland) *Selected Documents on American Foreign Policy, 1941-1951,* Dept. of State Publication 4245, released October 1951.

5. Halecki, Oscar. *Eugenio Pacelli: Pope of Peace.* New York, 1951.

6. Komarnicki, Waclaw. *Ustrój Państwowy Polski Współczesnej* (The System of Government in Present-day Poland), Wilno, 1937.

7. Kumaniecki, Kazimierz. *Ustrój Polityczny Polski.* (The Political System of Poland), Kraków, 1937.

8. Kuśnierz, Bronislaw. *Stalin and the Poles.* London, 1949.

9. Markham, Reuben H. *Communists Crush Churches in Eastern Europe.* Boston, 1950.

10. Vyshinsky, Andrei Y. *The Law of the Soviet State.* New York, 1948.

11. Woywood, Stanislaus, and Smith, Callistus. *A Practical Commentary on the Code of Canon Law.* Revised and enlarged edition. New York, 1948.

IV. Periodicals

1. *The Clergy Review.* London. May-June 1950, July 1950, December 1950.

2. *The Contemporary Review.* No. 1019, November 1950, *"Church and State in Poland"* by Cyryl Boldirev, London.

3. *Dziennik Polski.* (The Polish Daily), London, March 1 and 23, April 1, 1950.

4. *Glos Robotniczy.* (The *Voice of Labor),* Warsaw, October 23, 1951.

5. *Inter-Catholic Press Agency,* Nos. 12-15. New York, 1950, Oct. 7, 1953.

6. *New York Times.* New York, March 24, 1953.

7. *L'Osservatore Romano.* Vatican, 1950.

8. *Poland Today,* monthly, published by the Polish Research and Information Service Agency of the Polish Government. New York, April 1950, March 1951.

9. *Religious News Service.* New York, February 18, 1951.

10. *Rocznik Polityczny i Gospodarczy* (The Political and Economic Yearbook) *Czytelnik.* Łódź, 1948.

11. *Słowo Powszechne* (The Popular Word) Warsaw, January 27, 1951, April 1, 1952, June 3, 1952, November 8 and 9, 1952.

12. *Trybuna Ludu* (The People's Tribune) Warsaw, March 21, 1950, November 26, 1950, December 18, 1951, January 25, 1951, September 27, 1951, November 12, 1952, December 8, 1952, January 18, 1953, May 6-June 17, 1953, September 27, 953.

13. *Tygodnik Powszechny* (The Popular Weekly), Kraków, April and May 1950, February and December 1951.

14. *Wiadomości z Polski i o Polsce.* Report on Poland, published by the *Research and Publication Service, Polish R.I.C.,* National Committee for a Free Europe, Inc., New York, 1951-52.

15. *The Year Book of World Affairs, 1952,* "Church and State in Eastern Europe" by B. G. Ivanyi, (Collection of Documents), New York, 1952.

16. *Zbiór Domumentów/pod redakcją Juliana Makowskiego.* Warsaw, Issues Nos. 3/4, November 1945; Nos. 9/12, September 1946; Nos. 12/15, December 1946; Nos. 4/19, April 1947.

17. *Życie Warszawy* (Life of Warsaw), Warsaw, October 9, 1951, May 5, 1953.

Dr. George Rosu, Mircea Vasiliu and George Crisan

CHURCH AND STATE IN ROMANIA

Vladimir Gsovski, *editor*

CHURCH AND STATE IN ROMANIA

by Dr. George Rosu, Mircea Vasiliu and George Crisan

ABBREVIATIONS

M.O.—*Monitorul Oficial* (Official Gazette)

B.O.—*Buletinul Oficial* (Official Bulletin)

Note: The name of the *Monitorul Oficial* was changed to the *Buletinul Oficial,* beginning with the March 1, 1949 issue.

I. THE CHURCH IN ROMANIA PRIOR TO 1919

Available evidence indicates that Christianity was well established on the territory of present-day Romania in the second century. The region designated as Dacia, a province of the Roman Empire, had, between 106 A.D. and the end of the third century, an organized Church with an established hierarchy. A bishop of "Gothic Dacia," the name of this region after the withdrawal of the Roman legions, took part in the First Ecumenical Council at Nicaea in 325 A.D. Likewise, a Gothic Dacian bishop is mentioned among those present at the Second Ecumenical Council of Constantinople, 381 A.D. We do not possess any particular information concerning Christianity in this region for the period from the fifth until the thirteenth century. This was the time of barbarian invasions, which destroyed organized social life and forced the great majority of the population to seek refuge in the mountains.

The information available for the beginning of the thirteenth century shows the Church of Gothic Dacia as being part of the Eastern Orthodox Church. From that time until the second half of the nineteenth century the Romanian Eastern Orthodox Church was under the Ecumenical Patriarchate of Constantinople. This applies not only to canonical and dogmatic matters but also to the appointment of high dignitaries of the Church. The Romanian Church became independent from the Patriarchate only as a result of a long and complex process, which began when an independent Romanian State came into being in 1859 under the name of the United Romanian Principalities. The first constitution of the Kingdom of Romania of 1866 stated (Article 21) that "the Romanian Orthodox Church is independent." But recognition of its independence (autocephalous status) was not granted by the Patriarchate of Constantinople until 1885. Nevertheless, the Romanian Church has continued to maintain its unity with the Ecumenical Church of the East. This relation was, however, confined to purely religious matters. The Romanian Church considered it to be its duty whenever necessary to consult the Constantinople Patriarchate on questions of dogmas, canons, and cults.

The independence of the Romanian Church was a consequence of the political independence of the Romanian State.

The Romanian clergy took part in the governmental administration and in political life. Clergymen could be elected to the parliament and seats were reserved to them in some important governmental bodies. This was a continuation of an established tradition. In the past the representatives of the clergy had customarily been counselors of the *domnitor* (ruler) and members of the *sfatul tarii* (national assembly).

In general, since the establishment of the United Principalities in 1859 the Romanian Orthodox Church has been considered the predominant Church and has enjoyed a privileged position over all other denominations in the country. This situation continued in the Kingdom of Romania formed after 1866 (hereinafter called the Old Kingdom in contrast to the Romania which emerged after 1919). Nevertheless, the practice of religion by other denominations was unrestricted. The Romanian Orthodox Church did not consider itself universal, was not animated by a strong missionary spirit, and was rather passive and tolerant toward other creeds and cults. For this reason and because of the small number of persons professing other religions in the Kingdom of Romania, the situation did not call for any special legislation to regulate freedom of religion prior to World War I.

II. CHURCHES IN ROMANIA FROM WORLD WAR I TO THE END OF WORLD WAR II

A. *General Regime of Churches*

The Kingdom of Romania emerged from World War I with an enlarged territory. The newly integrated provinces had hitherto been governed by different laws. Hungarian law prevailed in the Banat and Maramuresh with some special provisions in force also in Transylvania; Austrian law was in force in Bukovina; and Russian law with some special local rules was in force in Bessarabia.

The population of the newly integrated provinces was predominantly Romanian of the Eastern Orthodox Church. Besides, there were other ethnic groups and a variety of Churches and sects.

Important segments of the population of Transylvania and the Banat, for instance, belonged to the Roman Catholic (Uniate) or Protestant Churches. Similarly, the population of Bukovina and Maramuresh professed principally the Orthodox and the Catholic (Uniate) faiths. There also existed a considerable Jewish minority. In addition to the Eastern Orthodox faith, there was in Bessarabia a conglomerate of creeds and cults, many of which originated in the seventeenth century and during subsequent reforms of the Russian Orthodox Church.

A new constitution was adopted in 1923, which proclaimed the principles of freedom of religion with the stipulation that they were to be subsequently developed in detail and enforced by special laws. This did not take place immediately. The Romanian Government gave priority to the unification and hierarchic reorganization of the Romanian Orthodox Church, which was effected in 1925 (see *infra*).

This step, in turn, made it necessary to define the status of

Religious affiliation according to the 1930 census

In percent

Distribution according to Provinces

	Total figures for population	Eastern Orthodox	Greek—Catholic	Roman Catholic	Reformed Calvinist	Evangelic Lutheran	Unitarian	Armeno—Gregorian	Armeno—Catholic	Lipovan or Old Rite	Adventist	Baptist	Jewish	Moslem	Other relig.	No religious affiliation	Not declared
Romania	18,057,028	72.6	7.9	6.8	3.9	2.2	0.4	*	*	0.3	*	0.3	4.2	1.0	*	*	*
Provinces:																	
Oltenia	1,513,175	99.0	*	0.4	*	*	*	*	*	*	*	*	0.2	*	*	*	*
Muntenia	4,029,008	94.8	0.4	1.3	0.3	0.4	*	*	*	*	0.1	*	2.3	*	*	*	*
Dobrudja	815,475	72.3	0.1	0.9	0.1	0.9	*	0.5	*	2.2	*	0.2	0.5	22.1	*	*	*
Moldavia	2,433,596	88.2	*	4.5	*	0.1	*	*	*	0.1	*	*	6.7	*	*	*	*
Bessarabia	2,864,402	87.6	*	0.5	*	2.6	*	*	*	1.1	*	0.7	7.2	*	0.1	*	*
Bukovina	853,009	71.9	2.3	11.5	*	2.4	*	*	*	0.4	0.1	0.1	10.9	*	*	0.1	*
Transylvania	3,217,988	27.8	31.1	12.8	15.5	7.6	2.1	*	*	—	*	0.3	2.5	*	*	*	*
Banat	939,958	51.6	3.6	34.2	2.2	1.5	*	*	—	*	*	0.7	1.5	*	*	*	*
Crisana & Maramuresh	1,390,417	36.8	25.2	15.3	12.8	1.1	*	*	*	*	0.1	1.5	7.0	*	*	*	*

* under 0.1 per cent

(From *Anuarul Statistic al Romaniei 1939 si 1940*—Romanian Yearly Statistics 1939 and 1940, pages 70-75)

the other denominations within the Romanian State and to clarify their relations with higher Church authorities having their seat abroad. This was accomplished by Law No. 54 on the General Regulation of Religious Denominations, enacted on April 22, 1928.

The State guaranteed equal freedom and protection to all denominations, provided that their practices did not endanger public order and were not contrary to law or morals. (This provision was repealed by Law No. 431 of 1943.) Any disturbance of the free practice of any religion was declared subject to punishment under the penal code. (This provision was later included in the Penal Code of March 18, 1936, which in Articles 308 to 312 provided severe penalties for those impeding the free practice of religious creeds recognized by the law.)

Other provisions of Law No. 54 of 1928 may be summarized as follows:

A person's religious belief does not prevent him from acquiring and exercising civil and political rights, nor does it relieve anyone from the obligations imposed upon him by law. National statutory law takes precedence over canon law. Political organizations of a sectarian nature are forbidden. No Church is allowed to entertain relations of dependency with any foreign Church authority or organization except relations imposed by the dogmatic and canonical principles of the Church. The jurisdiction of the national religious authorities does not extend beyond the frontiers of the country and, vice versa, no foreign Church may have jurisdictional powers over any denomination in Romania. Moreover, the Romanian Government was to be notified of any material support granted and accepted from abroad.

Clergymen, the heads of the religious organizations, and their officers must be Romanian citizens or they must apply for naturalization. A foreign citizen may be admitted only by special authorization; he must always be admitted when there is proof that the existence and the functioning of a religious community would otherwise be imperiled.

The heads of all religious denominations and their clergymen enjoy the same privilege as the Orthodox Church, namely, they must be tried for common and political offenses by the Romanian Supreme Court, not by ordinary courts. However, disciplinary cases in church matters shall be tried by their own synods.

The historical Churches *(infra)* are legal entities. The religious denominations administer their assets freely and establish and manage as many charitable and educational institutions as they wish or need. The same is true of divinity schools, which, however, must submit their curricula to the Ministry of Religious Affairs. Each Church has the right to give religious instruction to the youth of its denomination in either public or private schools as well as to men on active service in the armed forces.

The keeping of civil status records, which in some localities had been in the hands of the clergy, was assigned to civil authorities and thereby became uniformly regulated throughout Romania.

By the provisions of Law No. 54 of 1928, and its amendments (see *infra),* a general regime was established for the religious denominations. However, from the point of view of status the denominations were divided into several groups as follows:

1. National Churches. This term was applied to the Romanian Orthodox Church and the Greek Catholic (Uniate) Church.

2. Roman Catholic Church. It had its own status defined by the Concordat with the Holy See of 1927, which was also applied to the Uniate Church.

3. Historical but not national Churches: Calvinist, Evangelic Lutheran, Unitarian, Armenian-Gregorian, Jewish, and Mohammedan.

4. The so-called "religious associations," also called "minor denominations." This term was applied to a variety of sects. After 1933 this group was divided into two categories:

(a) those which acquired the status of a legal entity under the Law on Non-profit Corporations and which were officially recognized and allowed to function; and

(b) those which were considered dangerous to public order and morality and were therefore prohibited.

Law No. 54 of 1928 was applied to the Romanian Orthodox Church only insofar as its provisions were not contrary to the

Organic Law of this Church enacted in 1925 *(infra)*. Law No. 54 of 1928 also reserved the regulation of the status of the Roman Catholic Church (including the Uniate Church) to the Concordat, agreed upon in 1927 and ratified in 1929.

The Jewish religion had no central organization at the time Law No. 54 of 1928 was enacted. Thus the law postponed regulation of its status until such a central organization had been formed. This took place in 1930. The primary purpose of this organization was to obtain representation in the senate, inasmuch as the law provided that each national and historical Church should have such representation.

With these exceptions, Law No. 54 of 1928 was applicable to the Churches enumerated above under the category of historical Churches. It left open the possibility of recognition of other, or new, religious denominations, provided that they complied with the provisions of Law No. 54 of 1928 and, further, that their tenets and practices were not contrary to public order, the constitution, or to law and morals.

In principle the Government retained the right of supervision and control over all denominations. Their heads, whether elected or appointed, had to be confirmed by the king and take an oath of allegiance to him and to the constitution.

In addition to their own revenues the Churches were entitled to collect contributions from their parishioners to cover the expenses of maintenance. The State could supply the amounts required for specified needs; in this case it reserved the right to verify that these funds were lawfully used.

Articles 43 and 44 provided that, since the constitution guaranteed freedom of religion and conscience to all citizens, every individual had the right to belong to any religious denomination or to change his religion after he reached the age of eighteen years.

Law No. 54 of 1928 was amended several times before the end of World War II. The first amendment was occasioned by the fact that some sects carried on propaganda considered to affect public order. Thus by Decree No. 2752 of August 3, 1929, the Government introduced more severe penalties for clergymen who induced their congregations to disobey the laws of the country. The decree further granted power to authorities to withdraw recognition from a religious association for the same reasons.

These propaganda activities also induced the Government to provide a different treatment of the religious associations not classified as historical in Law No. 54 of 1928. Order *(Decisiune)* No. 114,119 of 1933 of the Ministry of Religious Affairs distinguished between authorized religious associations and those forbidden on the grounds of being dangerous to public order. The list of the latter was later expanded or reduced according to the evolution of the political concept of "public order." During World War II, for instance, several sects of the Russian Orthodox Church were forbidden because they had become tools of Soviet propaganda.

The second amendment was made by Decree No. 3286 of October 2, 1940, promulgated by Marshal Antonescu. By this act all religious orders and congregations not duly permitted to function at the time of the enactment of Law No. 54 of 1928 were banned. The primary purpose of these provisions was to outlaw the Jewish religion because the provisions of Law No. 54 of 1928 could be interpreted as not giving it a definite status. In addition, this act restated the requirement of Romanian citizenship for clergymen of all denominations and set a certain time limit within which the clergymen had either to comply with this requirement or leave the country. Finally, all religious associations became subject to registration with the Ministry of Religious Affairs, which had the right to refuse the registration of any one of these bodies.

A further amendment by Decree-Law No. 711 of March 21, 1941, forbade the admission of persons of Jewish faith to other denominations.

Law No. 927 of December 30, 1942, changed the procedure for the establishment of religious associations as provided for in Article 24 of Law No. 54 of 1928. An order of the Government was required for their establishment. No reasons had to be given in cases where the Cabinet decided to revoke an authorization previously granted.

Finally, the fight against sects (suspected of spying for the enemy) reached its climax in Law No. 431 of July 9, 1943, which forbade the practice of religions other than the "historical denominations" specified in Law No. 54 of 1928. The Government was empowered to suppress, by order of the Cabinet, the spreading of specific sectarian cults and to expropriate their assets.

The status of religious groups other than the Romanian Orthodox Church and the Roman Catholic Church acquired special significance after World War II. The historical background of these denominations is treated in Chapter F.

B. *Organization of the Romanian Orthodox Church*

After World War I the unification and reorganization of the Romanian Orthodox Church became a stringent necessity mainly because in addition to the Romanian Orthodox Church of the Old Kingdom there were several Orthodox Churches within the new frontiers governed by various hierarchical authorities. This reorganization was accomplished by Law No. 1402 of May 6, 1925. The law also stated that the Romanian Orthodox Church, being the Church of the majority of the Romanian people (72.6 percent, according to the 1920 census available at that time), should be regarded as the dominant Church of the country. It was declared autocephalous in its relations with the other Eastern Orthodox Churches, i.e., it was to be administratively independent. The law reaffirmed the role of the Romanian Orthodox Church as a national Church. The salaries of the clergy were paid by the State from budget appropriations.

The law dealt with the question of the Church's status as a legal entity in principle only. This status, however, was actually granted to the dioceses of the Orthodox Church by a separate law on May 3, 1928.

Article 21 of Law No. 1402 of 1925 (subsequently amended by Law No. 1002 of May 4, 1936) defined the status of the

Romanian Orthodox clergy. Since they were paid from the government treasury, the question has been raised as to whether the clergymen were government employees. The amendment specified that clergymen should enjoy the rights and benefits of government employees only as far as their remuneration is concerned. In all other respects (appointment, promotion, discipline, etc.) they remained under the rules of the Church law and the jurisdiction of the ecclesiastical authorities. The law also provided that the State should defray all other administrative expenses of the Orthodox Church.

C. *The Roman Catholic Church in Romania*

The Roman Catholic Church in Romania in the period after World War I embraced Churches of two rites: Catholics of the Latin Rite and the so-called Uniates or Greek Catholics with a different (Eastern) rite and organization (described in a separate chapter, *infra)*. Only the Latin rite of the Roman Catholic Church is treated in the present chapter. Some differences in the situation of the Catholic Church in the Old Kingdom and in the provinces incorporated from Hungary may be noted.

The Catholic Church of the Latin rite appeared for the first time toward the end of the 14th century in the Romanian provinces (Moldavia and Wallachia), but had no diocesan organization until the 17th century. Up to that time it consisted merely of several Catholic missions. In 1611 a diocese was established with a bishop in Yassy covering Moldavia, and later a diocese was organized for Wallachia. This diocese was governed by the Archbishop of Bucharest, who was regarded prior to 1919 as the highest Roman Catholic prelate in the Old Kingdom.

In the Old Kingdom Catholics formed a very small minority. Likewise, after World War I the Catholics of the Latin rite formed, according to the census of 1930, only 6.8 percent of the whole of Romania, and the Uniates only 7.9 percent. But in Transylvania and other provinces recovered from Hungary they represented a much larger group. (See table of religious census).

In Transylvania an organization of its own kind has developed within the Catholic Church. A Catholic diocese was established in Transylvania in the 11th century. In the 16th century Transylvania found itself partly isolated; indeed, from 1542 to 1716 the diocese in Transylvania had no bishop and no ordained clergy of the Latin rite. During this period the Roman Catholic laymen of the Latin rite organized parochial councils and a central council called the *Status Romano-Catholicus Transylvanicus.*

In 1918 Transylvania went to Romania. After prolonged negotiations between the Vatican and the Romanian Government, a Concordat was signed on May 10, 1927. It was ratified by the Parliament on May 29, 1929.

The most important provisions of this concordat are the following:

The Catholic Church in Romania is recognized as a legal entity, in conformity with the general laws of the country. This status is also granted to all Catholic organizations, including the orders and congregations which are legally established in accordance with both canon law and the laws of Romania.

The right of the Church to property of any kind is recognized and guaranteed by the State in conformity with the constitution and the laws of the country. The property and other assets assigned for religious, educational, charitable, and similar purposes must be used according to their initial designation, and the proceeds must be used exclusively within Romanian territory. The property may be transferred or mortgaged only in accordance with the rules established by the laws of Romania and canon law.

In conformity with the provisions of the Law on Legal Entities the government maintains the right of supervision of the material resources of the Catholic Church and the use made of them.

The Catholic Church is authorized to establish a "Sacred Diocesan Fund" in Romania, composed of the bonds belonging to the Church and its congregations and religious organizations. This fund is administered by the Diocesan Bishops' Council and serves to cover expenses incurred by religious and educational activities as well as salaries of the Catholic clergy. In case the fund should become insufficient to cover these expenses, the Romanian Government assumes the obligation of allocating the necessary subsidies from budgetary appropriations.

In addition to the "Sacred Fund," the status of a legal entity was also granted to two other funds, the General Catholic Fund for Religion and the General Catholic Fund for Education. The administration of properties belonging to schools, educational institutions, etc., was left to the Catholic diocesan authorities.

The Catholic Church had the right to open as many schools or charitable institutions of any kind as it desired. Since these schools had the right to issue publicly recognized diplomas, they were supervised by the Ministry of Education.

Religious instruction of Catholics in all kinds of schools including government schools was conducted according to directives issued by the Catholic bishop. The directives were to be submitted to the Ministry of Education. The bishop had the right to request the dismissal of teachers of the Catholic religion in public or private schools if he considered the teacher unqualified, even when such teachers were appointed and paid by the Government. Finally, the Catholic Church had the right to establish all kinds of seminaries for preparing Catholic clergymen. The curriculum of these schools was to be established by the competent Catholic Church authorities.

The Catholic bishops and their assistants, appointed by the Vatican, were required to be Romanian citizens and were obliged to take an oath of allegiance to the king, the constitution, and the laws of the country. Those who were not citizens were allowed to apply for citizenship within a reasonable period of time.

The appointment of the clergy was within the exclusive jurisdiction of the Church authorities. However, an appointment had to be communicated in advance to the Ministry of Religious Affairs.

Article 23, the last article of the concordat, stated that the two contracting parties reserved the right to denounce it upon service of an advance notice of six months.

An additional protocol was signed on May 30, 1932 (Official Gazette No. 180 of August 3, 1932) and ratified by Decree-Law

No. 659 (Official Gazette No. 52 of March 2, 1940) interpreting Article 9 of the concordat. Accordingly, the *Status Romano-Catholicus Transylvanicus* was transformed into a "Council of the Catholic Diocese of Latin Rite of Alba Julia" as an organ of the Diocese of Alba Julia. The Catholic Archbishop of the Latin Rite of Bucharest had the right to supervise and control the management of the income of the properties. The accord dealt in details with the administration of the different funds in accordance with their original designation. At the same time the protocol approved the by-laws of the Council.

The concordat granted the Catholic Church unlimited possibilities for religious propagation since it provided that the Romanian Government would not oppose the establishment of new Catholic parishes whenever this was requested by 400 worshippers or even less. According to these provisions as well as those of Law No. 54 of 1928, the Catholic Church was in fact treated as a national Church on an equal footing with the Romanian Orthodox Church.

The concordat also covered the status of the Armenian, Greek-Ruthenian, and Greek Catholic Churches in Romania.

D. *The Greek Catholic (Uniate) Church*

There are three Churches in Romania which, although initially founded as Churches of the Eastern Christian Orthodoxy, were ultimately united with the Roman Catholic Church under the supremacy of the Pope. These Churches, generally called Uniates, were:

1. The Romanian Uniates, called in Romania Greek Catholics.

2. The Russian, or rather Ukrainian Uniates, called in Romania Greek Ruthenians, mostly inhabiting Bukovina and part of Northern Bessarabia. The Russians are divided into three ethnological and linguistic groups. Among these are the Ukrainians or Little Russians (Malorossy) inhabiting southwestern Russia, Galicia, Northern Bukovina, and the Sub-Carpathian regions of Czechoslovakia. Outside Russia, namely in the former Austro-Hungarian Provinces, the Ukrainians (Little Russians) are also called Ruthenians.

3. The Armenian Uniates, also called Roman Catholics of the Armenian Rite.

All these Churches came under the primacy of the Pope at different times and under different circumstances. Only the Romanian Greek Catholics are dealt with in this chapter (for the others see *infra,* III, E.).

The union of the Greek Orthodox Church in Romania with the Roman Catholic Church was accomplished through an agreement concluded in 1698 between the Vatican and the Orthodox Bishopric of Alba-Julia. In joining the Catholic Church this faction of the Greek Orthodox Church reserved, among other things, the right to conduct its services in the Romanian language and the right of its clergy to marry. In exchange, the Uniates accepted four dogmatic points of the Catholics, including the Pope's primacy and the filioque creed.

This union was a compromise accepted by the Holy See in view of circumstances prevailing in Hungary, Transylvania, and the Banat in the 17th century. On the one side, the Hungarian kings were trying to convert their Romanian minority to Catholicism and thus detach it from the influence of the Romanian Principalities. On the other hand, the spread of Protestantism among the German minority in Transylvania presented a possibility of swaying the Romanians to the same religion.

The Greek Catholic segment was amalgamated into the Roman Catholic Church and subsequently became a rite within it. At first this Church was organized as a single diocese with the rank of bishopric; but later the number of dioceses was raised to three. Nevertheless, during a period of approximately ninety years from the date of the union the Uniate bishops were supervised and controlled by Jesuit priests sent from Rome. In 1855 the Greek Catholic Church was raised to the rank of a Metropolitanate and Jesuit control was withdrawn.

Until the Concordat of 1929 the status of this Church was based mainly on the provisions of the Act of Union of 1698. Both the constitution of 1923 and Law No. 54 of 1928 granted it a privileged status over the other religious minorities. It was reorganized after the conclusion of the Concordat and given all the rights and privileges of the Catholic Church. The prelates of the Greek Catholic Church were senators *ex officio* of the Romanian Parliament (as were those of the Roman Catholic Church), and its clergymen were paid by the State. This Church maintained three theological academies for the training of clergymen.

III. THE CHURCHES UNDER THE COMMUNIST GOVERNMENT

A. *Basic Provisions*

Soviet Russia has been the real ruler of Romania since its surrender on August 23, 1944. A Communist Cabinet was put in office on March 6, 1945. However, the period of the communist regime proper started on December 30, 1947, after the king's abdication, with the creation of the Romanian People's Republic and the enactment of the principal reforms.

Romania signed and ratified a peace treaty with the Allied and Associated Powers, binding herself to transform the main provisions of the treaty into national legislation. Article 3 of the peace treaty reads:

> Romania shall take all measures necessary to secure to all persons under Romanian jurisdiction, without distinction of race, sex, language, or *religion*, the enjoyment of human rights and the *fundamental freedoms*, including freedom of expression, of press and publication, of *religious worship* . . . [Italics supplied.]

Freedom of religious worship was, therefore, considered fundamental. The Romanian Government was under obligation to make no discrimination between the different Churches or denominations which existed in Romania.

The first attempt to carry out this obligation was made in the new Romanian constitution enacted on April 13, 1948. Article 27 reads:

>Freedom of conscience and freedom of *religious worship shall be guaranteed by the State.*
>
>*Religious denominations shall be free to organize themselves and may freely function, provided that their ritual and practice are not contrary to the constitution, public security, or morals.*
>
>No religious denomination, congregation, or community may open or maintain institutions for general education, but may *only operate special theological schools for training ministers* necessary to their religious service under State control.
>
>The Romanian Orthodox Church is autocephalous and unitary in its organization.
>
>The method of organization and the functioning of the religious denominations will be established by law.
>
>(Italics supplied)

Three principles are implied in these provisions:

1. Freedom of religious worship is guaranteed by the State;

2. The organization and functioning of religious denominations are, with specified exceptions, free;

3. The various creeds have the right to operate special schools for training their clergy.

However, these constitutional liberties were only nominal, serving purely for the purpose of propaganda. In practice, subsequent laws, and especially their administration, limited these constitutional liberties, placed all Churches under the strictest government control, and subordinated them to the Communist Party of Romania.

B.   *Status of the Religious Denominations in General*

1.   *General Survey*

Following World War II, the original law regulating religious denominations (Law No. 54 of 1928) underwent only one major amendment, by Law No. 62 of March 2, 1948. The main provisions of this law are as follows:

All recognized denominations are ordered to take detailed inventories of their assets and communicate them to the Ministry of Religious Affairs in order to enable the latter to exercise control over their material resources. Further, all denominations must hold religious services whenever the Government so orders.

The heads of the Churches, elected or appointed, shall be recognized only upon taking an oath of allegiance to the newly-established People's Republic. By this oath they promise not only to obey the laws, but also to enforce them, to compel their subordinates to obey them, and to defend the republic against "any enemies from within or without."

Finally, the Ministry of Religious Affairs was empowered to control and verify all Church assets and revenues as well as to supervise the use made of them.

It is clear that by this amendment the Government adopted a new attitude towards the Church. The existence of the Church is justified in the eyes of the Government and protected only insofar as the Church organizations enforce the law of the country and defend the existing political order. This virtually amounts to bestowing executive and police powers upon the Churches and forcing upon them the exercise of political rather than religious functions.

Besides, there is the novel provision according to which the Government has the right to control the use made by the Churches of their assets and revenues without drawing a distinction between the assets owned by the Church and the State subsidies, as did Law No. 54 of 1928.

Soon after these amendments were made, Law No. 54 of 1928 was repealed in its entirety by Decree No. 177 of August 4, 1948. This decree introduced new rules governing the practice of religion in Romania, presumably enforcing and interpreting principles established in the new constitution.

The first five articles of the decree proclaim that the State guarantees freedom of conscience and freedom of religion and punishes religious hatred. Religious belief does not excuse anyone from his duties and obligations under the law, nor is it an obstacle to acquiring and exercising civil and political rights. Yet no mention is made of the State's assuring equal protection under law to all religious denominations.

In contrast to Law No. 54 of 1928, no distinction is made between the national, the historical, and the minor denominations. Articles 6 through 9 of Decree No. 177 provide, in general, that all religious denominations are free to organize and function, provided that their practice and ritual are not contrary to the constitution, morals, and "public security or public order."

Religious denominations are free to establish or organize endowments, associations, orders, and congregations according to their own rules, teachings, canons, and traditions. Yet to be organized and to function, the religious denominations must be recognized and granted permission by decree of the Presidium of the Great National Assembly, upon the motion of the Cabinet. However, "in well-founded cases, recognition may be withdrawn in the same manner" (Article 13). Thus the existence of a religious denomination and its orders, congregations, et cetera, is left entirely to the discretion of the political authorities.

Only recognized religious denominations and their local organizations possess the status of legal entities. Such status may be granted to their civil associations and endowments with religious aims as well as to their orders and congregations, if they comply with the requirements provided by the law regulating legal entities (Article 28 of Decree No. 177).

All heads of religious denominations, dignitaries, and all other personnel must be Romanian citizens. They "enjoy fully the exercise of civil and political rights" (Article 20). No mention is made as to the position or fate of those who are not, or not as yet, citizens of Romania.

Enjoyment and full exercise of civil rights is clearly defined by the Civil Code. However, a different situation exists with regard to political rights. Although these rights are well defined in the statutory provisions, the final and only proof that a person enjoys political rights is that he was registered on the 1946 electoral lists and that his name has remained there since. In other words, only those clergymen and officers of the Church are permitted to serve their Churches who came successfully through all the purges conducted by the Communist Government since 1945. Since the beginning of 1949 the electoral lists have been checked annually by the local People's Councils. It stands to reason that no one is entered on the electoral lists who is not completely trusted by the Party. Other usual grounds for stripping a citizen of his political rights are having an "undemocratic attitude," being an "enemy of the people," or being a "traitor," et cetera. Therefore, political capacity is no longer a status granted to every citizen by the constitution, which may be withdrawn only in cases of great and precisely defined offenses against the State after due process of law. It may be taken away by decision of the Communist Party alone.

Moreover, Article 33 of Decree No. 177 provides that a clergyman of a recognized Church who shows an "anti-democratic attitude" may be deprived, totally or in part, of the right to draw salary.

The oath requirement established by Law No. 62 of 1948 is also kept in the decree. Every minister of religion or officer of a Church must take an oath before admission to office.

Article 25 provides that

> the Ministry of Religious Affairs shall suspend any decision, instruction, directive, or order [of a church authority] which has an ecclesiastical-administrative, cultural, educational, or charitable character or pertains to endowments, if it is contrary to the status of the denomination, to the act of its establishment, to *public security, public order,* or morals. Pastoral and circular letters shall be communicated *in advance* to the Ministry of Religious Affairs. [Italics supplied.]

The religious denominations and their endowments, associations, and the like, must submit a full report on their financial situation for verification and approval by the Ministry of Religious Affairs. The law provides that the salaries of clergymen and the officers of the Church shall be paid by the State. But in contrast to Law No. 1002 of 1936, Article 34 of Decree No. 177 suggests that these persons have in all respects the same standing as all other government employees. Article 34 reads:

> The placing on the payroll of clergymen and officers of the religious denominations shall be done according to the general rules.

The "general rules" of government employment referred to (Civil Service Code of 1946) make it clear that everyone who draws a salary from the government treasury has the rights and duties of a government employee. The Civil Service Code of 1946 was later abrogated and replaced by a new and stricter regulation for government employees in Romania (Decree No. 29, *M. O.* No. 24 of January 29, 1949).

Several provisions deal with the real estates and the assets of the church. Thus, where the members of a church quit their denominational Church and join another, the property and the assets shall be divided. In proportion with the number of the members who leave the Church the property shall be transferred to that Church which those members join. Where 75 percent of the total membership leave their denominational Church the entire property of the Church and its assets are transferred to the newly adopted Church. The implications of this rule are discussed *infra,* under III, E.

The religious denominations may maintain only such relations with other countries as are of a religious nature. Any communication may be conducted only on approval of the Ministry of Religious Affairs and through the medium of the Ministry for Foreign Affairs. The purpose of these provisions was obviously to interrupt the direct contact between the Roman Catholic Church in Romania and the Holy See, required by the Church's dogma and organization.

Any direct communication between Catholic prelates in Romania and the Holy See could thus be prosecuted under the provisions of the Decree of August 12, 1950, on State Security, which prescribes the death penalty for:

(a) "treason to the country, rendering service to the enemy, or causing prejudice to the power of the State;

(b) "procurement and transmission of State secrets to a foreign or enemy power . . ."

Briefly, the repealed Law No. 54 of 1928 was characterized by the absence of formalities and of obstacles for recognizing religious denominations; their status was determined by act of Parliament. Decree No. 177 of 1948 is, in contrast, characterized by three features:

(a) The rights acquired under Law 54 of 1928 are annulled, and all the old denominations are to meet the requirements set by the decree in order to continue their existence;

(b) It introduces a series of formalities, obstacles, and restrictions for the recognition, organization, and functioning of the religious denominations;

(c) The religious denominations are now entirely subject to the discretionary powers of the Government.

By Decree No. 178 (Official Gazette No. 178 of August 4, 1948) the Ministry of Religious Affairs was reorganized to fit the new tasks and was empowered to exert complete control over all religious denominations in the country. Subsequently, its administration was simplified by Decree No. 37 (Official Gazette No. 30 of February 5, 1949) carrying out a general order for dismissal of a number of public servants.

After this reduction in personnel the Ministry of Religious Affairs concentrated on control and secular matters and dissolved its sections dealing with spiritual questions, documentation, and studies.

The law regulating religious denominations was later implemented by Decree No. 243 (Official Gazette No. 217 of September 18, 1948), which established the number of dioceses for each recognized denomination on the basis of 750,000 worshipers per diocese, viz.,

Greek Orthodox	17 dioceses
Greek Catholic	2 ”
Roman Catholic	2 ”
Christians of the Old Rite	1 ”
Protestants	1 bishop and 1 superintendent

The remaining denominations were each to have one central organization.

2. Church Property

Decree No. 177 of 1948 on Religious Denominations grants the recognized denominations and their parishes the status of a legal entity. The institutions, orders, congregations, associations, and establishments organized by the Churches may, however, obtain such status only upon filing a special petition according to the procedure established for granting the status of a legal entity in general. It may also be observed that under Law No.

54 of 1928, the status of legal entity was extended automatically to a large group of Churches characterized therein as national or historical denominations. Decree No. 177 does not grant automatic recognition by operation of law to any denomination. Recognition of any denomination is within the unlimited discretion of the Government. Consequently, a denomination must petition to be recognized, and acquires the status of a legal entity only if the recognition is formally granted.

The most important point, however, lies in the expressly stated right of the Ministry of Religious Affairs "to verify and control" the inventory of all Church property and the Church budgets (Articles 29 and 30 of Decree No. 177).

In addition, it should be borne in mind that some Churches, the Roman Catholic Church in particular, were actually deprived of their assets. This was done ostensibly by legal means. Agricultural land still possessed by the Church after the land reform of 1919 was taken away in direct violation of Law No. 187 of March 23, 1945 on Agrarian Reform, which provided in Article 8 that:

> Agricultural land belonging to monasteries, metropolitanates, bishoprics, parishes, and clerical endowments shall be exempted from expropriation and left in the ownership of the present title holders.

Likewise, certain categories of land, such as vineyards and forests, were generally exempted from expropriation. Nevertheless, most Catholic landed property, including forests, vineyards, and the like, was seized by various "local committees" early in 1945 and thereafter subdivided into small holdings. The rest was seized by the Government in March 1949 without compensation. This time, the Government did not even take the trouble to issue a decree legalizing the seizure.

The "Sacred Fund" of the Catholic Church (see *supra*) was reduced to zero. It was composed almost exclusively of government bonds which were given to the religious bodies of the Catholic Church in Transylvania after 1919 in compensation for estates expropriated at that time. The inflation of 1944-1947 swept away their value. Then, just before the currency reform of August 14, 1947, government bonds were compulsorily called in and paid for in inflated *lei,* only an insignificant part of which was thereafter accepted for exchange in the currency reform. In this way, most of the material means of the Catholic Church for the support of its religious, educational, and charitable program disappeared. By the Law of November 3, 1948, all private health institutions were nationalized and a number of important Catholic hospitals and sanitariums were taken over by the State.

These successive expropriations have been extended to all religious denominations with the exception of the Russian Church (Christians of the Old Rite and the parishes later included in the Ukrainian Vicariate), which was exempted. If the Romanian Orthodox Church possesses today any material means, they are either subsequent grants by the Government or transfers by the Government from the seized assets of other religious denominations.

3. Church and School

The right to establish and operate schools of all kinds, granted to religious denominations by Law No. 54 of 1928, and to the Roman Catholic Church by the Concordat, was abolished. The same is true of the right to administer religious instruction in private and public schools. Communist policy in these matters was embodied in a series of decrees.

The first step was to suppress the denominational schools and those supported in part by Churches. The Government started by banning all foreign schools in Romania by Order No. 191,653 (Official Gazette No. 176 of August 2, 1948). Many of these schools were connected to a varying extent with religious denominations.

The next step was a reform of the school system enacted by Decrees No. 175 and No. 176 (Official Gazette No. 177 of August 3, 1948). By Article 35 of Decree 175 all denominational schools were taken over by the Government. Decree No. 176 provides:

> Art 1. For a better organization of public education and expansion and democratization of the educational system, all personal

and real properties which belonged to the churches, congregations, religious communities, nonprofit organizations and trade corporations and, in general, to individuals or legal entities, and were destined to support . . . denominational schools, shall pass into Government ownership and shall be used for educational needs.

This provision covers school buildings, dwellings for professors, boarding houses, and students' homes, as well as funds, estates, and legacies serving educational purposes. No compensation was to be paid for them. A list of over 2,000 denominational and private schools of all types from kindergartens to colleges, thus expropriated, was attached to Decree No. 176. The provisions quoted make it plain that no denominational school may be opened in the future. This conclusion is supported by the fact that a subsequent decree, No. 177 of August 4, 1948, regulating religious denominations, makes no mention of the right of Churches to open general schools. (It deals with schools in Chapter VI, but provides exclusively for theological schools.)

These decrees chiefly affected the Roman Catholic Church, which operated the majority of the denominational schools.

Decrees Nos. 175, 176, and 177 do not mention religious instruction in any way, nor does any other statute. There is no provision for a right of the Church to supervise religious instruction in case it should be given in the public schools.

The only schools the Church could hold are a very limited number of special theological seminaries for the training of clergymen. These are in all respects, including curriculum, under the supervision of the Ministries of Religious Affairs and of Education. The Ministry of Religious Affairs may, among other things, dismiss professors appointed by the Church whenever it deems that the "public order and the security of the state" so require.

Article 49 of Decree No. 177 limited the number of theological schools of college standing in the entire country to two for the Orthodox Church, one for the Catholic Church, and one for all Protestant Churches. A subsequent order of the Ministry of Religious Affairs, however, further reduced the number of divinity and clerical schools and did not provide for the establishment of any Roman Catholic divinity schools. This revealed the intention of the Government to bar all opportunity for the training of ministers of religion.

It must also be mentioned that no general education may be given at the church schools except in three special subjects of "general education," viz., the constitution and law of the Romanian People's Republic, the Russian language, and the history of Russian Theological literature.

Order No. 42,898 (Official Gazette No. 226 of November 15, 1948) approved curricula for the Church schools of the following Churches: Greek Orthodox, Protestant (including Evangelical, Reformed, and Unitarian), Jewish, Baptist, Adventist, and Moslem. No mention is made of any curricula for the Roman Catholic Church schools. The same is true of the Christian Church of the Old Rite, but for a different reason (see *infra*).

C.   *The Romanian Orthodox Church*

No new general law on the Romanian Orthodox Church has been enacted. It continues to be regulated by the provisions of the Law for Organization and Unification of May 6, 1925, No. 1402, as amended after 1947 (see *infra*). Yet an interesting question seems to remain open: Is the Orthodox Church still the dominant Church in the State ("National" Church)? As was pointed out previously, the Organic Law of 1925 provided that, since the Greek Orthodox creed is the religion of the majority of the Romanian people, the Romanian Orthodox Church is the dominant Church in the country. The amendments of Law No. 1402 of 1925 did not directly affect this provision. But this principle had been taken over from the constitution of 1923, which in Article 22 specifically stressed the position of the Romanian Orthodox Church as a national Church.

The constitution of 1923 was repealed and replaced by the Constitution of April 11, 1948, Article 27 of which provided only that "the Romanian Orthodox Church is autocephalous and unitary in its organization." Article 15 of Decree No. 177 of 1948 contains similar provisions. However, the new regulation failed to repeat the provisions of the repealed Law No. 54 of 1928 that the Romanian Orthodox Church shall be governed by its principles for internal organization provided that they are not contrary to the church's own organic statutes.

There is good reason to believe that the Romanian Orthodox Church is no longer considered a national Church in view of Article 84 of the new constitution of September 24, 1952. This follows very closely the pattern established by Article 27 of the constitution of 1948, but no longer contains the clause "the Romanian Orthodox Church is autocephalous and unitary in its organization." In other words, this Church is no longer mentioned in the constitution. This omission suggests that the Romanian Orthodox Church has no longer any privileged status and is placed on an equal footing with the other denominations.

The following two amendments to the Law of 1925 have been enacted thus far:

(a) Law No. 167 of May 30, 1947, changed the procedure in filling vacancies in the diocesan councils. These councils are the governing bodies of the dioceses and consist of clergymen and laymen, the latter elected by the council itself. Under Law No. 1402 of 1925 several candidates had to be nominated. Under Law No. 167 of 1947 only one candidate, who must have advance approval from the Ministry of Religious Affairs, is nominated. In this way, the Government succeeded in staffing these bodies with members who, in turn, elected such Church dignitaries as would be obedient to the political regime in power. Furthermore, the National Church Council which elects bishops, archbishops, and metropolitans, was enlarged to include all members of the Cabinet, undersecretaries, and members of the parliament from the districts of the diocese in which the vacancy occurred. The result has been that the secular members of the council outnumber the clergymen and thus can determine the outcome of the elections to the satisfaction of the regime.

(b) Law No. 60 of March 2, 1948, and Presidential Decree No. 133 of February 5, 1949, introduced only minor changes in the Church organization.

D. *The Roman Catholic Church*

As previously stated, the Roman Catholic Church, its organizations, congregations, institutions, and assets had been administered and managed according to the principles laid down in the Concordat of 1927 and subsequent acts enforcing it. The Roman Catholic Church administered, in 1939, 177 churches, 21 chapels, 669 parishes, 2,002 places of worship, 9 theology schools, 6 students' homes headed by nuns, 5 orphanages, 1 hospital, 32 monastic convents, 26 Franciscan monasteries, 56 nunneries, 18 high schools, 5 student homes, and 1 Ursuline Institute. (These figures are taken from an article by Professor Olimp Caciula, *"Cultele religioase"* in *Enciclopedia Romaniei,* vol. 2, Bucharest, 1939.) The Concordat set up definite limits to the supervision of the Catholic Church in Romania by the Romanian Government.

By Decree No. 151 (Official Gazette No. 164 of July 19, 1948) the Romanian Government denounced the Concordat and its additional protocols and briefly stated that the application of all these argreements ceased on the day of publication of the decree in the Official Gazette. This was a violation of Article 23 of the Concordat, which provided that its denunciation by either side must be preceded by a notice served six months in advance, and could mean only a breach of contract and rupture of relations.

Decree No. 151 did not mention whether the Catholic Church was to be guided by the provisions of the law regulating religious denominations in general or of any other law, and thus left it without regulation by law. This refers not only to the Roman Catholic Church but also to its rites, congregations, assests, et cetera. In fact, the steps subsequently taken by the Government have demonstrated that the decree was intended to deprive the the Catholic Church in Romania of legal protection. The Roman Catholic Church was practically barred from any educational activities and deprived of its funds (see *supra* III, B, 2 and 3). The expropriation of schools was followed by the disbanding of all Catholic organizations.

The first step was taken through Orders of the Cabinet Nos. 1677 and 1679 (Official Gazette No. 299 of December 25, 1948), by which eleven principal associations and endowments and their branches were suppressed and their assets transferred to the State. The same steps were taken by Order of the Cabinet No. 1770 (Official Gazette No. 10 of January 13, 1949) against eleven additional Roman Catholic and Reformed nonprofit organizations and their branches.

Order of the Cabinet No. 161 (Official Gazette No. 48 of February 26, 1949) suppressed sixteen other religious and professional Catholic associations and their district branches. Their assets were transferred to the Ministry of the Interior.

Finally, Order of the Cabinet No. 810 (Official Gazette No. 51 of August 1, 1949) suppressed the existing Roman Catholic Orders and Congregations and their dependent institutions, regardless of the form in which they were organized. Herein were included the eleven congregations and four orders of the Catholic Church in Romania. Only two monasteries and three convents were permitted where members of the disbanded congregations could choose to continue monastic life. Each member was obliged to communicate his decision in writing within twenty days to the Ministry for Religious Affairs. Those who were not Romanian citizens were summoned to appear before the local police authorities and arrange for their departure from the country. Those who refused to enter the permitted monasteries and convents were given the choice of admission to a public home for the aged or training in some trade and assignment to jobs by the Office for Distribution of Manpower.

Later, the Government took steps to sever the ties between the Catholic Church and the Holy See and to replace the authority of the Pope by that of a national Catholic organization. In September 1950 a meeting of several Catholic priests and members of the laity took place at Gheorgheni, at which the principles of such an organization were adopted. At a meeting held in Cluj on March 15, 1951, the so-called *Statusul Catolic* (Catholic directorate) was established. The directorate, which is supposed to act as the supreme governing body representing

Romanian Catholics, is headed by an executive council whose members are elected by the directorate, subject to Government approval.

E.   *The Greek Catholic (Uniate) Churches*
(Romanian, Ruthenian, Armenian)

As mentioned above (see Chapter D, II), there were three Uniate Churches in Romania. The origin and status of the so-called Greek Catholics, i.e., Romanian Uniates, were described there. Most of the adherents of this Church live in Transylvania. The members of the Armenian Uniate Church (Roman Catholics of Armenian Rite) also live in Transylvania (bishopric in Gherla). The third Uniate Church, called Greek Ruthenian, embraces only members of the Ukrainian, i.e., Ruthenian, population living in Bukovina and Marmuresh. Its origin dates back to the Brest Church Council of 1596, when the prelates of this Church, then within the confines of Poland, accepted union with the Holy See on conditions similar to those accepted by the Romanian Orthodox Church in 1698.

To this Church belonged the Ukrainian population of the northern part of Bukovina and Galicia, incorporated in the Soviet Union after World War II. (The Ukrainian and Byelorussian populations of the Soviet Union had also been in the Uniate Church until they were incorporated in the Russian Orthodox Church in 1839 by a decree of Emperor Nicholas I.)

Since all three Uniate Churches in Romania were, until recently, branches of the Roman Catholic Church, they found themselves without regulation by law when the Concordat was denounced. The members of all three Churches were forced by Government pressure to break with the Holy See and return, so to speak, to the Orthodox Church. Their disbandment, or rather their transformation into Orthodox parishes, was indirectly promoted by Order No. 39,380 of the Ministry of Religious Affairs (Official Gazette No. 242 of October 18, 1948). Under the earlier Decree No. 177 of 1948 if members of a parish chose another Church, they took with them a part of the assets of the parish proportionate to their number. If 75 per cent of the parishioners decided to join another Church, the church building was transferred to the newly adopted one. Order No. 39,380 provided that, in counting such members, only the heads of families were to be taken into account.

No decrees dealing specifically with the Armenian Uniate Church were discovered during this study.

On October 1, 1948, thirty-eight prelates, canons, and priests, allegedly delegated by the churchmen of the Uniate Church in Romania, assembled in Cluj and resolved to unite with the Romanian Orthodox Church. There is evidence that the campaign for unification before and after the congress was conducted under conditions of terror and intimidation, and that the assembled churchmen were not free agents. As a result of this action, separate Greek Catholic parishes ceased to exist, and churches and church premises were handed over to the Romanian Orthodox Church.

The reintegration of the Greek Catholic Church with the Orthodox Church in Romania was ultimately sanctioned by Decree No. 358 (Official Gazette No. 281 of December 2, 1948). Article 1 of the decree reads as follows:

> Subsequent to the reversion of the local Greek Catholic parishes to the Romanian Orthodox Church and in conformity with Article 13 of Decree 177/1948, its central organization and those provided by its constitution shall cease to exist.

The decree stipulates that the assets of the Greek Catholic Church shall become the property of the Romanian State without any compensation and shall be assigned partly or wholly to the Romanian Orthodox Church or to its constituent bodies.

The government obviously made use of the provisions of Article 13 of the Law on Religious Denominations of 1948 in withdrawing recognition from this Church, which after the denunciation of the Concordat lacked a definite status.

The fate of the Ukrainian (Ruthenian) Uniate Church was different. The Concordat of 1927 provided for the establishment of this Church as a separate diocese within the Roman Catholic Church. The seat was to be designated later.

It may be mentioned in this connection that the Uniate

Churches in Galicia and the northern part of Bukovina—now incorporated in the Soviet Union — were declared in 1947 and 1948 united with the Russian Church headed by the Moscow Patriarchate.

Subsequently, the Romanian Ministry of Religious Affairs issued Order No. 34,695 (Official Gazette No. 76 of December 2, 1949), which authorized the creation of a "Ukrainian Orthodox vicariate-general," whose task was to organize and have jurisdiction over all Ukrainian Orthodox parishes in Romania. (The original order mentioned a Ruthenian Vicariate but a note in the Official Gazette No. 81 of December 16, 1949, substituted the word "Ukrainian" for the word "Ruthenian.")

The Ukrainian vicariate is "an organization independent of any Orthodox diocese but dependent upon the Patriarchate of the Romanian Orthodox Church and governed by the provisions established by the Law on Organization and Functioning of the Romanian Orthodox Church [of 1925]" (Article 2). The organization of the vicariate is to be set up by the vicariate itself, subject to approval by the Romanian patriarchate and the Ministry of Religious Affairs.

It must be borne in mind that there are today no Ukrainian (or Ruthenian) Orthodox parishes in Romania other than the Uniate parishes. The Orthodox parishes with Ukrainian population existed only in Bessarabia and a few in Northern Bukovina, but these provinces are now within the Soviet Union. Thus, the vicariate will obviously embrace the Uniate parishes. In this way, the Ukrainian Uniate Church in Romania is detached from the Holy See and brought within the Romanian Orthodox Church in the same manner as the Uniates in Galicia and Northern Bukovina were brought into the Russian Orthodox Church.

F.   *Protestant Churches*

1.   *The Reformed Church (Calvinist)*

A definite organization of the Reformed Church (Calvinist) was first established in Bucharest in 1815. After 1919 this congregation merged with those of Transylvania.

In Transylvania the Reformed Church was founded soon after its establishment in Western Europe. The rulers of the province encouraged the movement and it found followers among Hungarian Catholics. In 1653 under the "Approved Constitution" (*Approbata Constitutio*) the rights were granted to the Reformed Church to organize itself according to its principles. Later, under Austrian Emperors and Hungarian Kings, such rights were recognized and maintained.

The modern constitution of the Reformed Church had been drawn in 1904, and was maintained by the Romanian Government after 1919. It had a bishopric at Cluj. Another was organized at Oradea. A theological seminary was functioning at Cluj.

The Reformed Church believers represent 3.9 percent of the whole of Romania.

2. The Evangelic Lutheran Church

Very early historically the Princes of Moldavia and Wallachia granted freedom to the Lutheran movement. Gaspar Peucer, Melanchthon's son-in-law, had been appointed professor at the Law Academy of Cotnar in Moldavia in 1561-1563. The first Evangelic Lutheran Church was organized in 1753 in Wallachia and was followed in 1813 by a church in Moldavia.

In Transylvania, the Saxons have always had ties with their former homeland, and the Lutheran Church was organized soon after its establishment in Germany, in 1542, by Honterus, a Lutheran priest. Thereafter the whole Saxon group embraced the new concept.

The Saxon settlements in Transylvania had a privileged status enjoying local autonomy and had freedom to organize the Lutheran Church.

After 1919, Romanian administration maintained the status of the Evangelic Lutheran Church in Transylvania with a bishop at Sibiu, to which, the Evangelic Lutheran Churches from the Old Kingdom joined. A theological seminary was functioning at Brasov. According to the 1930 census 2.2 percent of the whole population of Romania were Evangelic Lutherans.

3. The Unitarian Church

This church found a few adherents in Transylvania only. The first Church was established and organized by the Prince of Transylvania in 1568. It had a bishop and a theological seminary at Cluj. The Unitarians represented 0.4 percent of the total population of Romania according to 1930 census.

4. The Baptist Church

In the Old Kingdom the Baptists began to thrive about 1910, especially among German-speaking people. Up to 1919 there were known only five organized Baptist Churches.

In Transylvania and Bukovina the Baptists established the first churches soon after the 1848 revolution. Its growth had been noticeable. Hungarian and Austrian administrations granted it religious freedom.

After 1919, when Transylvania and Bukovina joined the old kingdom of Romania, a large number of Romanian emigrants came back home from America. Many of them had embraced the Baptist faith, and propagated it in Romania. According to the 1930 census there were 51,000 Baptists in Romania. Their number had grown to 200,000 by 1947.

The Baptist Church is organized into Communities and Associations of Communities. A theological seminary has been functioning at Bucharest since 1923.

5. The Seventh Day Adventists Church

This movement penetrated Romania toward 1870. Its believers are scattered all over the country but in very small communities. According to the 1930 census there were about 15,000 believers of this kind.

The Protestant Churches existing in Romania, came under Government supervision through Decree No. 177 of August 4, 1948, on the Organization of Denominations, and Decree No. 37 of February 5, 1949, on the Ministry of Religious Affairs.

The Reformed and Protestant Churches continue to have dioceses at Sibiu, Cluj, and Oradia, and a theological college at Cluj.

The Neo-Protestant Churches so-called Evangelicals (Advent-
ists, Baptists, Pentecostals) joined together in a federation, which
received an official status. According to the Communist newspaper *Universul,* of September 28, 1951, the role of the federation was to "integrate them [the Neo-Protestant Churches] into
the new rhythm of democratic life" or, in plain language, to use
them to further the Communist order.

G. *The Christians of the Old Rite*

The term "Christians of the Old Rite" applies to a group of
dissenters who originally belonged to the Russian Orthodox
Church, broke away from it to some extent in the seventeenth
century and because of persecution left Russia to settle at various
times on the territory of present-day Romania. They are generally called *Lipovani* (probably after the name of the Bessarabian
town of Lipova) or *muscali.* In their new place of settlement,
they preserved their language, dress, habits, and customs. The
split was the result of the revision of the Church books undertaken in the middle of the seventeenth century by Nicon the
patriarch of Moscow. The revision was intended to amend the
liturgical books then in circulation in Russia with respect to
erroneous deviations from the books used in other Eastern Orthodox Churches and to correct some local departures from the
established ritual. Originally there were no dogmatic or canonical
differences. But, in time, those adhering to the old ritual became
divided into a number of sects, some of which departed from
the teachings of the Orthodox Church. There are among them
sects which completely deny priesthood, sacraments, or obligations toward the State such as taxes and military service. In
any event, those who settled abroad broke all administrative
connection with the Moscow hierarchy but joined no other Eastern Orthodox Church. Only a number of those remaining in
Russia reunited in the 1830's with the official Russian Orthodox
Church.

However, those who settled in the Romanian eastern provinces
and their descendants continued their life in religious communi-

ties separately from the Romanian environment and the Russian Church. Being opposed to assimilation or unification with the Romanian Orthodox Church, they were always treated as a separate religious denomination. Religious freedom has been granted by documents on several occasions.

This Church succeeded in organizing closed religious communities in parishes, and it managed to build Churches, establish monasteries, and among some sects even to establish a certain hierarchy. But it had no divinity schools of its own, and many of its sects were not willing to train their priests in Romanian or Russian schools.

After the enactment of Law No. 54 of 1928 the dignitaries of the Church of the Old Rite prepared a constitution and by-laws for their Church and submitted it to the Romanian Government for approval in order to obtain recognition as a denomination. Until 1942 they repeatedly tried to get this recognition and thus transform a *de facto* existence into a *de jure* status. Because of political reasons and suspicions of disloyalty, recognition was never granted.

After World War II, Russia showed interest in this Russian minority in Romania and its organization, and helped it become recognized by the Romanian Government, although not all of the Lipovan communities were then willing to act under Soviet tutelage. Recognition was extended by Law No. 728 of 1946 (Official Gazette No. 212 of September 13, 1946).

Furthermore, the status of a legal entity was granted to all hierarchical organizations of Christians of the Old Rite, including their monasteries.

On the other hand, this law states that, in contrast to the statutory provisions of Law No. 54 of 1928, the Romanian State does not grant any kind of subsidy to this denomination, either for maintaining its organization and institutions or for paying its clergy.

It must be borne in mind that under the present set-up the government, by assuming the financial support of the denominations, makes all Churches thereby dependent upon itself. Therefore, the above-mentioned provision of Law No. 728 of 1946 may be considered a privilege of the Lipovan Church and a token of its independence from the government.

Besides enjoying hierarchical independence, this Church is able to establish and operate parish schools with teachers appointed by the parish assemblies. These schools are neither controlled by the Ministries of Education and of Religious Affairs nor obligated to submit their curricula for approval (Article 73). Thus, unlike all other denominations the Christian Church of the Old Rite is free from the control of the Ministry of Religious Affairs over its organization and rites.

Its assets and financial state are not checked by the Government. It is permitted to establish and manage denominational schools free of any kind of supervision exercised by the Ministry of Education. No other denomination enjoys these rights.

In view of the Soviet interest in this denomination, it may be assumed that its status, like any other matter of interest to the Soviets, is no longer subject to Romanian law.

H.   Other Churches

The Moslems in Dobrogea have a *muftiat* (diocese) at Constantza and a theological school at Medgidia. All Jewish religious groups have also been united in a Federation of the Mosaic Cults to facilitate government control (*Universul,* September 28, 1951).

I.   Atheistic Propaganda

In 1949, on the initiative of the Romanian Workers' (Communist) Party, the Society for the Popularization of Science and Culture (SRSC) was created after the model of a similar Association in the USSR. The aim of this society is to "propagate among the laboring masses political and scientific knowledge to fight obscurantism, superstition, mysticism, and all other influences of bourgeois ideologies" (*Universul,* February 7, 1951). Religion was identified with the ideology of the bourgeoisie, and the proletarian outlook was identified with atheism. The society is directed by a presidium composed of prominent Communist intellectuals. In 1951 it had twenty-eight regional organizations, branches in thirty-seven *raions* (districts), and lecture circles in all other districts. The society employed 3,000 propagandists and organized 42,000 lectures with an attendance of 7 million. The SRSC concentrates its efforts on the laboring masses and workers' clubs and organizations must reserve at least one day a month for its activities (*Universul,* February 7, 1951).

However the people and their spiritual leaders are staunch in their loyalty to the Christian belief. By the end of 1952 the Communist regime felt the necessity to open a new special concentration camp for orthodox priests who refuse to submit to the regime and cooperate with the so-called "Patriotic Priests Movement." There were already by that time about 300 priests interned in this camp. (*New York Times,* January 7, 1953)

TABLE OF STATUTES

ADDITIONAL SOURCES

BIBLIOGRAPHY

Anuarul Statistic al Romaniei 1939 si 1940, Institutul Central de Statistica
(Statistical Year Book of Romania 1939 and 1940, Central Institut for statistics), Bucuresti, Splaiul Unirii, 1940,

Attwater, Donald, The Catholic Eastern Churches, Milwaukee, Wis., Bruce Publ. Co., 1935 (p. 308).

Attwater, Donald, The Christian Churches of the East, 2 vol. Milwaukee, Wise., Bruce Publ. Co., 1947-48.

Attwater, Donald, The Dissident Eastern Churches, Milwaukee, Wis. Bruce Publ. Co. (pp. 111-118).

Boroianu, D.G., *Dreptul Bisericesc* (Church Law), Craiova, 1903.

Buletinul Oficial (Official Bulletin), Bucuresti, 1949-1951.

Buletinul Statistic pe anul 1920 (Romanian Bulletin of Statistics for 1920), Bucuresti, 1920.

Buletinul Statistic al Romaniei pe anul 1930 (Romanian Bulletin of Statistics for 1930), Bucuresti, 1930.

Consiliul Legislativ, Colectiune de Legi si Regulamente, (Legislative Council, Collection of laws and ordinances), Vols. I-XXX, 1916-1942, Bucuresti.

Enciclopedia Romaniei, (Romanian Encyclopedia) Vol. II., Bucuresti, 1939.

Fortescue, Adrian, The Orthodox Eastern Church, London, Catholic Truth Society, 1916 (Chap. X. pp. 328-334).

Hamangiu, C., *Codul General al Romaniei, Legi uzuale,* (General Code of Romania, Common Laws), Vols. I-XXX, Bucuresti, 1907-1942.

Kidd, Rev. B.J., The Churches of Eastern Christendom, From A.D. 451 to the present time, London, Faith Press. 1947. (Chap. XIV. pp. 345-351).

Monitorul Oficial, (Official Gazette), Bucuresti, 1866-1949.

Romanian National Committee, Persecution of Religion in Romania, Washington, 1949.

Scott, The Rev. Sidney Herbert, The Eastern Churches and the Papacy, London, Sheed & Ward, 1928 (p. 404).

Torbet, Robert, A History of the Baptists, Judson Press, Philadelphia, 1950. (pp. 208-209).

TSankov, Stefan, The Eastern Orthodox Church, Milwaukee, Wisc., Morehouse Publ. Co., 1930.

"Universul" February 7, 1951, September 28, 1951, Bucuresti.

Zernov, Nicolas, The Church of Eastern Christians, New York, MacMillan, 1942.

English Sources on Eastern Orthodox Church

Attwater, Donald, The Christian Churches of the East, 2 vol., Milwaukee, Wis., Bruce Pub. Co., 1947-48.

Attwater, Donald, The Catholic Eastern Churches, Milwaukee, Wis., . Bruce Publ. Co., 1935. (p. 308).

Attwater, Donald, The Dissident Eastern Churches, Milwaukee, Wis., Bruce Publ. Co. (pp. 111-118).

Fortescue, Adrian, The Orthodox Eastern Church, London, Catholic Truth Society, 1916. (Ch. X. pp. 328-334)

Kidd, Rev. B.J. The Churches of Eastern Christendom, from A.D. 451 to the present time, London, Faith Press, Ltd., 1947 (Ch. XIV. pp. 345-351).

Romanian National Committee, Persecution of Religion in Romania, Washington, 1949.

Scott, The Rev. Sidney Herbert, The Eastern Churches and the Papacy, London, Sheed & Ward, 1928 (p. 404).

Torbet, Robert, A History of the Baptists, Philadelphia, Judson Press, 1950. (pp. 208-209)

TSankov, Stefan, The Eastern Orthodox Church. Milwaukee, Wisc., Morehouse Pub. Co., 1930.

Zernov, Nicolas, The Church of Eastern Christians, New York, MacMillan, 1942.

INDEX

Figures indicate pages; letters in front of figures indicate the country; C—Czechoslovakia; H—Hungary; P—Poland; R—Romania; S—Soviet Union.

A

Abbreviations, C 5, H 75, P 163, R 256

Ábrahám, Mózes, H 149, notes 131, 134; 150 note 142

Acheson, Dean, H 127

Act of Union of 1698, R 270

Adamski, Stanisław, Bishop, P 215

Adventist Church, Seventh Day, R 260, 281, 289, 290

Agaphangel Metropolitan, S xxi-xxiii

Alba-Julia, the Diocese of, R 269, 270

Alekseev, S xxiv and Note 61 to Introduction

Alexii—bishop later, Moscow Patriarch, P 239; S xv, xxii

Ambord, P. Beat, S. J., H 150 note 160

Andreev, S xxiv and Note 61 to Introduction

Annabring, Mathias, H 91

Andrew II, King, H 91

Antireligious propaganda, S xi-xviii, xxiv

Antireligious correspondence course institute, S xi-xii

Aprobatat Constitutio, R 288

Archives, Expropriation of, H 90

Armenian-Gregorian Church, R 260, 262, 263

Armenian Uniates (Catholic), H 83; R 260, 269, 270, 285, 286

Armistice of January 20, 1948, H 111

Army Chaplains, appointment, C 19, P 235

Art, Works of, H 90, 101, S xix. *See also* Church Property

Associations, Religious. *See* Religious Associations

Atheism, C 21, R 292, 293, P 180, 189; S xi-xviii, xxv

Augsburg Evangelical Church or Augsburg Church of Evangelicals, C 12, 13, H 80, 83, P 240

Augsburg Protestant Church of Poland, P 239, 240

Austrian Laws, in Bukovina, R 259; in

Czech lands, C 7, 18; in Czechoslovakia, C 15; in former German area, C 7

Autocephalous churches. *See* under the name of the particular church

Autocephalous Status, H 82, P 238, 239, R 257, 265, 281

Az Ember, H 97

B

Badarik, Bartalan Bishop, H 143, 144

Balogh, Jenő, H 138

Banat, R 259, 270

Baptist Church, C 12, H 83, R 260, 281, 289, 290

Baziak, Archbishop, formerly Metropolitan of Lwów, P 217

Beale, Joseph Henry, H 150 note 159

Bednorz, Filip, Rev. — Capitular Vicar, P 245

Bednorz, Herbert, Aux. Bishop, P 215

Bessarabia, R 259, 269, 287

Bibliographies, C 67, H 156, 157, P 250-252, R 298, 299

Bieniek, Juliusz, Aux. Bishop, P 215

Bierut, Bolesław, P 203, 223, 228

Bishops, archbishops, *See under* Roman Catholic Church, Russian Orthodox Church

Bliss Lane, Arthur, U. S. Ambassador, P 226. *See also* United States of America

Bohemia, C 7, 9-11, 14, 30. *See also* Czech Lands

Brasov, Lutheran Seminary at, R 288

Breitinger, Fr.—as Archbishop of Gniezno and Poznań, P 174

Brikchev, S xxi and note 42 to Introduction

Brest, Church Council 1596 (Uniates), R 285

Bucharest, Baptist Theological Seminary in, R 289; Catholic Archbishop of,

301

Forthcoming Studies of the Mid-European Law Project at the Library of Congress

NATIONALITY LEGISLATION IN EASTERN EUROPE

Vladimir Gsovski, Chief Editor

This book covers nationality legislation in Bulgaria, Czechoslovakia, Hungary, Poland, Romania, Yugoslavia, Estonia, Latvia and Lithuania.

Since 1918 the area of Eastern and Central Europe has been subject to numerous territorial and political rearrangements, with consequent changes in the nationality of its inhabitants. Numerous international treaties governing the question of nationality in the new countries which emerged on former German, Austrian and Russian territories were concluded. World War II, with the German and Soviet territorial expansion and annexation by the Soviet Union of several nations, with a new type of legislation depriving entire social groups of their nationality, has created a high degree of uncertainty and confusion.

This volume presents the developments in the field of nationality legislation during and since World War II set against the background of earlier legislation, and supplies translations of most important laws.

$5.00

(*No. 27 of Praeger Publications in Russian History and World Communism*)

BIBLIOGRAPHY OF LEGAL SOURCES IN EASTERN EUROPE

Vladimir Gsovski, Chief Editor

With the establishment of Communist governments in Eastern and Central Europe, a reform of laws was initiated in the countries affected which was largely inspired by the Soviet legal system and resulted in the adoption of new codes and statutes. These developments are reflected in the discontinuation of the old legal publications and the issuance of new periodicals, collections of laws and a large number of legal studies. Moreover, the legal history of those countries is not widely known. In order to provide an essential tool for the study of their laws, both old and new, these bibliographical studies were prepared. The bibliographical listing is preceded by an introduction giving the legal history of each country in brief, the roots of the national legislative system, and gradual transition to the present system under the Communist government. The more important legislation currently in force, including constitutional and administrative law, administration of justice, civil, commercial, penal, labor and economic laws, military law, and legislation governing education, taxation and finance are listed. A description of the main legal sources follows in each case. The bibliography is subdivided into works and studies published in English, French, German and other languages. The following nine studies will be published:

1. Bulgaria	4. Poland	7. Estonia
2. Czechoslovakia	5. Romania	8. Latvia
3. Hungary	6. Yugoslavia	9. Lithuania

Price per volume $3.50   Price per set $20.00

(*Nos.* 18 *to* 26 *of Praeger Publications in Russian History and World Communism*) ..

Other Praeger Publications in Russian
History and World Communism

FROM LENIN TO MALENKOV
The History of World Communism
Hugh Seton-Watson

The first full-dress history and analysis of communism as a world-wide movement. It dissects the common pattern of Communist behavior and the application of Communist long-range strategy and local tactics to different social, economic, and intellectual climates.

"A remarkable achievement. His analysis of the social factors that favor or hinder Communist movements is brilliant,"
The New York Times

Hugh Seton-Watson is the author of four major works on Russian history, Eastern Europe, and world communism. He is professor of Russian History at the University of London. (No. 10 in the series)

Trade ed. $6.00   Text ed. $5.00

THE EAST EUROPEAN REVOLUTION
Hugh Seton-Watson

Second Revised Edition

The basic background book on the social structure, politics, history and economics of the Balkan areas and the sovietization of the satellite countries. "It would be difficult to praise too strongly the immense scholarship, careful observation and fairmindedness that has gone into this remarkable book." *The New York Times*. (No. 1 in the series)
$5.50

THE DECLINE OF IMPERIAL RUSSIA
Hugh Seton-Watson

A universally-acclaimed history of Russia from 1855 to 1914. "A clear, scholarly, and thoughtful account of an important period," Michael Karpovich, *American Historical Review*. (No. 3 in the series)
Trade ed. $7.50   Text ed. $6.00

COMMUNIST GUERILLA WARFARE
C. Aubrey Dixon and Otto Heilbrunn

Guerilla warfare, as developed by Mao Tse-Tung and perfected by Stalin during the German campaign, has revolutionized the concept of war. This is the first scientific study of guerilla warfare and an outstanding contribution to military science. Brigadier Dixon and Dr. Heilbrunn based their work on their own observations, on numerous German and Russian documents, and on analyses of the testimony of Wehrmacht officers. (No. 11 in the series) $4.50

THE COMMUNIST THEORY OF LAW
Hans Kelsen

This is the first comprehensive study of the theory of law based on the "materialistic" or economic interpretation of society inaugurated by Karl Marx. It examines the communist doctrine that the law is an ideological superstructure with the relationships of economic production as its real basis and points up the doctrine's contradictions.

Professor Hans Kelsen is the most eminent international jurist of our time. His many and brilliant works in international and constitutional law are considered classics in their fields. (No. 12 in the series)

$5.00

THE TRAGEDY OF THE BALTIC STATES
J. A. Swettenham

This is a vivid but scholarly description of the little known history of the three Baltic states—Latvia, Lithuania and Estonia—from the time of their liberation in 1917 until the present. The author was formerly a member of the Displaced Persons Division of the British Control Commission for Germany. (No. 15 in the series) $3.50

MUSIC UNDER THE SOVIETS: The Agony of an Art
Andrey Olkhovsky

A critical and revealing study of the fate of music under a totalitarian political system. The author takes up the major aspects of music in the Soviet Union as a profession and an art, and provides an account of the historical background of Soviet music, the organization of Soviet musical life, education and publishing, and the development of specifically Soviet forms of music.

The author, an eminent Russian teacher and composer, left the Soviet Union in 1942 and has lived in the United States since 1949 studying and teaching music. (No. 32 in the series) $6.00

THE HISTORY OF A COLLECTIVE FARM
Fedor Belov

Soviet admission of a crisis in its agriculture has focussed attention on this key sector of the Soviet economy. This is a full account of the operations of a typical collective farm by a man who was its chairman for three years (1947-1949). It discusses in detail the establishment of the farm, its relations with governmental and other agencies, its system of inducements and coercion, and the economic and social position of its members to give a remarkably complete picture of the functioning of the collective farm system in the Soviet economy.

THE HISTORY OF A COLLECTIVE FARM was written under a grant from the Research Program on the U.S.S.R. (No. 36 in the series) $6.00

RUSSIA'S DANUBIAN EMPIRE
Gordon Shepherd

From his vantage point as a high official of the Allied Commission, and then as a newspaper correspondent, Gordon Shepherd has prepared this definitive study of Russia's acquisition of an empire along the Danube since the end of World War II. (No. 14 in the series) $4.50

LENIN AND HIS RIVALS
The Struggle for Russia's Future, 1898-1906
Donald W. Treadgold

A study of the political thought and action of the Russian intelligentsia in the decade up to and including the Revolution of 1905-6. It is focussed on the emergence, starting in 1898, of the major political parties in Russia, parties headed by persons such as Chernov, Lenin, Martov and Miliukov. The book features personal interviews with survivors of these political struggles and tells the story of the first attempt at a popular front between Bolsheviks and other political groups for what were assumed to be common ends. The author was formerly in charge of the Russia in Asia project at the University of Washington. (No. 33 in the series) $5.00

THE COMMUNIST MENACE IN MALAYA
Harry Miller

"Sound, thorough and absorbingly interesting . . . Mr. Miller's facts are provocative and he lets them speak for themselves," *New York Times*. (No. 16 in the series) $3.50

A CHRISTIAN COMMENTARY ON COMMUNISM
Edward Rogers

A learned and comprehensive commentary on the various forms of communism, theoretical and practical, from Plato to Stalin. "A penetrating and convincing critique of the Communist program . . . ," *Christian Century*. (No. 5 in the series) $3.50

SATELLITE AGRICULTURE IN CRISIS
A Study of Land Policy in the Soviet Sphere

A study of the application of the Soviet land system to the satellites which traces the rise of state and collectivized agriculture in Eastern Europe from 1945 to now. Prepared by the Research Staff of Free Europe Press, a division of the Free Europe Committee. (No. 13 in the series)

Clothbound $3.50   Paperbound $2.50

COMMUNISM AND DEMOCRACY IN AUSTRALIA
L. C. Webb

A study of a democratic community grappling with the communist problem as well as a lively presentation of Australian democracy in action. The author discusses party politics in Australia, the Australian parliamentary system and the relationship between the churches and politics. The focal point of the study is the 1951 referendum. Professor Webb is head of the Political Science Department of the Australian National University. (No. 34 in the series) $5.00

THE PEOPLES OF THE SOVIET FAR EAST
Walter Kolarz

The first account of the policies which the Soviet Government has pursued towards the many nationalities inhabiting her vast Far Eastern possessions.

The author is an expert in Soviet colonial and nationalities policies. (No. 8 in the series) $4.50

RUSSIA AND HER COLONIES
Walter Kolarz

The best major work to deal with Moscow's colonial and nationalities policy in all parts of its empire except for those in the Pacific. "Warmly recommended as the first clear guide through the tangle of Soviet policy in the treatment of national minorities," *Saturday Review*. (No. 4 in the series) $6.00

CURRENT SOVIET POLICIES
Leo Gruliow, Editor

The most important reference tool available on Soviet policies today. "Permanently valuable to the student of Soviet policy," *Catholic World.* (No. 6 in the series)

Trade ed. $6.00   Text ed. $5.00

LABOR IN THE SOVIET UNION
Solomon M. Schwarz

"A valuable, scholarly, and much-needed study of Soviet labor policy and its impact on the lives of Russian workers by an astute, veteran observer of Soviet affairs," *Foreign Affairs.* (No. 2 in the series)

$6.00

COURTS, LAWYERS AND TRIALS
UNDER THE LAST THREE TSARS
Samuel Kucherov

Preface by Michael Karpovich

An examination of the fundamental principles of the Judicial Reform of 1864 and the institutions which it created by a great scholar of law and Russian practices. (No. 7 in the series) $6.00

Forthcoming in the Series

COMMUNIST CHINA TODAY
Domestic and Foreign Policies
Peter S. H. Tang

This is a comprehensive study of all major aspects of Communist China today, its political structure and history, its personalities and plans. Dr. Tang analyzes the impact of Marxism and Leninism on China, China's role in the world communist movement, the various periods of the communist drive for conquest of China until the postwar triumph of 1949. He brings the reader up to late 1954 with full details of the Moscow-Peiping axis and the prospects of Chinese Titoism.

Peter S. H. Tang is a leading scholar and authority on Chinese communism. During the war, he was attache at the Chinese Embassy in Moscow. He has written extensively in his main field. (No. 35 in the series) $6.00

A HISTORY OF BOLSHEVIST RUSSIA
Georg von Rauch

A great scholar's masterfully-drawn history of Soviet Russia from the Revolution to the end of 1954. Professor von Rauch, one of Germany's most eminent Russian historians, traces the Russian road to world power—describing Soviet personalities and factions, Soviet internal and foreign programs, ideological, economic and sociological developments —in a highly readable, dispassionate treatment. (No. 9 in the series)

$6.00

THE DIALECTICAL MATERIALISM OF THE SOVIET UNION
Father Gustavus Wetter

This is the classic work on the history and theory of dialectical materialism, the core of Soviet ideology and the philosophical basis of all Soviet science. Its author is the world's leading Catholic authority on communist ideology and Jesuit Superior of the Collegium Russicum in Rome. (No. 31 in the series)   ca $10.00

COMMUNISM AND NATIONALISM IN THE MIDDLE EAST
W. Z. Laqueur

This is the first definitive study on the history of Communism in the Middle East, its sources, impact on policy, and prospects. The author traces the roots of the new Arab nationalism and surveys the relations between the Communists and extreme nationalists. Particular study is made of country by country—in Egypt, Israel, Jordan, Syria, Lebanon, Iraq and Turkey—from 1919 to 1954.

Walter Z. Laqueur has written extensively on middle-eastern affairs, and is a frequent contributor to the *New Leader*. (No. 28 in the series)

$4.50